Max Weber

ON CHARISMA AND INSTITUTION BUILDING

THE HERITAGE OF SOCIOLOGY

A Series Edited by Morris Janowitz

Max Weber

ON CHARISMA AND

INSTITUTION BUILDING

Selected Papers

Edited and with an Introduction by
S. N. EISENSTADT

THE UNIVERSITY OF CHICAGO PRESS
CHICAGO AND LONDON

THE UNIVERSITY OF CHICAGO PRESS, CHICAGO 60637
The University of Chicago Press, Ltd., London

© *1968 by The University of Chicago. All rights reserved.*
Published 1968
Printed in the United States of America

01 00 99 98 97 96 95 94 93 92   7 8 9 10 11

ISBN: 0-226-87724-8 (paperbound)
Library of Congress Catalog Card Number: 68–54202

Contents

VII. CHARISMA AND INSTITU-TIONALIZATION IN THE SPHERE OF RELIGION AND CULTURE

Acknowledgements

I would like to thank the following persons, who helped me in the preparation of this volume: Professor Morris Janowitz, editor of the series, for suggesting the volume and for his detailed comments on my manuscript; Mrs. R. Shako, who helped prepare the manuscript for publication; and Mrs. Y. Atzmon and Professor Edward Shils for their comments on the Introduction.

S. N. EISENSTADT

Introduction

Charisma and Institution Building:

Max Weber and Modern Sociology

I

THE CENTRAL THEMES of this essay are that the concept of charisma as developed by Weber and its possible further extensions are of crucial importance for understanding of the processes of institution building; that this concept was already implicit—and to some extent even explicit—in Weber's own writings; and that the explication of the relations between charisma and institution building is perhaps the most important challenge which Weber's work poses for modern sociology. In much of existing sociological literature it has been assumed that a deep chasm exists between the charismatic aspects and the more ordinary, routine aspects of social organization and the organized, continuous life of social institutions—and that Weber himself stressed this dichotomy. It seems to me, however, that this is a mistaken view and that the best clue to understanding Weber's work, and especially his significance for modern sociology, lies in the attempt to combine the two and to analyze how they are continuously interrelated in the fabric of social life and in the processes of social change. I shall accordingly first present a brief analysis of Weber's major intellectual and scientific concerns and attempt to show how these are related to the concept of charisma and how the analysis of this concept brings us to the consideration of the place of the charismatic in the processes of institution building and of social and historical change and transformation. Last, I shall attempt to show the implications of this analysis for Weber's analysis of the nature and problems of modern society.

II

Weber's work does not need an introduction to the English-speaking sociological world. Most of his major works—all the *Aufsätze für Religionsoziologie*,[1] his *General Economic History*,[2] many of his essays on methodology of the social sciences,[3] and large parts of his monumental *Wirtschaft und Gesellschaft* have been translated in special collections, in the *Theory of Social and Economic Organization*,[4] in parts of *Essays from Max Weber*,[5] in *The Sociology of Religion*,[6] and in *The City*[7] and in the volume *On Law*,[8] to be followed by a full-fledged translation by G. Roth. So also have several of his essays—the famous essays on politics and science as vocation, as well as some of his articles on economic history.[9] The major works missing in English are most of his empirical researches, collected in his *Gesammelte*

[1]   *The Protestant Ethic and the Spirit of Capitalism*, trans. by Talcott Parsons (London: Allen & Unwin, 1930); *The Religion of China: Confucianism and Taoism*, trans. and ed. by H. H. Gerth (Glencoe, Ill.: Free Press, 1951); *Ancient Judaism*, trans. and ed. by H. H. Gerth and Don Martindale (Glencoe, Ill.: Free Press, 1952); *The Religion of India: The Sociology of Hinduism and Buddhism*, trans. and ed. by H. H. Gerth and Don Martindale (Glencoe, Ill.: Free Press, 1952); *The Sociology of Religion*, trans. by Ephraim Fischoff (Boston: Beacon Press, 1963) (mostly from *Wirtschaft u. Gesellschaft*).
[2]   *General Economic History*, trans. by Frank H. Knight (Glencoe, Ill.: Free Press, 1927).
[3]   *Max Weber on the Methodology of the Social Sciences*, trans. and ed. by Edward A. Shils and Henry A. Finch (Glencoe, Ill.: Free Press, 1949).
[4]   Trans. by R. A. Henderson and Talcott Parsons, ed. by Talcott Parsons (New York: Oxford University Press, 1947).
[5]   *Essays from Max Weber*, trans. and ed. by H. H. Gerth and C. Wright Mills (New York: Oxford University Press, 1946).
[6]   *Sociology of Religion*.
[7]   *The City*, trans. and ed. by Don Martindale and Gertrud Neuwirth (Glencoe, Ill.: Free Press, 1958).
[8]   *On Law in Economy and Society*, trans. by Edward A. Shils and Max Rheinstein (Cambridge, Mass.: Harvard University Press, 1954).
[9]   *Essays from Max Weber*.

Aufsätze zur Soziologie und Sozialpolitik[10] and several of the concrete historical analyses, mostly collected in his *Gesammelte Aufsätze zur Sozial und Wirtschaftsgeschichte.*[11]

Even before most of these translations became available his work was introduced to the English-speaking and, especially to the American sociological world through the writings of Talcott Parsons.[12] In Parsons' *Structure of Social Action* he fully explored the place of Weber in the development of modern sociological thought and analysis and at the same time presented a very detailed examination of most of the major aspects of Weber's work. In further works and essays, especially in his introductions to the *Theory of Social and Economic Organization* and to the *Sociology of Religion*, Parsons has continued to explore the significance of Weber's work for the development of sociological theory in general and for various fields of sociology in particular. Perhaps the most succinct presentation of Weber's place in the history of sociology can be found in Parsons' recent paper "Unity and Diversity in the Modern Intellectual Disciplines: The Role of the Social Sciences."[13]

Aside from Parsons' works, exposition of Weber's works could be found in the thirties and forties in the historical exposition of Barnes and Becker,[14] in A. Salomon's articles in *Social Research*,[15] in several articles by Edward A. Shils,[16] and in the comprehensive

10   Tübingen, J. C. B. Mohr, 1924.

11   Tübingen, J. C. B. Mohr, 1924.

12   E.g., Introduction to Weber's *Theory of Social and Economic Organization*, pp. 1–70; *The Structure of Social Action* (New York: Free Press, 1968); Introduction to Weber's *Sociology of Religion*, pp. ix–lxvii; "Unity and Diversity in the Modern Intellectual Disciplines: The Role of the Social Sciences," *Daedalus*, vol. 94 (Winter, 1965).

13   *Ibid.*, especially pp. 55–61.

14   H. E. Barnes and H. Becker, *Social Thought from Lore to Science* (New York: Dover Publications, 1952, originally published in 1936).

15   "Max Weber's Methodology," *Social Research*, 1 (1934) 147–68; "Max Weber's Sociology," *ibid.*, 2 (1935):60–73; "Max Weber's Political Ideas," *ibid.*, pp. 368–84.

16   "Some Remarks on the Theory of Social and Economic Organization," *Economica*, 15 (1948):36–50; *Foreword* to *Max Weber on the Methodology of the Social Sciences*, pp. iii–x; "Charisma, Order and Status," *American Sociological Review*, 30 (1965):199–213.

presentation of his work and intellectual orientation given by
R. Bendix in *Max Weber—An Intellectual Portrait*.[17] In connection with the centenary of Weber's birth in 1964 additional analyses of his significance in the history of sociology and of German
cultural life have appeared.[18]

All this does not mean, of course, that there is no place for
further detailed analysis of Weber's work in sociology and comparative history and of his place in European *Geistesgeschichte*
in general and in German social and political thought in the late
nineteenth and early twentieth century in particular. The study
of his influence in all these areas poses problems of research
mainly for the historian of social thought, for those concerned
with any of the many concrete fields of research in which Weber
worked, and for the historian of German intellectual life in the
nineteenth and twentieth centuries.

The importance of Weber, however, is not only as a major
figure in the history of sociology or in the *Geistesgeschichte* of
the nineteenth and twentieth centuries. Nor is Weber's work of
significance today only as a mine of varied concrete hypotheses
and analyses—many of them unsurpassed in the study of bureaucracy, of sociology of law, and sociology of religion or in the analysis of different types of capitalism. True enough, in many fields of
sociology—the more analytical inquiry into the nature of social
relations, general methodological writings, the analysis of social
organization or social systems, the analysis of economic sociology,
the study of bureaucracy and of different types of political systems, and to a lesser degree several aspects of sociology of religion
and of law—sociological analysis has reached a stage in which,
while building on Weber it may soon go beyond him—if not in

[17]   R. Bendix, *Max Weber—An Intellectual Portrait* (New York:
Doubleday, 1960).

[18]   E.g., Wolfgang Mommsen, *Max Weber und die deutsche Politik,
1890–1920* (Tübingen: J. C. B. Mohr, 1959); Otto Stammer, ed., *Max
Weber und die Soziologie heute: Verdhandlungen des 15. deutschen Sozio-
logentages* (Tübingen: J. C. B. Mohr, 1965); the April, 1965, issue of *The
American Sociological Review* (vol. 30); Karl Engisch, Bernhard Pfister,
and Johannes Winckelmann, eds., *Max Weber: Gedächtnisschrift der
Ludwig-Maximilians Universität München* (Berlin, 1966).

the richness of details, then at least in analytical and conceptual elaboration. Thereby sociology may perhaps be able, in Whitehead's famous formulation, to forget its founders.

All the developments in these fields, important as they are, do not, however, yet confront us with the basic substantive and analytical problems which Weber's manifold analysis has posed, even if sometimes only implicitly, before sociological analysis and theory. This implicitness is due mostly to Weber's general reluctance to engage in full, systemic, formal analysis of social relations, to his predilection for pursuing thoroughly a single line of thought, and to his preoccupation with many current political and ideological issues in their unique contemporary historical setting. Therefore, in order to explore his contribution to central problems of sociological analysis, we shall not concentrate on the exposition of his conceptual and methodological approaches, which has already been abundantly treated in the literature.[19] Instead, we shall concentrate on the exposition of some of the major substantive problems implied in his analysis, and the purpose both of the selections from Weber's work included here and of this brief introduction is to attempt to present and analyze some of these problems.

III

The best way to explicate the central problems implied in Weber's work is through the confrontation of his major substantive contribution to sociology, on the one hand, and his major philosophical, "value," or intellectual orientations which directed his scientific analysis, on the other. From the point of view of substantive contribution, Weber's greatness and uniqueness lay in the manner in which he combined historical and sociological analysis. The unparalleled richness and variety of the materials which he mastered and his training in legal, economic, and social

19   See, for example, Alexander von Schelting, *Max Weber's Wissenschaftslehre* (Tübingen, J. C. B. Mohr, 1934) ; R. Bendix, *Max Weber— An Intellectual Portrait* (New York, 1960) ; Talcott Parsons, *The Structure of Social Action* (New York: Free Press, 1968).

history made him fully aware of the various methodological problems of each of these fields. His ability to master the history of far-away religions and civilizations made him stand out among all sociologists—and such mastery in itself could be enough to assure him a unique place in their company. But his greatest contribution to comparative historical sociology lay in the ways in which he made use of this great richness. He did not use it to erect great evolutionary schemes of world history or of the progress of the human mind—although, as we shall yet see later, many of the concerns or preoccupations of the evolutionary schools and of German *Geistesgeschichte* and *Kulturgeschichte* were very close to Weber's heart. Neither did he use it to illustrate or elaborate a classificatory schema of different types of social activities and organizations—an approach which was very much in vogue in German sociology at the period of Weber's activity— although here again some of the central problems of such classification and typology were also very close to his concerns. Rather Weber employed all this richness to analyze systematically the great variety of human creativity in its social context, to analyze the most salient of the common characteristics and problems of different spheres of human endeavor, and to explore the conditions of emergence, continuity, change, and stagnation of different types of social organization and cultural creativity.

Analytically, his greatest contribution to comparative studies was based on the application of general categories to the systematic study of whole societies both inside and outside Europe. But he did not use these rich historical materials to "illustrate" his broad analytical categories. He used the broad analytical categories either to explain, on a comparative canvas, some of the distinct characteristics of a single society or to analyze some broader types of societies, institutions, collectivities, and patterns of behavior. It was this continuous use of both these approaches and their continuous combination in his work that constitute the uniqueness and strength of his work.

But the wide range and great vitality of his historical and comparative analysis can be fully understood only when we examine how it was related to his basic philosophical or value orientations and concerns. The foci of these concerns were the problems and predicaments of human freedom, creativity, and personal responsibility in social life in general and in modern society in particular. In this respect he was not, of course, unique among modern sociologists. All the classical figures of modern sociology —Marx, Tocqueville, Lorenz von Stein, Durkheim—were deeply concerned with these problems. The rise of sociological analysis has often been attributed to the growing awareness of the specific ways in which these problems became manifest in the context of modern society. The uniqueness of Weber—and his importance for the development of systematic sociological analysis—lies in the way in which he dealt with these problems and related them to his scientific analysis. While deeply concerned with analyzing the condition of freedom, he did not conceive the search for freedom—or its suppression—as the only constituent of social life or as the only mainspring of human motivation; nor did he construct grandiose developmental or historical schemes which assured, as it were, the ultimate victory of freedom.

True enough, the problem of alienation—central in Marx's early thought—was of no less concern to Weber. He did not, however, see alienation as derived from only one aspect of social relations, but rather as immanent in all such relations in all institutional fields.[20] Weber perceived that it is possible for alienation to be rooted in several basic aspects of social and cultural life. By its very nature, social life imposes on those who participate in it the possibility or even the necessity of gradual withdrawal from the mainsprings of social and cultural creativity and thereby creates not only the possibility of their losing contact with these mainsprings, but also the possibility of hatred towards those who represent such creativity either in their own persons or in the offices of which they are incumbents. It is here that the close and paradoxical relation between creativity, freedom, and organized social life stands out most fully.

[20]   S. M. Lipset stresses this point in "Social Class," an article in the *International Encyclopaedia of the Social Sciences* (New York: Macmillan, 1968).

IV

For Weber, freedom, creativity, and personal responsibility did not lie outside the scope of society, of social relations and activities. On the contrary, interpersonal relations, organizations, institutional structures, and the macrosocietal setting constituted the arena in which freedom, creativity, and responsibility could become manifest. But they also imposed severe limitations and constrictions on such creativity, thus creating the possibility of alienation not only in the economic sphere, but in all spheres of social relations. Hence his most general concern, permeating all his work, was with what may be called, in the terminology of modern sociology, the processes of institution building, social transformation, and cultural creativity. These processes involve crystallization, continuity, and change of major types of institutions, cultural symbols, and macrosocietal settings, and the analysis of the possibilities (and limits) of transforming existing institutional and cultural complexes and building new ones.

On the one hand, Weber perceived face-to-face relations, social groups and organizations, and macrosocial and cultural frameworks as massive organizational and structural forces within which human beings enjoy but little freedom and few possibilities of creative change and activity, or even of full development and exercise of personal responsibility. On the other hand, however, face-to-face relations, organizations, institutions, the societal macrostructure, and cultural creations alike emerge as the result of the common endeavor of people in society, even if the ultimate outcome of such endeavor differs greatly from the original aims of their perpetrators.

These creations may be of at least two different kinds. First, they may be the result of the accretion or accumulation of long series of activities of many people in different walks of life in peripheral spheres of society, each of whom takes up something from the tradition he inherits and changes it imperceptibly by living in it and by transmitting it to new generations. Second, they may be the fruits of great dramatic innovations in the society or cultural organization or of innovations in the more peripheral spheres of society which succeed to impinge on such centers. Great religions and religious organizations and new types of legal norms and systems, of political leadership, of economic organization, and of artistic expression—all these are among such great, dramatic expressions of human creativity.

Thus, on all these levels of social life, the possibility of creativity and freedom does not exist outside the institutional framework; it is rather to be found in certain aspects of social relations and organization, of institution building and—paradoxically enough—very often in the process of destruction of institutions. But this very creativity is not lacking in structure. It is subject to organizational limitations and structural exigencies and itself creates possibilities of new organizational pressure and constriction. It contains within itself tendencies toward constriction and rigidity, and toward the destruction of institutions, symbols, and macrosocietal settings.

These constrictions and destructive tendencies may be rooted, first, in the fact that once an innovation is accepted it may as a result become routine, "deflated," more and more removed from its original impetus. Those who participate in its perpetuation—its originators and their initial close collaborators—tend to become less interested in it; indeed, their whole relation to these mainsprings of creativity may become attenuated. But such constrictions may also be rooted in the fact that the originators of these cultural innovations—of great religions, of new political systems, or of new economic enterprises—may become afraid of the further spread of the spirit of such free creativity, may attempt to impose limitations on such spread, on the attempts of other people or groups to participate in such creativity or to extend its scope. In this way the innovators may engender among such outside groups hostility and alienation toward the very acts of creativity and toward the destruction of institutions. It is this continuous tension between what may be called the constrictive and the creative aspects of institutions and of social organization that is of central interest to Weber.

According to Weber, this tension was closely related, as we

shall yet see in greater detail later, to the whole process of rationalization and of demystification (*Entzauberung*) of modern social life. Hence the possibility of attaining freedom, creativity, and personal responsibility seemed very doubtful and problematic to him, particularly under modern conditions. Weber certainly did not share the optimism which much later Karl Mannheim expressed in his last works on the possibility of democratic planning.[21] But his deep pessimism was matched only by the depth of his concerns with these problems and by his attempts to evaluate soberly yet passionately the possibilities of creativity and freedom in different types of social relations and organizations. And it was through the continuous confrontation of this concern with his analytical apparatus on the one hand and his vast comparative sociological and historical knowledge on the other that Weber reformulated and transformed some of the basic problems of sociology.

V

Weber developed his study of the problem of individual freedom and creativity around the concept of *charisma*. As is well known, his most explicit definition of charisma was presented with regard to different types of legitimation of authority but, as we shall see, this definition is not really confined to the political sphere but stretches far behind it. Weber describes charisma as "a certain quality of an individual personality by virtue of which he is set apart from ordinary men and treated as endowed with supernatural, superhuman, or at least specifically exceptional qualities."[22] It is essential that the charismatic individual be recognized or regarded as such; "this recognition is a matter of complete personal devotion arising out of enthusiasm, or of despair and hope."[23]

Hence social or political systems based on charismatic legiti-

[21]   *Freedom, Power and Democratic Planning* (London: Routledge & Kegan Paul, 1951).

[22]   *Theory of Social and Economic Organization*, p. 329.

[23]   *Ibid.*, p. 359.

mation exhibit certain characteristics which reflect the intense and personal nature of the response to charisma. First, recognition of the leader is an especially compelling duty, even if it be formally voluntary. As Parsons puts it, "the authority of the leader does not express the 'will' of his followers, but rather their duty or obligation."[24] Consequently, there is a distinctive moral fervor that is sharply opposed to the forms of traditional morality and sober rational calculation. Charismatic groups do not have elaborate systems of roles, rules, and procedures to guide the performance of administrative functions. They disdain "everyday economizing," the attainment of a regular income by continuous economic activity devoted to this end.[25] Thus it has been claimed that the charismatic situation is the total antithesis of "routine," of organized social institutions and relations. It is not only that charismatic authority is formally contrasted with "traditional" and "rational" authorities. Beyond this formal distinction, pure charisma has some inherent antinomian and anti-institutional predispositions. Given the absolutistic moral fervor, the revolutionary disdain of formal procedures, and the inherent instability of the lack of provision for succession, charismatic activities and orientations, because of their close relation to the very sources of social and cultural creativity, contain strong tendencies toward the destruction and decomposition of institutions.

This charismatic fervor is rooted in the attempt to come into contact with the very essence of being, to go to the very roots of existence, of cosmic, social, and cultural order, to what is seen as sacred and fundamental. But this attempt may also contain a strong predisposition to sacrilege: to the denial of the validity of the sacred, and of what is accepted in any given society as sacred. The very attempt to reestablish direct contact with these roots of cosmic and of sociopolitical order may breed both opposition to more attenuated and formalized forms of this order, as well as fear of, and hence opposition to, the sacred itself.

It is these tendencies that constitute the focus of both the

---

24   *Theory of Social and Economic Organization*, p. 65.
25   *Ibid.*, p. 332.

creative and destructive tendencies of charisma. If, on the one hand, the charisma may lead to excesses of derangement and deviance, on the other hand charismatic personalities or collectivities may be the bearers of great cultural social innovations and creativity, religious, political, or economic. It is in the charismatic act that the potential creativity of the human spirit—a creativity which may perhaps in some cases be deranged or evil —is manifest; and it is not only the potential derangement, but such creativity by its very nature and orientation tends to undermine and destroy existing institutions and to burst the limits set by them. Similarly, on the personal level, charismatic predispositions may arise from the darkest recesses and excesses of the human soul, from its utter depravity and irresponsibility of its most intensive antinomian tendencies; while, on the other hand, charisma is the source of the fullest creative power and internal responsibility of the human personality.[26]

And yet the antithesis between the regular flow of organized social relations and of institutional frameworks on the one hand, and of charismatic qualities and activities on the other, is not as extreme or total as might be deduced from the foregoing discussion. While analytically this distinction between "organized" (traditional, legal, or bureaucratic) routine and charisma is sharp, this certainly does not imply total dichotomy between concrete sitations. True enough, in some very special situations— extreme social change, breakdowns and attempts to transform such crumbling frameworks—this dichotomy between orderly institutional life and the destructive or the innovative and constructive potentials of charismatic activities could become sharply articulated.

But even in such situations the analytical distinction between the charismatic and the routine is not complete or extreme. Throughout his discussion of charisma Weber emphasizes not so much the charismatic leader, but the charismatic group or band, be it the religious sect or the followers of a new political leader.

[26]   This aspect of charisma has been especially stressed by Wolfgang Mommsen in "Max Weber's Political Sociology and his Philosophy of World History," *International Social Science Journal,* 17 (1965):23–46.

The first meeting point between the charismatic predisposition toward the destruction of institutions and the exigencies of orderly social organization is demonstrated in the necessity of the charismatic leader or group to assure some continuity for this very group, that is, to assure the succession of its leadership and the continuity of its organization. Such transformation of a great charismatic upsurge and vision into some more continuous social organization and institutional framework constitutes the first step in the routinization of charisma. But routinization of charisma does not necessarily imply only the process through which a great upsurge of charismatic vision loses, as it were, its initial impetus and becomes flattened, diffused, and in a sense obliterated. There is another equally important aspect to this process, the key to which lies in the concepts of "charisma of the office" (*Amtcharisma*), of kinship (*Geltilcharisma*), of hereditary charisma (*Erbcharisma*),[27] or of "contact charisma."[28] As is well known, these concepts, especially that of the charisma of the office, have been used by Weber to denote the process through which the charismatic characteristics are transferred from the unique personality or the unstructured group to orderly institutional reality.

The very coining of these terms indicates that the test of any great charismatic leader lies not only in his ability to create a single event or great movement, but also in his ability to leave a continuous impact on an institutional structure—to transform any given institutional setting by infusing into it some of his charismatic vision, by investing the regular, orderly offices, or aspects of social organization, with some of his charismatic qualities and aura. Thus here the dichotomy between the charismatic and the orderly regular routine of social organization seems to be obliterated—to be revived again only in situations of extreme and intensive social disorganization and change.

The obliteration of this dichotomy which seems to take place is deceptive. Thus the concepts of charisma of the office, of kinship,

---

27   Max Weber, *Theory of Social and Economic Organization*, pp. 334–42. *See also* chapter 2 below.
28   This concept has first been used by Shils in "Charisma, Order and Status," p. 201.

of hereditary or contact charisma, constitute the first step in the replacement of the classification which defines purely charismatic and purely routine actions or structures as pure and incompatible by a classification which sees charismatic activities and orientations as analytical elements which are inherent, even if in varying degrees, in all social relations and organizations.

Thus we face the necessity of defining the nature of the charismatic quality of activities and orientations in a way that can account for both its distinctness from ordinary, routine activities as well as the possibility of its interweaving in concrete situations.

VI

Perhaps the best way to approach the resolution of this problem is through the analysis of the appeal of the charismatic, of the desire to participate in the charismatic act and group, and of the nature of the social situation in which people may become especially sensitized to such appeal. What is it in the charismatic that appeals to people, that makes them willing to follow a charismatic leader, to accept his call to give up some of their resources —wealth, time, energy, or existing social bonds and commitments —for the implementation of his vision? And when are people most willing to follow his appeal?

In Weber's own writings this problem is not explicitly dealt with. For the most part, he takes for granted the nature of the appeal of the charismatic. This taking for granted of the appeal of the charismatic is even more common—without Weber's insights —in subsequent analyses. One approach, often employed in sociological and psychological research, stresses the general abnormality of the predisposition to the charismatic, an interpretation in line with Weber's emphasis on the extraordinary character of charisma. These analyses often attribute the predisposition to acceptance of charismatic leadership to some semipathological or sociopsychological cause. Weber's own formulation could seemingly lend itself to such an interpretation; he suggests that charisma "may involve a subjective or internal reorientation born out of suffering, conflicts or enthusiasm," and that this may take place "in times of psychic, physical, economic, ethical, religious, political distress."[29] Thus it may seem that it is mainly the disturbed, the disoriented, the alienated that tend to respond to such appeals—and they necessarily will become most prominent in extreme situations of social change and disturbances. It is in situations of stress or, to use Durkheim's term, of anomie, that more and more people tend to feel helpless, alienated, and disoriented and feel that the society in which they live is meaningless and normless; thus their own pathogenic tendencies become strengthened and the more pathological personalities may become prominent and find a wider scope for their activities.

Several trends of sociological research tended indeed to emphasize this approach. For instance, many of the earlier attempts to apply psychoanalytic theory to social phenomena seemed to imply that any predilection to some identification with charismatic symbols was rooted in early deformations of some "natural" familial relations—especially those between parents and children.[30]

Many of the more recent studies of social and religious movements or of processes of conversion have followed a similar line; likewise, many studies of political leaderships, attitudes, and ideologies, for instance, the studies of "authoritarian personality."[31]

---

29   *Theory of Social and Economic Organization*, p. 333.

30   See for instance, Harold D. Lasswell, *The Analysis of Political Behaviour* (London: Routledge & Kegan Paul, 1948), pp. 180–245.

31   See, among others, T. W. Adorno, *The Authoritarian Personality* (New York: Harper & Row, 1950) ; Norman Cohn, *The Pursuit of the Millenium* (New York: Harper & Row, 1961) , Leon Festinger, Henry W. Riecken, and Stanley Schachter, *When Prophecy Fails* (Minneapolis: University of Minnesota Press, 1946) ; Yonina Talmon, "Pursuit of the Millenium—the Relation between Religious and Social Change," *European Journal of Sociology*, 3 (1962) :125–49; *idem.*, "Millenarian Movements," *ibid.*, to be published; Anthony F. Wallace, "Revitalisation Movements," *American Anthropologist*, 58 (1956) ; and *idem.*, *Culture and Personality* (New York: Random House, 1962).

Even much of the recent usage[32] of the term charisma in the literature on new countries has tended to emphasize the importance of charismatic symbols and personality in abnormal situations, in situations of crisis or of stress and tended to interpret the charismatic saviors, symbols, and leaders as a panacea for the disturbed situations in which these countries found themselves.

True enough, many of these studies, especially the latter ones, do indeed contain many important insights into our problem. And yet their implicit tendency to see the predisposition to the acceptance of the charismatic as rooted in some pathological state cannot explain the potentially continuous appeal of the charismatic in seemingly orderly and routine situations. Does charisma appeal only to some pathological predispositions potentially always present among all or most people? Even if we assume that some such pathological tendencies do really always exist, does any charismatic quality appeal equally to all of them? And what does this appeal mean? Does it simply feed these pathological tendencies, reinforcing them, or does it attempt to resolve some of them? And what does such resolution entail? Does any situation of stress or of anomie intensify such pathological tendencies? What are the conditions under which leaders arise who possess only those charismatic qualities which are destructive of institutions, as against those who are also capable of building up new institutions?

All these problems have in some way constituted foci of diverse trends of research in the social sciences from Weber on. But as yet our knowledge about all these problems is limited— and not only because of the naturally intermittent and haphazard course of any scientific enterprise. It is also because the crucial differentiating variables relevant to these problems have not been fully and explicitly stated and formulated. Perhaps the most important missing link in this whole area was the lack of systematic exploration of the nature of the charismatic orientation and bond

---

[32]   See, for instance, David Apter, *The Politics of Modernization* (Chicago: University of Chicago Press, 1966) ; and for a critical appraisal of the uses of this concept in this context see Claude Ake, "Charismatic Legitimation and Political Integration," *Comparative Studies in Society and History*, 9 (1966) :1–13.

as a distinct type of social action. It is only when it is fully recognized that this bond is not something abnormal, that the differences between the more extreme and the more routine expressions of charisma can be more fully recognized and systematically studied. This has lately been done by Edward A. Shils.[33] We may quote here from him:

The charismatic quality of an individual as perceived by others, or himself, lies in what is thought to be his connection with (including possession by or embedment of) some *very central* feature of man's existence and the cosmos in which he lives. The centrality, coupled with intensity, makes it extraordinary. The centrality is constituted by its formative power in initiating, creating, governing, transforming, maintaining, or destroying what is vital in man's life. That central power has often, in the course of man's existence, been conceived of as God, the ruling power or creator of the universe, or some divine or other transcendent power controlling or markedly influencing human life and the cosmos within which it exists. The central power might be a fundamental principle or principles, a law or laws governing the universe, the underlying and driving force of the universe. It might be thought to reside in the ultimate principles of law which should govern man's conduct, arising from or derived from the nature of the universe and essential to human existence, discerned or elucidated by the exercise of man's most fundamental rational and expressive powers. Scientific discovery, ethical promulgation, artistic creativity, political and organizational authority (*authoritatem, auctor,* authorship) and in fact all forms of genius, in the original sense of the word as permeation by the "spirit," are as much instances of the category of charismatic things as in religious prophecy. . . .

This extended conception of a charismatic property (as perceived by one who is responsive to it, including the "charismatic person" himself) refers to a vital, "serious," ultimately symbolic event, of which divinity is one of many forms. Presumptive contact with the divine, possession by the divine, the possession of magical powers, are only modes of being charismatic. Contact with this class of vital, "serious" events may be attained through reflective wisdom or through disciplined scientific penetration, or artistic expression, or forceful and confident reality-transforming action. All these are also

[33]   "Charisma, Order and Status," pp. 199–213.

modes of contact with, or embodiment of, something very "serious" in Durkheim's sense, which is thought to be, and therewith becomes, central or fundamental to man's existence. . . .

Most human beings, because their endowment is inferior or because they lack opportunities to develop the relevant capacities, do not attain that intensity of contact. But most of those who are unable to attain it themselves are, at least intermittently, responsive to its manifestations in the words, actions, and products of others who have done so. They are capable of such appreciation and occasionally feel a need for . . . Through the culture they acquire and through their interaction with and perception of those more "closely connected" with the cosmically and socially central, their own weaker responsiveness is fortified and heightened.

All of these charismatic "connections" may be manifested intensely in the qualities, words, actions and products of individual personalities. This was emphasized by Weber and it has entered into contemporary sociology. But they may also become resident, in varying degrees of intensity, in institutions—in the qualities, norms, and beliefs to which members are expected to adhere or are expected to possess—and in an attenuated form, in categories of strata of the members of a society. . . .

Here the gap between the charismatic as an extraordinary event or quality and as a constituent element of any orderly social life is at least partially bridged. The search for meaning, consistency, and order is not always something extraordinary, something which exists only in extreme disruptive situations or among pathological personalities, but also in all stable social situations even if it is necessarily focused within some specific parts of the social structure and of an individual's life space.

VII

This general contention is borne out by various researches in the social sciences which—although they were not consciously dealing with these problems and not even fully aware of them—do yet touch on them; and if reexamined in the light of our questions may indeed contribute to their elucidation. Two kinds of research are of special importance from this point of view: first, anthropological studies bearing on the place of rituals in social life, and second, studies of communication in modern societies.

Different as the nature of the problems with which these two kinds of research are concerned, they seem to point to parallel conclusions with regard to the nature of the social situations in which the appeal to the charismatic becomes especially articulated and the predisposition to respond to some charismatic symbols becomes especially intensive.

Anthropological literature shows first how charismatic symbols are especially articulated in those ritual occasions most closely related to individual and collective rites of passage—birth, initiation, marriage, and death, or various collective ceremonies. Second it shows how receptiveness to such charismatic qualities and activities permeates more routine types of social activities—economic or community affairs or regular political or administrative activities—but especially on those occasions or situations in which their routine is to some extent broken or disturbed.

This becomes even more fully borne out from modern studies of communication, a field which may seem to have little to do with charisma. Some of the initial approaches implicit in these studies shared the assumption to which we have previously alluded, namely, that a sensitivity to charismatic forms of communication is of a semipathological nature, rooted in psychic stress and deformation.[34] The results of these researches indicated that such

34   See, for instance, Rudolph Arnheim, "The World of Daytime Serial," in Paul F. Lazarsfeld and Frank K. Stanton, eds., *Radio Research 1942–43* (New York: Duell, Sloan and Pearce, 1943), pp. 507–48; Eliot Freidson, "Communications Research and the Concept of the Mass," in W. L. Schramm, ed., *Process and Effects of Mass Communications* (Urbana: University of Illinois Press, 1954), pp. 380–89; Joseph T. Klapper, *The Effects of Mass Media: A Report to the Public Library Inquiry* (New York: Bureau of Applied Social Research, Columbia University, 1949); Ernst Kris and Nathan Leites, "Trends in Twentieth Century Propaganda," in Bernard Berelson and Morris Janowitz, eds., *Reader in Public Opinion and Communication* (Glencoe, Ill.: Free Press, 1950), pp. 278–88; Lloyd Warner and William Henry, "The Radio Daytime Serial: A Symbolic Analysis," in Berelson and Janowitz, *Public Opinion and Communication*, pp. 423–34. For instances of more differentiated approaches to the problem see Robert K. Merton, "Mass Persuasion: The Moral Dimension," in Berelson and Janowitz, *ibid.*, pp. 465–68; Hans Speier, "The Future of Psychological Warfare," in Berelson and Janowitz, *ibid.*, pp. 381–96.

predispositions are not something abnormal, that they do not arise only in very extraordinary circumstances, but that they become articulated in certain definite types of social situations.[35]

An analysis of these various researches indicates that the most important among such situations are (a) those in which there takes place some transition from one institutional sphere to another, or situations of simultaneous activity in several institutional spheres, or in several subsystems of a society; (b) situations in which such various subsystems have to be directly connected with the central values and activities of a society; (c) situations in which people are faced with a choice among various roles; (d) situations in which the routine of a given role or group is endangered or disrupted. In all such cases the individual is placed in potentially ambiguous, undefined, and conflicting situations in which his identity and status image and continuity of the perception of other actions are endangered. The common denominator of these various situations, of the more structured individual and collective rites of passage reported in anthropological studies, and of the less structured "communicative situations" of modern societies, is that people or groups participating in them experience some shattering of the existing social and cultural order to which they are bound. Hence in such situations they become more sensitive to those symbols or messages which attempt to symbolize such order, and more ready to respond to people who are able to present to them new symbols which could give meaning to their experiences in terms of some fundamental cosmic, social, or political order, to prescribe the proper norms of behavior, to relate the individual to collective identification, and to reassure him of his status and of his place in a given collectivity.[36]

Moreover, all these studies indicate that such situations do not arise only in catastrophic conditions, but that they constitute part of any orderly social life—of the life of individuals as they pass from one stage in their lifespan to another, or from one sphere of

---

[35]   See S. N. Eisenstadt, "Conditions of Communicative Receptivity," *Public Opinion Quarterly*, 17 (Fall 1953):363–75 and "Communication and Reference-Group Behavior," in his *Essays in Comparative Institutions* (New York: John Wiley, 1965), pp. 309–43.

[36]   *Ibid.*

activities to another, and of the organization of groups and societies. But the recognition of the fact that some predisposition to the acceptance of charismatic appeals and some quest for meaning and order exists in most social situations does not only pose again the problem of the relations between the charismatic and the ordinary in the structure of any social relation, organization, and institution, but adds a new dimension to this problem. Especially, it raises more sharply the problem of the different foci of the charismatic in the institutional structure. The preceding analysis of the processes of institutionalization of the charismatic and of the nature of the situations in which people are especially sensitized to the appeal of the charismatic has mainly been focused on more dispersed, microsocietal situations. And yet the most common emphasis in Weber's own work, as well as in much of the subsequent sociological analysis, was that the charismatic tends to become more fully embedded in more central societal locations and in the broader macrosocietal frameworks and that these frameworks tend to become directed by the charismatic symbols. Hence it is necessary to analyze in greater detail the problem of the nature of the broader macrosocietal, institutional frameworks or foci within which the charismatic orientations, symbols, or activities are centered.

As is well known, sociological analysis has continuously stressed that it is the religious and the political spheres that are the most natural foci or institutional abodes of such charismatic qualities and symbols. This contention has often been presented in a rather routine way as deriving mainly from the specific organizational needs of these spheres for legitimation or for keeping people quiet and obedient, thus reinforcing the "semi-conspiratorial" theory of charisma or of ideology.

Once again, Shils' expositions provide the most important developments beyond this line of analysis, especially his exposition of the "center" as a distinct aspect of any institutional framework, and as the structural locus of the macrosocietal institutionalization of charisma. To quote Shils again:[37]

37   "Centre and Periphery" in *The Logic of Personal Knowledge: Essays Presented to Michael Polanyi* (London: Routledge & Kegan Paul, 1961), pp. 117–31.

Society has a center. There is a central zone in the structure of society. This central zone impinges in various ways on those who live within the ecological domain in which the society exists. Membership in the society, in more than the ecological sense of being located in a bounded territory and of adapting to an environment affected or made up by other persons located in the same territory, is constituted by relationship to this central zone.

The central zone is not, *as such*, a spatially located phenomenon. It almost always has a more or less definite location within the bounded territory in which the society lives. Its centrality has, how-ever, nothing to do with geometry and little with geography.

The center, or the central zone, is a phenomenon of the realm of values and beliefs. It is the center of the order of symbols. of values and beliefs, which govern the society. It is the center because it is the ultimate and irreducible; and it is felt to be such by many who can-not give explicit articulation to its irreducibility. The central zone partakes of the nature of the sacred. In this sense, every society has an "official" religion, even when that society or its exponents and in-terpreters conceive of it, more or less correctly, as a secular, plural-istic, and tolerant society. The principle of the Counter-Reformation: *Cuius regio, eius religio*, although its rigor has been loosened and its harshness mollified, retains a core of permanent truth.

The center is also a phenomenon of the realm of action. It is a structure of activities, of roles and persons, within the network of institutions. It is in these roles that the values and beliefs which are central are embodied and propounded.

This close relation between the charismatic and the center is rooted in the fact that both are concerned with the maintenance of order and with the provision of some meaningful symbolic and institutional order. But this close relation between the two does not imply their total identity. Rather, it raises many new questions and problems. What is the structure of such centers and what are their structural relations to the periphery? How many centers which embody such charismatic orientation are there in a society, for instance, political, cultural, religious or ideological, and other centers? What is the relation between the "ordering" and "mean-ing-giving" (charismatic) functions of such centers, on the one hand, and of their more organizational and administrative activ-ities, on the other?

Especially it brings us to the problem of the ways in which both the symbolic and the organizational aspects of routinization of charisma vary among the major institutional spheres of a social order. Given that the quest for order is evident throughout the major spheres of a society and that it is not something purely abstract or symbolic, but closely related to the organizational needs and problems of these spheres, it necessarily follows that the process of routinization of charisma and the charismatic qualities may differ greatly among different institutional spheres. This problem of the different charismatic qualities which are appropriate to different types of institutional spheres has been dealt with by Weber only indirectly, by way of illustration or by analysis of some aspects of charismatic leadership in the different spheres of social life. He has drawn the fullest "ideal-typical" description of charismatic personalities and activities from the religious and political spheres,[38] and has presented there some of the obvious differences between the charismatic qualities or orientations in these two spheres. Thus, the prophet or the mysta-gogue, different as they are in their basic orientations, have to be able especially to organize purely symbolic-emotive spheres and to restructure the emotional components of personality, while the political leader has to exhibit different qualities or orientations, in combining a symbolic ordering of the *social* stability with more detailed daily problems of administration.[39]

Similarly, although less explicitly, we find allusions to or illus-trations of the charismatic qualities needed by the innovator in the legal or economic fields. Throughout his work on sociology of law, Weber's analysis points out the specific characteristic of the legal conception of order as differing in both its symbolic and organizational implications from the political or the religious, although they are, of course, often very closely interrelated.[40] Perhaps of special interest here are Weber's analyses of the eco-nomic entrepreneur, in general, and of the modern capitalist, in particular. Through his analysis of the relation between Protes-tantism and capitalism, he attempts to show that even in this

---

38   See chapters 2 and 6 below.
39   See chapter 6 below.
40   See chapter 3 below.

seemingly most "material" of all social spheres, real change, innovation, or transformation are greatly dependent not only on the objective forces of the market or of production but on a charismatic reformulation of the *meaning* of economic activities.[41] All these are only allusions or indications for further research. But they point out in a general way that such differences between the charismatic qualities most appropriate to different institutional spheres, are rooted both in the difference in the organizational needs and problems of these spheres as well as in the specific symbolic problems, or problems of symbolic order inherent in each such sphere. One major structural meeting point between these two is the nature of the quest for participation in the central aspects of each such institutional sphere, that is of participation in those aspects of such spheres which seem to be most fundamental, most closely related to the essence of cosmic, cultural, or social order.

Weber's works also point out that the nature of the symbolic and organizational problems, and hence the nature of the charismatic qualities necessary for finding new appropriate answers to these problems, differs not only between different institutional spheres but also in different types of societies, between a primitive country and a great historical Empire, between a traditional religious community and a modern scientific organization. Moreover, the nature of these problems may well change under the very impact of such different charismatic personalities, and of the new institutional settings set up by them. All these constitute problems for further research, problems with regard to which sociological research has not yet fully taken up Weber's challenge.

VIII

But whatever the results of such researches will be concerning such differences between different institutional spheres and between different societies, the very formulation of this problem implies the existence of some quest for such order and

41   *The Protestant Ethic and the Spirit of Capitalism.*

for participation in those symbols, organizations, and frameworks in which this order may be embedded. This in turn raises the questions of the nature of the quest for such participation and of the relations between the center or centers and the periphery, especially in terms of the aspiration of members of a society to participate in such centers and the possibilities of access to them. In Weber's own work the nature of such centrality has not, paradoxically enough, been fully explored in its relation to the political and religious fields. In a way, Weber took it for granted. He took up more fully the structural aspects and implications of such centrality in his analysis of social stratification. Although greatly influenced by Weber, subsequent analyses of stratification have not fully caught up with the implications of his work. The central concept in later sociological analysis of stratification, largely derived from Weber, is that of prestige.[42] As is well known, prestige has been presented in most analyses of stratification as one of the three major dimensions of stratification, power and wealth being the other two. But at the same time prestige was the least analytically specified dimension. Both the bases (or criteria) of prestige and the structural implications of its differential distribution have been abundantly described but not fully explored in their basic analytical implications. They were to some extent taken for granted, often subsumed under, or related to, the concept of "style of life," which often served, like the concept of prestige itself, as a sort of general residual category in the studies of stratification.

However, important implications for these problems can be derived from Weber's own work and from the preceding analysis of charisma. Among the most important of these implications is that the sources of prestige, of the deference which people render to others, are rooted not only in their organizational (power, economic, etc.) positions, but also in their differential proximity to those areas which constitute the institutional foci of charisma, that is, the various types of centers (political, cultural, etc.) and in the degree of their participation in those areas. But if the

[42]   Max Weber, *Theory of Social and Economic Organization*, pp. 393–94.

roots of prestige are to a large extent defined through such differential and varied participation in the charismatic foci of institutions and symbols, then the *control* of the degree of such participation, of the access to these centers, becomes a crucial aspect of
social structure in general and of stratification in particular. In
this way prestige is no longer manifest only in symbolic difference
and behavior, as many analysts other than Weber have sometimes
assumed, but in addition, it implies control of the differential
access to participation in such centers. Hence, such participation
is not only a goal in its own right and may also become a medium
of exchange through which other goals, other media, such as
money or power, may be obtained. This insight opens up many
additional problems in sociological analysis which may be elucidated by further research.

IX

Throughout the preceding discussion I have continuously
alluded to the distinction between the ordinary and the charismatic, a distinction which seems to be implicit in Weber's approach and in the later derivations from it, and have assumed that
both are basic components of any concrete social relation, organization, or macrosociety, and that both are present in any process
of institution building. I have not, however, explicated the nature
of this distinction between the ordinary and the charismatic and
of the relations between them. We may start perhaps by attempting
to see what was Weber's own approach to this problem.

Weber's most general exposition of the relations between the
ordinary and the charismatic was probably given in his definition
of the relations between "interests" and ideas. In Mommsen's
translation:[43]

"Interests" (material and ideal) directly govern the acts of men.
Nevertheless, "views of life" created by ideas, have frequently, as
pointed, indicated the lines along which the dynamic power of interest propels action. The "view of life" will determine from what and
for what one wants to be—be it said—can be "saved." Whether from
political or social bondage to some messianic future kingdom, or from

43   *International Social Science Journal*, p. 30.

some absolute evil and bondage to some Messianic future Kingdom on this side of the grave, or from absolute evil or bondage to sin into a perpetual free state of bliss in the bosom of some divine Father; or from the chains of the finite and the threat of Hell manifested in pain, disease and death into ever-lasting bliss in some earthly or paradisal future existence?

A somewhat more detailed definition of the various ordinary or routine aspects of social relations can be found in those parts of Weber's work, in the well-known passages in *Wirtschaft u. Gesellschaft,* translated in *Theory of Social and Economic Organization,* in which are given his conceptions of human activity in general and of social relations in particular, which were of such crucial importance in the development of sociological thought. "Social" action is defined by him as "action oriented to the past, present or future behaviour of others," while "social relationships denotes the behavior of a plurality of actors in so far as, in its meaningful content, the action of each takes account of that of others and is oriented in these terms."[44] From this relatively simple yet basic conception, Weber's analysis of social relations and organization gradually branches out in two complementary directions. One is the analysis of the nature of what may be called, in more recent sociological parlance, the systemic properties and exigencies of social relations, organizations, and institutions. The other is the analysis of the major analytical aspects or types of social relations, what we call today the major institutional spheres of a society—economic, political, legal, stratificational, and religious or cultural spheres. Weber builds into his definition the various aspects of social relations in such a way as to bring out the different elements of more complex continuous and stable social relations. It is here that he develops the major orientations of action: *Zweckrational* and *Wertrational,* affective and traditional ones; their crystallization into different types of uniformities, customs, fashion, convention, etc.; the analysis of the major types of solidarity, communal, and associational relations.[45] In a similar vein he brings out the second aspect of

---

44   *Theory of Social and Economic Organization,* pp. 102–7.
45   *Theory of Social and Economic Organization,* pp. 104–5; and chapter 1 below.

organized social relations, that is, the definition of the different institutional fields of social activity—economic, political, religious. Thus, for instance, "Action will be said to be 'economically oriented' in so far as according to its subjective meaning . . . it is concerned with the satisfaction of a desire for 'utilities.' Economic action is a peaceful use of actor's control over resources which is primarily economically oriented."[46] Then he shows how each such aspect of social behavior, each institutional sphere, creates, beyond the very general needs or systemic problems which are inherent in any social relation or organization as such, the specific problems of each type of social relation or institutional sphere. Thus, in economic relationships the organizational problems of division of labor, of mobilization and processing of resources, and of marketing the products of economic activities are most predominant. In political relations it is the assurance of loyalty and of administrative expertise that are of crucial importance; likewise with regard to other major spheres of society, religion, culture, education, or social stratification. The specificity of each such aspect or sphere lies in the nature of its systemic interdependence on the other sphere or aspects. Any such aspect constitutes a problem from the point of view of its own sphere, as for instance the maintenance of order or of obedience for the political sphere constitutes a prerequisite from the point of view of economic activities.

True enough, with regard to all these problems, we do not find in Weber's work a systematic analysis of the "nature" or "problems" of social organization or system in terms of "systemic" needs or exigencies, and it is perhaps in this field of the exploration of the systemic qualities of social relations that the greatest advances and progress beyond Weber have been attained in sociological analysis.[47] But it is out of these indications that the

[46]   *Ibid.*, p. 145. For the definition of the political action, of "imperative control," see *ibid.*, p. 139.

[47]   See especially Talcott Parsons, *The Structure of Social Action;* *idem., The Social System* (Glencoe, Ill.: Free Press, 1951); Talcott Parsons, Robert F. Bales, and Edward A. Shils, *Working Papers in the Theory of Action* (Glencoe, Ill.: Free Press, 1953).

nature of the distinction between the charismatic and the ordinary can be brought out. The non-charismatic or the ordinary activity seems to compromise those activities which are oriented to various discrete, segregated goals not connected together in some great pattern or "grand design," which are oriented mostly to goals which are instrumental to other goals or aims, and which are also mostly oriented toward adaptation to any given natural or human social environment and to persistence and survival within it.

A very large part of the daily activities of human beings in society is probably organized in such a way and oriented to such goals. The implementation of such goals necessitates the development of many specific organizations and structures which tend to coalesce into varied institutional patterns. In a sense, it is they that constitute the crux of the institutional nexus wihin any society. And yet, as we have seen above, all these goals and patterns tend also to become somehow related to a broader, fundamental order, rooted in the charismatic and focused around the different situations and centers in which the charismatic is more fully embedded and symbolized. True enough, in these various "orderly" activities oriented to discrete, instrumental, and adaptive goals, the charismatic orientations may become greatly attenuated; they may become very distant and the various concrete goals may be perceived as rather distant from the sources of the charismatic. And yet some such relation or orientation to the charismatic tends somehow to persist in these activities, even if in the most attenuated and passive form.

This persistence of the charismatic is rooted in some of the basic characteristics of the major institutional spheres which have been stressed by Weber. Throughout his work he indicated that the political, economic, legal, religious, and stratification spheres are not only organizational aspects of any relatively stable social relations or institutions; they do not only constitute means for the attainment of goals which are, as it were, outside of them. They constitute also realms of goals, of "ends" of potentially broader, overall "meanings" toward which the activities of the participants are oriented. They constitute part of, to use Geertz's nomenclature,[48] the "symbolic" templates for the organization of social psychological processes.

X

It is this double aspect of social institutions—their organizational exigencies on the one hand, and their potential close relations to the realm of meaning on the other—which may provide us with clues as to how the ordinary and the charismatic are continuously interwoven in the process of institution building. New organizations and institutions are built up through the varied responses and interactions between people or groups who, in order to implement their varied goals, undertake processes of exchange with other people or groups.[49] But the individuals or groups who engage in such exchange are not randomly distributed in any society. Such exchange takes place between people placed in structurally different positions, that is, in different cultural, political, family, or economic positions which in themselves may be outcomes of former processes of institutional exchange. Their very aspirations and goals are greatly influenced by their differential placement in the social structure and the power they can thereby exercise. The resources that are at their disposal—for instance manpower, money, political support, or religious identification—are determined by these institutional positions and vary according to the specific characteristics of the different institutional spheres. These resources serve as means for the implementation of various individual goals, and they may in themselves become goals or objects of individual endeavors. Such resources always evince some tendency to become organized in specific, autonomous ways, according to the specific features of their different institutional spheres; this can be seen, for instance, in the fact that the exchange

[48]   C. Geertz, "Ideology as a Cultural System," in D. Apter, ed., *Ideology and Discontent* (Glencoe, Ill.: Free Press, 1964), pp. 62–63.
[49]   S. N. Eisenstadt, "The Study of Processes of Institutionalization, Institutional Change and Comparative Institutions," in his *Essays on Comparative Institutions* (New York: John Wiley, 1965), especially pp. 16–40.

of economic resources is organized in any society in different ways than that of political or religious resources.

But the terms of exchange, that is, the criteria of what is regarded as valuable or of which goals or means are equivalent, are at least partially derived from the charismatically charged goals and norms, from the broader and more fundamental conceptions of order. Hence, in the crystallization of institutional frameworks a crucial part is played by those people who evince a special capacity to set up broad orientations, to propound new norms, and to articulate new goals. In other words, institution building is based not only on the direct or indirect exchange of various institutional resources between individuals or groups which attempt to use these resources for the implementation of their discrete, instrumental goals but in addition also necessarily includes interaction between, on the one hand, those individuals or groups who are able to articulate varied collective goals and crystallize acceptable norms and, on the other, those individuals, groups, or strata that are willing to accept such regulations and norms. The crystallization and upholding of such norms seemingly provides some sort of response to a felt need for some general stability and order and attests to the ability to provide some broader meaning to more varied specific needs which may arise in different situations. Hence, the capacity to create and crystallize such broader symbolic orientations and norms, to articulate various goals, to establish organizational frameworks, and to mobilize the resources necessary for all these purposes (for example, the readiness to invest in the appropriate activities) is a basic aspect or constituent of the flow of institution building in any society.

It is presumably people in such positions or aspiring to them who are especially sensitive to what may be called societal "needs," and who may be oriented to taking care of those activities and problems which may be necessary for the maintenance and continuity of given social organizations and institutions. But they are always interested in the maintenance and continuity not only, or mainly, of the society in general, but of some specific type of organization which best suits their own orientation and goals.

The concrete institutional framework which emerges in any given situation is thus the outcome not only of some general appropriateness of a given solution proposed by such people to the groups acting in this situation but also of the relative success of different competing groups of such leaders and entrepreneurs who attempt to impose, through a mixture of coercive, manipulative, and persuasive techniques, their own particular solution on a given situation.[50]

But the availability of such people, or their concrete orientation and activities, is not always assured or determined by the development of the varying needs among different groups in a society. Moreover, even if some such groups or entrepreneurs do emerge, the ways in which they will act and the type of institutions they will build are not given or predetermined because the concrete broad orientations and goals which they may develop may vary greatly. The development of such "charismatic" personalities or groups constitutes perhaps the closest social analogy to "mutation," and the degree of their ability to forge out a viable symbolic and institutional order may be an important factor in the process of survival, or selection of different societies or cultural creations. This analysis brings out again the fact that a crucial aspect of the charismatic personality or group is not only the possession of some extraordinary, exhilarating qualities, but also the ability, through these qualities, to reorder and reorganize both the symbolic and cognitive order which is potentially inherent in such orientations and goals and the institutional order in which these orientations become embodied; and that the process of routinization of charisma is focused around the ability to combine the reordering of these two spheres of human existence and of social life.

We know as yet very little either about conditions of development of such entrepreneurial, charismatic people, of their psychological and behavioral attributes, and about the conditions under which they may be capable of implementing their vision. There exist several descriptive studies and data, but as yet but relatively

[50]   S. N. Eisenstadt, "The Study of Processes of Institutionalization."

few systematic analyses,[51] which deal with this problem or with the nature of the processes through which specific charismatic symbols and orientations become embedded in the more ordinary institutional activities and exchange. All these aspects still constitute an essential part of the challenge of Weber's work for modern sociological analysis—and problems for further analysis and research.

XI

The preceding reformulation of the nature of the charismatic and of its relations to the process of institution building implies a reorientation of the major questions about the nature of the social order. Instead of assuming that such order is given by some external force imposed on the individuals and on their own wishes, or that order is only an outcome of their rational premeditated selfish evaluation of their interests or of the exigencies of social economic division of labor engendered by these interests, this formulation emphasizes that the existence of some quest for some such order, not only in organizational but also in symbolic terms, is among the basic wishes or orientations of people.[52] In other words, this implies that among the "egoistical" wishes of human beings a very important part is comprised by their quest for and conception of the symbolic order, of the "good society," and of the quest for participation in such an order. This quest constitutes a basic, although differential, component in the whole panorama of social and cultural activities, orientations, and goals. It calls for rather special response from those able to respond to this quest, and this response tends to be located in specific, distinct

51   See, for one attempt in this direction, David C. McClelland, *The Achieving Society* (Princeton, N.J.: Princeton University Press, 1961) and also the various works on religious and social movements cited above.
52   Talcott Parsons, "Culture and the Social System: Introduction," in Talcott Parsons, *et al.*, *Theories of Society* (Glencoe, Ill.: Fress Press, 1961), 2:963–93 and S. N. Eisenstadt, "Sociological Theory," in *International Encyclopaedia of Social Sciences* (New York: Macmillan, 1968).

parts or aspects of the social structure. The structural focus of this quest is to be found in the charismatic activity, group symbol, or institutional focus.[53]

But this quest for participation in such order does not necessarily constitute a focus of consensus—it may easily become a focus of dissension, conflict, and change. As we have seen, the initial assumption of many of the sociological analyses of charisma has stressed its disruptive effects, that is, its contribution to the destruction of existing institutions and to social change. The recognition that charismatic activities or symbols constitute also a part or aspect of the solidary institutional framework does not negate this basic insight; it only enables us to approach the relation between charisma and social change and transformation in a much more differentiated and systematic way. It enables us to see that the very quest for participation in a meaningful order may be related to processes of change and transformation; that it may indeed constitute, at least in certain circumstances, the very focus of processes of social transformation.

The starting point of this approach is the recognition of the inherent tension that the charismatic builds into any social system. Bendix has put this succinctly in the following words:

> . . . each system of domination remains "valid" only within limits, and when these are ignored or exceeded for too long, the type of domination either changes its form or loses its original, authoritative character altogether. Charisma is a "supernatural quality of a personality," which in its original meaning proved itself by miracles, thereby gaining recognition from the ruled and in turn making that recognition their sacred duty. True, charismatic authority unconditionally demands acceptance of its claims to legitimacy, but the belief in its legitimacy is by no means unconditional. For, if the test of this claim remains forever wanting, then the "person favoured by the gift

---

53   This is, of course, not dissimilar from Durkheim's exposition of the "social" as distinct from the "individual" volitions, except that his very emphasis on this distinction did not facilitate the perception of the commitment to the social order as *one* among the individuals' "egoistical" wishes. See Emile Durkheim, *The Elementary Forms of Religious Life* (Glencoe, Ill.: Free Press, 1954) ; *idem., Sociological Philosophy* (Glencoe, Ill.: Free Press, 1953).

of grace is shown to be forsaken by his God or his magic or heroic powers."

Seen from the point of view of the ruled, this means that their belief in the lawful claims of this authority may well spring from "enthusiasm" or "necessity and hope" [*Begeisterung oder Not und Hoffnung*] but that secretly they desire or hope for tests which will confirm its legitimacy. It is certainly characteristic of charismatic domination that the ruler interprets these desires or hopes as disbelief and demands unconditional acceptance of this interpretation. But the desire of the ruler for signs of confirmation remains. The same applies to the other types. The legitimacy of traditional domination rests on the "sanctity of established structures and powers of command" [*Heiligkeit altüberkommener Ordnungen und Herrengewalten*]; accordingly, authority is exercised by the person of the ruler, not by means of status. However, the commands of a ruler are legal not only when they conform to tradition but also when they proceed from the "arbitrary will of the master. Hence, traditional domination possesses a charismatic duality of rule that is tradition bound as well as free from tradition." This freedom from tradition refers to the arbitrary will of the personal ruler, who may have the right to ignore tradition since his will is absolute, but who can thereby imperil his own traditional authority. . . .[54]

Perhaps the most important aspect of this analysis is that such tensions or conflicts are rooted not only in the clashes of different interests in a society, but in the differential distribution of the charismatic in the symbolic and organizational aspects of any institutional system, and that it is the combination of this differential distribution and conflicts of interests that may indeed constitute a major focus both of continuity and of potential changes in any social system.

Whatever the success of the attempt of any institutional entrepreneurs to establish and legitimize common norms in terms of common values and symbols, these norms are probably never fully accepted by the entire society. Most groups tend to exhibit some autonomy in terms of their attitudes toward these norms and in terms of their willingness or ability to provide the resources

[54]   R. Bendix, "Max Weber's Sociology Today," *International Social Science Journal*, 17 (1965) :19–20.

demanded by the given institutionalized system. For very long periods of time a great majority of the members of a given society or parts thereof may be identified to some degree with the values and norms of the given system and willing to provide it with the resources it needs; however, other tendencies also develop.[55] Some groups may be greatly opposed to the very premises of the institutionalization of a given system, may share its values and symbols only to a very small extent, and may accept these norms only as the least among evils and as binding on them only in a very limited sense. Others may share these values and symbols and accept the norms to a greater degree, but may look on themselves as the more truthful depositories of these same values. They may oppose the concrete levels at which the symbols are institutionalized by the élite in power, and may attempt to interpret them in different ways. Others may develop new interpretations of existing symbols and norms and strive for a change in the very bases of the institutional order. Hence, any institutional system is never fully "homogeneous" in the sense of being fully accepted or accepted to the same degree by all those participating in it. These different orientations to the central symbolic spheres may all become foci of conflict and of potential institutional change.

Even more important is the fact, that whatever the initial attitudes of any given group to the basic premises of the institutional system, these may greatly change after the initial institutionalization of the system. Any institutionalization necessarily entails efforts to maintain, through continuous attempts to mobilize resources from different groups and individuals, the boundaries of the system, and to maintain the legitimacy of its values, symbols, and norms. But continuous implementation of these policies may affect the positions of various groups in the society, and give rise to continuous shifts both in the balance of power among them and in their orientations to the existing institutional system. Thus, the very nature of the setting up of an institutional system; of the differential distribution in a society of the major charismatic

---

[55]   For further exposition see S. N. Eisenstadt, "Institutionalization and Change," *American Sociological Review*, 29 (April 1964) :235–47.

symbols and centers and of differential access to them, creates
the possibility that "anti-systems" may develop within the system;
and while such anti-systems may often remain latent for very long
periods, they may also constitute important foci of change under
propitious conditions. The existence of such contradictions or
conflicts among the different symbolic centers and institutional
spheres and among different groups in their relations to these
centers does not, of course, preclude the possibility that the system
will maintain its internal subboundaries more or less continuously, and achieve accommodation or partial insulation of different subsystems. But the possibility of conflict and potential change
is always present, rooted in the very process of crystallization and
maintenance of institutional systems, of the structure of their
symbolic and organizational centers, of the relations of these
centers to the periphery's conceptions of centrality. These various
forces naturally differ between different institutional spheres and
between different societies—and should constitute foci of further
research—but the very sensitivity of these forces and the tendency
to change are inherent in all of them.

XII

It is here that we come to what is probably the central
focus of the analysis of the relations between charisma and social
change—the analysis of the self-transformative power of charismatic symbols and activities and of their power to transform the
societies in which they are embedded. In what respect does such
transformation differ from simple secular trends of structural or
demographic change? What types of charisma are able to transform societies, and under what conditions? As with regard to so
many other fields, although this problem is inherent in his work,
Weber himself did not explicate it fully. However, the preceding
analysis of some of the implications of his work may indeed help
us in identifying the central characteristics of such transformation.

A central aspect of any process of social transformation is the
recrystallization of the centers of any society—not only of the
rates of access to such centers but of the very content and the

definition of the central charismatic symbols and of the modes of participation in them. It is perhaps this dimension which constitutes the difference between stychic, structural, or demographic change on the one hand, and the transformation of social systems on the other. Throughout his studies Weber looked for those movements which are indeed capable of effecting such far-reaching institutional transformation. Which types of charismatic activities and orientations do indeed have such transformative powers, and under what conditions are they effective? In all his studies of systems—political, legal, or religious—Weber dealt with this problem. But only in his famous treatment of the problem of the Protestant Ethic did he come close to a full systematic exposition of this problem, although even here most of the broader analytical implications have to be extrapolated from Weber's presentation.

What is it in the Protestant Ethic or symbolic system and in the social setting of its bearers that facilitated its development in the direction of such transformation? On the basis of both Weber's analysis and of later work in this field,[56] it may be suggested that the aspects of the Protestant value orientation which are most important from the point of view of our discussion are: (1) its strong combination of "this-worldliness" and transcendentalism —a combination which orients the individual behavior to activities within this world but at the same time does not ritually sanctify any of them, either through a mystic union or any ritual act, as the final point of religious consummation or worthiness; (2) the strong emphasis on individual activism and responsibility; (3) the unmediated, direct relation of the individual to the sacred and to the sacred tradition, an attitude which, while strongly emphasizing the importance and direct relevance of the sacred and of tradition, yet minimizes the extent to which this relation and individual commitment to the sacred can be mediated by any ritual institutions, organization, or professional textual exegesis.

[56] S. N. Eisenstadt, "The Protestant Ethic Thesis in an Analytical and Comparative Framework" in S. N. Eisenstadt, ed., *The Protestant Ethic and Modernization* (New York: Basic Books, 1968) and the various essays in this collection.

Hence it opens up the possibility of continuous redefinition and reformulation of the nature and scope of such tradition—a possibility which is further enhanced by the strong transcendental attitude which minimizes the sacredness of any "here and now."

These religious orientations of Protestantism and Protestants, especially Calvinists, were not, however, confined only to the realm of the sacred. They were closely related to, and manifest in two major orientations in most Protestant groups' conception of the social reality and of their own place in it, that is, in what may be called their status images and orientations. Most of the Protestant groups developed a combination of these two types of orientations. First was their openness toward the wider social structure, rooted in their "this-worldly" orientation which was not limited only to the economic sphere but which also, as we shall see later, could be expressed in other social fields. Second, they were characterized by a certain autonomy and self-sufficiency from the point of view of their status orientation. They were relatively little dependent for the validity of their own status symbols and identity on the existing political and religious centers. These aspects of the Protestant Ethic were conducive to its great transformative capacities and the ability of the Protestant groups to influence the behavior of people and the shape of institutions.

But the extent to which these beliefs could indeed become influential depended to no small degree on the social organization of their bearers and of the broader social setting within which they were operative. Here, in general, it seems that such transformative tendencies of religious and ideological systems and movements tend to be greater the more they are borne and promoted by relatively cohesive élites with a strong sense of self-identity, and especially by secondary élites which, while somewhat distant from the central ruling one, yet maintain positive solidary orientations to the center and are not entirely alienated from the preexisting élites and from some of the broader groups of the society. Similarly, the effects of such transformative potentials of the religious and ideological movements tend to be greater insofar as the existing social structure in its totality or in those of its parts within which these religious and ideological developments are intensive, is characterized by some extent of autonomy or distinctiveness of the social, cultural, and political orders, and by relatively strong cohesiveness of the more active broader strata. Similarly, the existence within broader social strata and family groups of relatively strong internal cohesion of some status-autonomy and flexibility, together with openness toward the center, may greatly facilitate the internal transformation of these groups and the development within them of positive orientations to the new centers and of willingness to provide these centers with the support and resources they need. Conversely, insofar as such autonomy is small, and the self-closeness of wider social groups is great, they can, through withdrawal of resources and through the development of intensive unregulated demands on the center, undermine the very conditions of the functioning of these new institutional centers.

It was by virtue of the combination of these value orientation and structural characteristics that there emerged within the Protestant countries some psychosocial mechanisms through which the influence of ideas on behavior became operative. The most important of these seems to have been a new type of personal identity that has a degree of reference to a given collective identity. This identity generated a very strong, although flexible, emphasis on the personal commitment to do something for the community. At the same time, this identity was not entirely bound up with any one political system, state, or community. In addition, it entailed a strong connection between personal commitment, personal identity, and several types of institutional exchange activities—economic, political, administrative. In this way it opened up the connections between these personal and collective identities to a great variety of concrete, "this-worldly" activities.

Thus, if we look closely at Weber's Protestant Ethic thesis, we see that, whatever the correctness of its details, it is an attempt to explain the transformation of a whole social or cultural system through a change in the type of relations between personal and collective identities, on the one hand, and between them and various concrete institutional activities on the other hand. And it was this symbolic transformation which thus facilitated, even if it did not cause, the emergence of some new institutional developments. This review of Weber's Protestant Ethic thesis shows us that it contains important indications, not only about the particular historical problem it deals with, but also for the analysis of processes of transformation of social structures in general and for the relative importance in such processes of the charismatic push as against the purely secular or stychic structural organizational or demographic change.[57]

XIII

The preceding analysis brings us to the problem of the relation between charisma and social change in comparative and historical perspective and to the problems of charisma in the modern world. Weber based his vast comparative work on great concern with problems of historical development in general and with the historical development of Western civilization in particular. Moreover, one of his major analytical contributions to sociological-historical studies lay in the way in which he was able to insert the temporal dimension as a category inherent in the very structure of social systems and of social life—not as something irrelevant to the major forms of social organization, or as an external force directing the destiny of societies. He saw that within social systems there is some inherent tendency to change over time and to perceive such change as an element of their cosmic, social, or cultural order. Did he, however, find beyond the great variety of concrete instances of change any guiding principles according to which the variety of different types of institutionalized relations, groups, or collectivities tend to develop in different societies?

True enough, Weber's analytical and methodological work was to a large extent oriented against much of current idealistic

[57]   In Weber's own work perhaps the most interesting analysis of this problem is that of the causes of decline of the Ancient World. See Max Weber, "Die sozialen Gründe des Untergangs der antiken Kultur," in his *Gesammelte Aufsätze zur Sozial- und Wirtschaftsgeschichte* (Tübingen, 1924), pp. 289–311.

German *Geistesgeschichte,* historical materialism, and evolutionism alike; out of this reaction he developed a rather negative attitude to any overall scheme of human history—and this negative attitude became transferred to much of modern sociological theory. Therefore, it may seem as if many of the concrete types of social organizations which he classified in this grandiose enterprise of explanation of the nature of historical development, built allegedly in his "ideal-typical" way, are constructed either in a "random," "ad-hoc" way, or in terms of the historical uniqueness of each society, without there being any more general guiding principle in the classification of these types. However, this would be only a partial view. Just as he was opposed to any definite and comprehensive schemes of universal history, so he was also opposed to historicism.[58] Hence, beyond the great variety of the concrete types with which he dealt, there tend to emerge some broader and more inclusive considerations and orientations. On the one hand, most of the major types which he constructs in almost all institutional spheres are distinguished according to what may be called the extent or scope of their structural differentiation. Thus, for instance, he distinguishes between primitive and historical communities, between small patrimonial and larger more complex historical bureaucratic structures. Moreover, a close examination of Weber's writings, especially his *Sociology of Religion* or in his studies in political sociology,[59] readily reveals that he draws most of his illustrations of the development of charismatic types and of their institutionalization from periods of what may be called breakthroughs from one stage of social differentiation to another. In all these studies he indeed fully recognized the importance of structural differentiation in creating the conditions under which new problems of order and meaning emerge and in creating, through some charismatic innovation or transformation, the possibilities of breakthroughs to new types of social organization. But at the same time he was fully aware that

[58]   For a somewhat different view see R. Bendix, "Max Weber's Sociology Today," *International Social Science Journal,* 17 (1965):9–22.
[59]   See Talcott Parsons, introduction to Max Weber, *Sociology of Religion.*

neither the general possibilities of the institutionalization of such breakthroughs nor their concrete contours are fixed simply through the very process of structural differentiation. Nor did he assume that there will necessarily be any similarity in the nature of the contents of the charismatic innovation which may develop in different societies at similar stages of differentiation. However, he certainly did not negate the possibility of comparing such contents. Indeed, it can be legitimately claimed that most of his historical-sociological work was devoted to such comparisons. Although the starting points of many of his comparisons were rooted in specific historical situations, this did not negate the comparability of the problems and the wider comparative applicability of the concepts he developed—rather it emphasized such applicability.

It is in this context that the general problem of the contents of the various charismatic symbols and orders as they evolve in different types of societies and in human history becomes pertinent. Are the different types of charismatic activities and symbols which tend to develop in different types of societies purely random and accidental, or can one discern here also some more general pattern or trend? Or, to use again more modern sociological parlance, can one discern some trends or comparable developments, not only with regard to the process of structural differentiation, but also with regard to the principles of integrative order that tend to develop at similar stages of differentiation? It seems that Weber did indeed assume that some such comparable developments and problems can be discussed in a meaningful way. He focused this comparison in his work around the concepts of rationality and *Entzauberung*.[60]

The concept of rationality, as developed by Weber, has, as is well known, at least two different, even if interrelated, meanings or aspects. One is the more formal, organizational meaning, the *Zweckrationalität*, later designated by Mannheim as "functional

---

[60]   *Entzauberung* refers mainly to the "contents" aspects of culture and describes the demystification of the conception of the world connected with growing secularism, with the rise of science, and with growing routinization of education and culture.

rationality.''[61] This aspect of rationality is very closely related to the process of structural differentiation and complexity; in many ways the possibility of the extension of such rationality is largely necessitated by the very process of structural differentiation. But rationality pertains also to the realm of meaning, of values, of *Wertrationalität*, of what has been called in Mannheim's terminology "substantive rationality." This rationality can be manifest and its scope may continuously expand in all spheres of human endeavor, of culture, and of social organization—in religion, education, and scientific endeavor, in political life, and in social and interpersonal relations. The broadening of the' scope of substantive rationality becomes especially evident at the most crucial breakthroughs from one level of social differentiation to another. It becomes evident in the nature of the problems posed and answers given in all these spheres of human endeavor and social organization. At each such breakthrough there emerges the tendency, or at least the potentiality, to extend the scope of rationality in posing the basic problems of the major symbolic and cultural spheres in a more rational way, that is, in terms of growing abstraction in their formulation, of growing logical coherence and general phrasing, and to some extent also in the ranges of answers attempted to these problems.[62] Such possibilities of extension of rationality are to a very large extent tantamount to the extension of the potential of human creativity and ranges of human freedom. True enough, Weber does not succumb to the optimistic postulate that all charismatic answers (or types of order) which develop at the time of any such breakthroughs are always necessarily rational. On the contrary, in several parts of his work, and especially in his *Sociology of Religion* and in the analysis of modern political developments, he does most clearly postulate the

[61]   K. Mannheim, *Man and Society in an Age of Reconstruction* (London: K. Paul, Trench, & Trubner, 1940).

[62]   Weber did not assume that the concrete contents of the questions raised, and especially of the answers given, in such situations was necessarily the same in different societies. But at the same time his work does imply the comparability of such answers and questions in terms of extension of rationality.

possibility of what may be called irrational answers—magical, demonic, constrictive of freedom, and "alienated"—to such new problems. But although the establishment of such rational ordering is not automatically assured in any situation of growing social differentiation, yet the possibility of such development indeed lies within it. Such extension of substantive rationality is not confined to articulation of abstract ideas. It has some very definite structural-organizational consequences implied in the preceding analysis of the nature of the charismatic in general and of the routinization of charisma as a major aspect of institution building in particular.

Seemingly charismatic qualities, with their emphasis on the extraordinary, constitute the very opposite of any rationality. But it is indeed within the realm of meaning that the greatest potentials for the extension of substantive rationality are to be found. Therefore, given the basic affinity of the charismatic to the provisions of order and of meaning, such extension of rationality may indeed be very often the outcome of charismatic activities of personalities and groups who evolve new conceptions of order and goals and who are able to routinize these charismatic qualities and orientations through the crystallization of new societal centers and institutional frameworks.

But this charismatic, transformative extension of substantive rationality contains also many paradoxes, especially in its relations to problems of creativity and freedom in general and in modern societies in particular. According to many prevalent views, the most important constrictions on such freedom and creativity, and hence also the most important sources of change, instability, and alienation in societies in general and in modern societies in particular, are rooted in the contradiction between the structural implications of the two types of rationality. According to such views, these constrictions are rooted in the contradiction between the liberating or creative potential given in the extension of substantive rationality as against the potentials for constriction and compulsion inherent in the organizational extension of functional rationality most clearly seen in the growing tendencies to bureaucratization inherent in modern societies. This contradiction, which has sometimes been seen as parallel to that between the liberating power of charisma as against the more constrictive tendencies of the process of its routinization, is not abated by the fact that often it is the very extension of substantive rationality (as evident, for instance, in the broadening of the scope of the political community, or in the extension of scientific knowledge) that creates the conditions for the intensification of the more constrictive tendencies inherent in extension of functional rationality in almost all spheres of human endeavor and of social life.

And yet, these more constrictive conflict-oriented tendencies which develop in modern societies are not only rooted in the extension of functional rationality and in its structural effects. They may also be rooted, especially in the modern world, in some of the aspects or consequences of the very extension of substantive rationality—and especially in those aspects of this expansion which are most closely related to *Entzauberung*—a concept which denotes the demystification and secularization of the world, the attenuation of charisma, and a sort of charismatic neutralism. The tendencies to such *Entzauberung* are rooted not only in the encounter between the dynamic qualities of charisma on the one hand and the organizational exigencies of its selective institutionalization in the social structure on the other hand, but also in some of the very basic implications of the transformation of the creative, charismatic qualities of the centers and of the quest for participation in these centers as they developed in modern societies.

Weber indicated, even if often only implicitly, that modern societies are characterized not only by certain structural characteristics such as growing differentiation and specialization, which necessarily lead to specialization of bureaucratization, but also by far-reaching changes in the structure of the social centers, in the pattern of participation in them, and of access to them. Modern societies are also characterized by a growing differentiation and autonomy of various centers, growing demands for access to them, and for participation in them, culminating in tendencies toward the obliteration of the symbolic difference between center and periphery. He sensed, even if he did not make it fully explicit, that, while in the first stages of modernity most social tensions and conflicts evolved around the broadening of the scope of participation and channels of access to the centers, later, when many of these goals may have indeed been attained, a new series of problems, tensions, and conflicts may arise. These problems are focused around the possibility of development of growing apathy toward the very central values, symbols, and centers, not because of the lack of possibility of access to them but because of, in a sense, overaccess to them. Thus the demystification of the world may come about in the phenomenon that the attainment of participation in many centers may indeed be meaningless, that the centers may lose their mystery, that the King may be naked indeed. This process may, of course, be greatly intensified by the increase of bureaucratization and of growing specialization in modern societies. But it would be erroneous to assume that these trends in themselves would produce such new problems and tensions. Rather it is the combination of these trends to bureaucratization with the changing structure of participation in the centers that may account for these results of demystification and of the routinization of the charismatic in modern settings.

This approach may add a new dimension to studies of change and conflict and may throw an additional light both on the study of the great social and political trends and problems of the twentieth century and on various contemporary phenomena, such as the new types of revolt of youth, or the transformation of problems of leisure. The common denominator of all these phenomena is in the attempts to dissociate one's predisposition to the charismatic from the societal centers and from the traditions of the larger culture and to associate it more and more only with the sphere of private, face-to-face relations and activities—and even here to emphasize tendencies toward secularization, negation of purity, and dissociation of seriousness and any normative commitment. Here again all these are only preliminary illustrations or indications. But they, as all the other preliminary indications outlined in the preceding paragraphs, are derived from that reformu-

lation of the basic problems of social order which can be derived
from a reexamination of Weber's work. They all constitute a challenge and guide line for further sociological analysis.

S. N. Eisenstadt

Introduction to the Selections from Weber's Writings

The following selections from Weber's writings focus
on the problems presented in the introductory essay, especially
that of the relations between charisma and institutionalization.
Accordingly I shall first present Weber's general conception of
social action, social relations, and social organization and his
general conception of charisma and of its institutional implications, that is, the relation between charisma and routinization of
charisma or charisma and discipline. Next follow excerpts from
his writings dealing with the major institutional spheres—the
political sphere (in which the most general definition of charisma
can be found), the legal and the economic spheres, the sphere of
social stratification and organization (with special emphasis on
the city), and the spheres of religion and culture.

In each of these spheres I shall attempt to present Weber's
conception of the nature of the specific organizational problems
of this sphere, of the ways in which the charismatic elements may
become incorporated into the organization, and of the ways in
which charisma becomes related to the major developments of and
changes in these spheres throughout the history of human society
up to the specific problems of modernity.

I. Charisma and the Structure of Social Relations

In order to understand the place of charisma in institution building according to Weber's theory, it is first necessary to present the basic concepts he uses in the analysis of the structure of the social action, social relations, social organization, and legitimate order. Thus Weber's concept of charisma is first examined in relation to more regular social relations.

1

GENERAL DEFINITIONS
OF SOCIAL ACTION
AND SOCIAL RELATIONSHIP

The Definitions of Sociology and of Social Action

SOCIOLOGY (in the sense in which this highly ambiguous word is used here) is a science which attempts the interpretive understanding of social action in order thereby to arrive at a causal explanation of its course and effects. In "action" is included all human behaviour when and in so far as the acting individual attaches a subjective meaning to it. Action in this sense may be either overt or purely inward or subjective; it may consist of positive intervention in a situation, or deliberately refraining from such intervention or passively acquiescing in the situation. Action is social in so far as, by virtue of the subjective meaning attached to it by the acting individual (or individuals), it takes account of the behaviour of others and is thereby oriented in its course.[1]

Reprinted by permission of The Macmillan Company from *Theory of Social and Economic Organization* by Max Weber, trans. A. R. Henderson and Talcott Parsons. Copyright 1947 by Talcott Parsons.

[1]   In this series of definitions Weber employs several important terms which need discussion. In addition to *Verstehen*, which has already been commented upon, there are four important ones: *Deuten, Sinn, Handeln,* and *Verhalten. Deuten* has generally been translated as "interpret." As used by Weber in this context it refers to the interpretation of subjective states of mind and the meanings which can be imputed as intended by an actor. Any other meaning of the word "interpretation" is irrelevant to Weber's discussion. The term *Sinn* has generally been translated as "meaning"; and its variations, particularly the corresponding adjectives,

Social action, which includes failure to act and passive acquiescence, may be oriented to the past, present or expected future behaviour of others. Thus it may be motivated by revenge for a past attack, defence against present, or measures of defence against future aggression. The "others" may be individual persons, and may be known to the actor as such, or may constitute an indefinite plurality and may be entirely unknown as individuals. Thus "money" is a means of exchange which the actor accepts in payment because he orients his action to the expectation that a large but unknown number of individuals he is personally unacquainted with will be ready to accept it in exchange on some future occasion.

Not every kind of action, even of overt action, is "social" in the sense of the present discussion. Overt action is non-social if it is oriented solely to the behaviour of inanimate objects. Subjective attitudes constitute social action only so far as they are oriented to the behaviour of others. For example, religious behaviour is not social if it is simply a matter of contemplation or of solitary prayer. The economic activity of an individual is only social if, and then only in so far as, it takes account of the behaviour of someone else. Thus very generally in formal terms it becomes social in so far as the actor's actual control over economic goods is respected by others. Concretely it is social, for instance, if in

---

sinnhaft, sinnvoll, sinnfremd, have been dealt with by appropriately modifying the term meaning. The reference here again is always to features of the content of subjective states of mind or of symbolic systems which are ultimately referable to such states of mind.

The terms *Handeln* and *Verhalten* are directly related. *Verhalten* is the broader term referring to any mode of behaviour of human individuals, regardless of the frame of reference in terms of which it is analyzed. "Behaviour" has seemed to be the most appropriate English equivalent. *Handeln,* on the other hand, refers to the concrete phenomenon of human behaviour only in so far as it is capable of "understanding," in Weber's technical sense, in terms of subjective categories. The most appropriate English equivalent has seemed to be "action." This corresponds to the editor's usage in *The Structure of Social Action* and would seem to be fairly well established. "Conduct" is also closely similar and has sometimes been used. *Deuten, Verstehen,* and *Sinn* are thus applicable to human behaviour only in so far as it constitutes action or conduct in this specific sense.—T. PARSONS

relation to the actor's own consumption the future wants of others are taken into account and this becomes one consideration affecting the actor's own saving. Or, in another connexion, production may be oriented to the future wants of other people.

Not every type of contact of human beings has a social character; this is rather confined to cases where the actor's behaviour is meaningfully oriented to that of others. For example, a mere collision of two cyclists may be compared to a natural event. On the other hand, their attempt to avoid hitting each other, or whatever insults, blows, or friendly discussion might follow the collision, would constitute "social action."

Social action is not identical either with the similar actions of many persons or with action influenced by other persons. Some types of reaction are only made possible by the mere fact that the individual acts as part of a crowd. Others become more difficult under these conditions. Hence it is possible that a particular event or mode of human behaviour can give rise to the most diverse kinds of feeling—gaiety, anger, enthusiasm, despair, and passions of all sorts—in a crowd situation which would not occur at all or not nearly so readily if the individual were alone. But for this to happen there need not, at least in many cases, be any meaningful relation between the behaviour of the individual and the fact that he is a member of a crowd. It is not proposed in the present sense to call action "social" when it is merely a result of the effect on the individual of the existence of a crowd as such and the action is not oriented to that fact on the level of meaning. At the same time the borderline is naturally highly indefinite. In such cases as that of the influence of the demagogue, there may be a wide variation in the extent to which his mass clientele is affected by a meaningful reaction to the fact of its large numbers; and whatever this relation may be, it is open to varying interpretations.

But furthermore, mere "imitation" of the action of others, such as that on which Tarde has rightly laid emphasis, will not be considered a case of specifically social action if it is purely reactive so that there is no meaningful orientation to the actor imitated. The borderline is, however, so indefinite that it is often hardly possible to discriminate. . . .

The Types of Social Action

Social action, like other forms of action, may be classified in the following four types according to its mode of orientation (1) in terms of rational orientation to a system of discrete individual ends (*zweckrational*), that is, through expectations as to the behaviour of objects in the external situation and of other human individuals, making use of these expectations as "conditions" or "means" for the successful attainment of the actor's own rationally chosen ends; (2) in terms of rational orientation to an absolute value (*wertrational*); involving a conscious belief in the absolute value of some ethical, aesthetic, religious, or other form of behaviour, entirely for its own sake and independently of any prospects of external success; (3) in terms of affectual orientation, especially emotional, determined by the specific affects and states of feeling of the actor; (4) traditionally oriented, through the habituation of long practice.[2] . . .

2   The two terms *zweckrational* and *wertrational* are of central significance to Weber's theory, but at the same time present one of the most difficult problems to the translator. Perhaps the keynote of the distinction lies in the absoluteness with which the values involved in *Wertrationalitaet* are held. The sole important consideration to the actor becomes the realization of the value. In so far as it involves ends, rational considerations, such as those of efficiency, are involved in the choice of means. But there is no question either of rational weighing of this end against others, nor is there a question of "counting the cost" in the sense of taking account of possible results other than the attainment of the absolute end. In the case of *Zweckrationalitaet*, on the other hand, Weber conceives action as motivated by a plurality of relatively independent ends, none of which is absolute. Hence, rationality involves on the one hand the weighing of the relative importance of their realization, on the other hand, consideration of whether undesirable consequences would outweigh the benefits to be derived from the projected course of action. It has not seemed possible to find English terms which would express this distinction succinctly. Hence the attempt has been made to express the ideas as clearly as possible without specific terms.

It should also be pointed out that, as Weber's analysis proceeds, there is a tendency of the meaning of these terms to shift, so that *Wertrationalitaet* comes to refer to a system of ultimate ends, regardless of the degree of their absoluteness, while *Zweckrationalitaet* refers primarily

The Concept of Social Relationship

The term "social relationship" will be used to denote the behaviour of a plurality of actors in so far as, in its meaningful content, the action of each takes account of that of the others and is oriented in these terms. The social relationship thus *consists* entirely and exclusively in the existence of a *probability* that there will be, in some meaningfully understandable sense, a course of social action. For purposes of definition there is no attempt to specify the basis of this probability.

Thus, as a defining criterion, it is essential that there should be at least a minimum of mutual orientation of the action of each to that of the others. Its content may be of the most varied nature; conflict, hostility, sexual attraction, friendship, loyalty, or economic exchange. It may involve the fulfilment, the evasion, or the denunciation of the terms of an agreement; economic, erotic, or some other form of "competition"; common membership in national or class groups or those sharing a common tradition of status. In the latter cases mere group membership may or may not extend to include social action; this will be discussed later. The definition, furthermore, does not specify whether the relation of the actors is "solidary" or the opposite. . . .

Modes of Orientation of Social Action

It is possible in the field of social action to observe certain empirical uniformities. Certain types, that is, of action which correspond to a typically appropriate subjective meaning attribu-

---

to considerations respecting the choice of means and ends which are in turn means to further ends, such as money. What seems to have happened is that Weber shifted from a classification of ideal types of action to one of elements in the structure of action. In the latter context "expediency" is often an adequate rendering of *Zweckrationalitaet*. This process has been analyzed in the editor's *Structure of Social Action*, chap. xvi.

The other two terms *affektuell* and *traditional* do not present any difficulty of translation. The term affectual has come into English psychological usage from the German largely through the influence of psychoanalysis.

table to the same actors, are found to be wide-spread, being frequently repeated by the same individual or simultaneously performed by many different ones. Sociological investigation is concerned with these typical modes of action. Thereby it differs from history, the subject of which is rather the causal explanation of important individual events; important, that is, in having an influence on human destiny.

An actually existent probability of a uniformity in the orientation of social action will be called "usage" (*Brauch*), if and in so far as the probability of its maintenance among a group of persons is determined entirely by its actual practice. Usage will be called "custom" (*Sitte*) if the actual performance rests on long familiarity. On the other hand, a uniformity of action may be said to be "determined by the exploitation of the opportunities of his situation in the self-interest of the actor." This type of uniformity exists in so far as the probability of its empirical performance is determined by the purely rational (*zweckrational*) orientation of the actors to similar ulterior expectations.[3] . . .

The Concept of Conflict

A social relationship will be referred to as "conflict" in so far as action within it is oriented intentionally to carrying out

3   In the above classification as well as in some of those which follow, the terminology is not standardized either in German or in English. Hence, just as there is a certain arbitrariness in Weber's definitions, the same is true of any corresponding set of definitions in English. It should be kept in mind that all of them are modes of orientation of action to patterns which contain a normative element. "Usage" has seemed to be the most appropriate translation of *Brauch* since, according to Weber's own definition, the principal criterion is that "it is done to conform with the pattern." There would also seem to be good precedent for the translation of *Sitte* by "custom." The contrast with fashion, which Weber takes up in his first comment, is essentially the same in both languages. The term *Interessenlage* presents greater difficulty. It involves two components: the motivation in terms of self-interest and orientation to the opportunities presented by the situation. It has not seemed possible to use any single term to convey this meaning in English and hence, a more roundabout expression has had to be resorted to.—T. PARSONS

the actor's own will against the resistance of the other party or parties. The term "peaceful" conflict will be applied to cases in which actual physical violence is not employed. A peaceful conflict is "competition" in so far as it consists in a formally peaceful attempt to attain control over opportunities and advantages[4] which are also desired by others. A competitive process is "regulated" competition to the extent that its ends and means are oriented to an order. The struggle, often latent, which takes place between human individuals or types of social status, for advantages and for survival, but without a meaningful mutual orientation in terms of conflict, will be called "selection." In so far as it is a matter of the relative opportunities of individuals during their own lifetime, it is "social selection"; in so far as it concerns differential chances for the survival of inherited characteristics, "biological selection." . . .

Types of Solidary Social Relationships

A social relationship will be called "communal"[5] if and so far as the orientation of social action, whether in the individual case, on the average or in the pure type, is based on a subjective feeling of the parties, whether affectual or traditional, that they belong together. A social relationship will, on the other hand, be called "associative" if and in so far as the orientation of social

4   *Chancen.* This usage of the term is to be distinguished from that translated as probability or likelihood.

5   The two types of relationship which Weber distinguishes in this section he himself calls *Vergemeinschaftung* and *Vergesellschaftung.* His own usage here is an adaptation of the well-known terms of Tœnnies, *Gemeinschaft* and *Gesellschaft,* and has been directly influenced by Tœnnies' work. Though there has been much discussion of them in English, it is safe to say that no satisfactory equivalent of Tœnnies' terms have been found. In particular, "community" and either "society" or "association" are unsatisfactory, since these terms have quite different connotations in English. In the context, however, in which Weber uses his slightly altered terms, that of action within a social relationship, the adjective forms "communal" and "associative" do not seem to be objectionable. Their exact meanings should become clear from Weber's definitions and comments.—T. PARSONS

action within it rests on a rationally motivated adjustment of interests or a similarly motivated agreement, whether the basis of rational judgment be absolute values or reasons of expediency. It is especially common, though by no means inevitable, for the associative type of relationship to rest on a rational agreement by mutual consent. In that case the corresponding action is, at the pole of rationality, oriented either to a rational belief in the binding validity of the obligation to adhere to it, or to a rational expectation that the other party will live up to it.[6] . . .

A social relationship, regardless of whether it is communal or associative in character, will be spoken of as "open" to outsiders if and in so far as participation in the mutually oriented social action relevant to its subjective meaning is, according to its system of order, not denied to anyone who wishes to participate and who is actually in a position to do so. A relationship will, on the other hand, be called "closed" against outsiders so far as, according to its subjective meaning and the binding rules of its order, participation of certain persons is excluded, limited or subjected to conditions. Whether a relationship is open or closed may be determined traditionally, affectually, or rationally in terms of values or of expediency. It is especially likely to be closed, for rational reasons, in the following type of situation: a social relationship may provide the parties to it with opportunities for the satisfaction of various interests, whether the satisfactions be spiritual or material, whether the interest be in the end of the relationship as such or in some ulterior consequence of participation, or whether it is achieved through co-operative action or by a compromise of interests. If the participants expect that the admission of others will lead to an improvement of their situation, an improvement in degree, in kind, in the security or the value of the satisfaction, their interest will be in keeping the relationship open. If, on the other hand, their expectations are of improving their position by monopolistic tactics, their interest is in a closed relationship. . . .

[6]   This terminology is similar to the distinction made by Ferdinand Toennies in his pioneering work, *Gemeinschaft und Gesellschaft;* but for his purposes, Toennies has given this distinction a rather more specific meaning than would be convenient for purposes of the present discussion.

2

THE CONCEPT OF
LEGITIMATE ORDER

The Concept of Legitimate Order

ACTION, especially social action which involves social relationships, may be oriented by the actors to a *belief* (*Vorstellung*) in the existence of a "legitimate order." The probability that action will actually empirically be so oriented, will be called the "validity" (*Geltung*) of the order in question.[1] The legitimacy of an order may be guaranteed or upheld in two principal ways (1) from purely disinterested motives,[2] which may in turn be (a) purely affectual, consisting in an emotionally determined loyalty; or (b) may derive from a rational belief in the absolute validity of the order as an expression of ultimate values,[3] whether they be moral, aesthetic or of any other type; or (c) may originate

---

[1]   The term *Gelten* has already been dealt with. From the very use of the term in this context it is clear that by "order" (*Ordnung*) Weber here means a *normative* system. The pattern for the concept of "order" is not, as in the law of gravitation, the "order of nature," but the order involved in a system of law.

[2]   The antithesis *innerlich-aeusserlich* as applied to elements of motivation does not have any direct English counterpart. The aspect of *innerlich*, however, which is most important in the present context seems to be adequately expressed by the term "disinterested." The essential point is that the object of such motivation is valued for its own sake or as a direct expression of ultimate values rather than as a means to some "ulterior" end.—T. PARSONS

[3]   *Wertrational.*

in religious attitudes, through the belief in the dependence of some condition of religious salvation on conformity with the order; (2) also or entirely by self-interest, that is, through expectations of specific ulterior consequences, but consequences which are, to be sure, of a particular kind.

A system of order will be called *convention* so far as its validity is externally guaranteed by the probability that deviation from it within a given social group will result in a relatively general and practically significant reaction of disapproval. Such an order will be called *law* when conformity with it is upheld by the probability that deviant action will be met by physical or psychic sanctions aimed to compel conformity or to punish disobedience, and applied by a group of men especially empowered to carry out this function.[4] . . .

The Bases of Legitimacy of an Order

Legitimacy may be ascribed to an order by those acting subject to it in the following ways:—

(a) By tradition; a belief in the legitimacy of what has always existed; (b) by virtue of affectual attitudes, especially emotional, legitimising the validity of what is newly revealed or a model to imitate; (c) by virtue of a rational belief in its absolute value,[5] thus lending it the validity of an absolute and final commitment; (d) because it has been established in a manner which is recognized to be *legal*. This legality may be treated as legitimate in either of two ways: on the one hand, it may derive from a voluntary agreement of the interested parties on the relevant terms. On the other hand, it may be imposed on the basis of what is held to be a legitimate authority over the relevant persons and a corresponding claim to their obedience.

Representation and Responsibility

The order which governs a social relationship by tradition or by virtue of its legal establishment, may determine that certain

4   On the concept of convention, see beside Ihering, op. cit., and Weigelin, op. cit., F. Toennies, *Die Sitte.*
5   *Wertrational.*

types of action of some of the parties to the relationship will have consequences which affect the others. It may be that all are held responsible for the action of *any* one. In that case they will be spoken of as "solidary" members. Or, on the other hand, the action of certain members, the "representatives," may be binding upon the others. That is, the resulting advantages will go to them, they will enjoy the benefits, or conversely bear the resulting losses.

Representative authority[6] may be conferred in accordance with the binding order in such a way (a) that it is completely appropriated in all its forms—the case of "independent" authority; or (b) it may be conferred in accordance with particular criteria, permanently or for a limited term; or (c) it may be conferred by specific acts of the members or of outside persons, again permanently or for a limited term—the case of appointment. There are many different conditions which determine the ways in which social relationships, communal or associative, develop relations of solidarity, or of representation. In general terms, it is possible only to say that one of the most decisive is the extent to which the action of the group is oriented to violent conflict or to peaceful exchange as its end. Besides these, many special circumstances, which can only be discussed in a detailed analysis, may be of crucial importance. It is not surprising that this development is least conspicuous in groups which pursue purely ideal ends by peaceful means. Often the degree of closure against outsiders is closely related to the development of solidarity or of representation. But this is by no means always the case. . . .

The Concept of "Corporate Group" and Its Types

A social relationship which is either closed or limits the admission of outsiders by rules, will be called a "corporate group" (*Verband*)[7] so far as its order is enforced by the action of specific individuals whose regular function this is, of a chief or "head"

---

6   *Vertretungsgewalt.*

7   The term *Verband*, which is one of the most important in Weber's scheme has, in the technical sense defined in this paragraph, been translated as "corporate group." "Association" has not been used because it does not imply the formal differentiation between a head or chief and

(*Leiter*) and usually also an administrative staff. These function-aries will normally also have representative authority. The incum-bency of a directing position or participation in the functions of the administrative staff constitute "governing authority" (*Regier-ungsgewalt*). This may be appropriated, or it may be assigned in accordance with the binding rules of the association according to specific criteria or procedures. It may be assigned permanently, for a term, or for dealing with a specific situation. "Corporate action" is either the action of the administrative staff, which by virtue of its governing or representative authority is oriented to carrying out the terms of its order, or it is the action of the members as directed by the administrative staff.

It is indifferent, so far as the concept is concerned, whether the relationship is of a communal or associative character. It is sufficient for there to be a person or persons in authority—the head of a family, the executive committee of an association, a managing director, a prince, a president, the head of a church—whose action is concerned with carrying into effect the order governing the corporate group. This criterion is decisive because it is not merely a matter of action which is *oriented* to an order, but which is specifically directed to its *enforcement*. Sociologically this adds to the concept of a closed social relationship, a further element, which is of far-reaching empirical importance. For by no means every closed communal or associative relationship is a corporate group. For instance, this is not true of an erotic relationship or of a kinship group without a formalized system of authority. . . .

Types of Order and Organization Governing Action in Corporate Groups

A system of order which governs corporate action as such, will be called an "administrative" order (*Verwaltungsordnung*).

---

ordinary members. A "corporation" is, from this point of view, one specific kind of corporate group. The term *Leiter* is not readily trans-latable. "Chief" has most frequently been used because it seems to have less objectionable connotations than any alternative. Thus we speak of the "chief" of the medical staff of a hospital and use the term in other similar connexions.

A system of order which governs other kinds of social action and thereby protects the actors in enjoyment of the benefits derived from their relation to the order, will be called a "regulative" order (*Regulierungsordnung*). So far as a corporate group is solely oriented to the first type of order, it will be called an "administrative" group (*Verwaltungsverband*). So far as it is oriented to the second type, a "regulative" group. . . .

An "organization" (*Betrieb*) is a system of continuous purposive activity of a specified kind. A "corporate organization" (*Betriebsverband*) is an associative social relationship characterized by an administrative staff devoted to such continuous purposive activity.

A "voluntary association" (*Verein*) is a corporate group originating in a voluntary agreement and in which the established order claims authority over the members only by virtue of a personal act of adherence.

A "compulsory association" (*Anstalt*) is a corporate group the established order of which has, within a given specific sphere of activity, been successfully imposed on every individual who conforms with certain specific criteria.[8] . . .

Power, Authority, and Imperative Control

"Power" (*Macht*) is the probability that one actor within a social relationship will be in a position to carry out his own will despite resistance, regardless of the basis on which this probability rests.

"Imperative control" (*Herrschaft*)[9] is the probability that a

[8] *Betrieb* is a word which in German has a number of different meanings in different contexts. It is only in the present technical use that it will be translated by "organization." It should, however, be recognized that the term "organization" is here also used in a technical sense which conforms with Weber's explicit definition. The distinction of *Verein* and *Anstalt* is one of far-reaching sociological importance, which has not become established in English usage. The terms "voluntary" and "compulsory" association seem to be as adequate any available terms. They should, however, not be interpreted on a common-sense basis but referred to Weber's explicit definitions.—T. PARSONS

[9] As has already been noted, the term *Herrschaft* has no satisfactory English equivalent. The term "imperative control," however, as used by

command with a given specific content will be obeyed by a given group of persons. "Discipline" is the probability that by virtue of habituation a command will receive prompt and automatic obedience in stereotyped forms, on the part of a given group of persons.

1. The concept of power is highly comprehensive from the point of view of sociology. All conceivable qualities of a person and all conceivable combinations of circumstances may put him in a position to impose his will in a given situation. The sociological concept of imperative control must hence be more precise and can only mean the probability that a *command* will be obeyed.

2. The concept of "discipline" includes the "habituation" characteristic of uncritical and unresisting mass obedience.

The existence of imperative control turns only on the actual presence of one person successfully issuing orders to others; it does not necessarily imply either the existence of an administrative staff, or, for that matter, of a corporate group. It is, however, uncommon to find it not associated with at least one of these. A corporate group, the members of which are by virtue of their membership subjected to the legitimate exercise of imperative control, that is to "authority," will be called an "imperatively co-ordinated" group[10] (*Herrschaftsverband*). . . .

It goes without saying that the use of physical force is neither the sole, nor even the most usual, method of administration of political corporate groups. On the contrary, their heads have employed all conceivable means to bring about their ends. But, at the same time, the threat of force, and in case of need its actual use, is the method which is specific to political associations and is

---

N. S. Timasheff in his *Introduction to the Sociology of Law* is close to Weber's meaning and has been borrowed for the most general purposes. In a majority of instances, however, Weber is concerned with *legitime Herrschaft*, and in these cases "authority" is both an accurate and a far less awkward translation. *Macht*, as Weber uses it, seems to be quite adequately rendered by "power."—T. PARSONS

10   In this case imperative control is confined to the legitimate type, but it is not possible in English to speak here of an "authoritarian" group. The citizens of any state, no matter how "democratic" are "imperatively controlled" because they are subject to law.—T. PARSONS

always the last resort when others have failed. Conversely, physical force is by no means limited to political groups even as a legitimate method of enforcement. It has been freely used by kinship groups, household groups, the medieval guilds under certain circumstances, and everywhere by all those entitled to bear arms. In addition to the fact that it uses, among other means, physical force to enforce its system of order, the political group is further characterized by the fact that the authority of its administrative staff is claimed as binding within a territorial area and this claim is upheld by force. Whenever corporate groups which make use of force are also characterized by the claim to territorial jurisdiction, such as village communities or even some household groups, federations of guilds or of trade unions, they are by definition to that extent political groups.

3

THE SOCIOLOGY OF
CHARISMATIC AUTHORITY

The General Character of Charisma

BUREAUCRATIC AND patriarchal structures are antagonistic in many ways, yet they have in common a most important peculiarity: permanence. In this respect they are both institutions of daily routine. Patriarchal power especially is rooted in the provisioning of recurrent and normal needs of the workaday life. Patriarchal authority thus has its original locus in the economy, that is, in those branches of the economy that can be satisfied by means of normal routine. The patriarch is the 'natural leader' of the daily routine. And in this respect, the bureaucratic structure is only the counter-image of patriarchalism transposed into rationality. As a permanent structure with a system of rational rules, bureaucracy is fashioned to meet calculable and recurrent needs by means of a normal routine.

The provisioning of all demands that go beyond those of everyday routine has had, in principle, an entirely heterogeneous, namely, a *charismatic*, foundation; the further back we look in history, the more we find this to be the case. This means that the 'natural' leaders—in times of psychic, physical, economic, ethical, religious, political distress—have been neither officeholders nor incumbents of an 'occupation' in the present sense of the word, that is, men who have acquired expert knowledge and who serve

From *Max Weber: Essays in Sociology*, edited and translated by H. H. Gerth and C. Wright Mills. Copyright 1946 by Oxford University Press, Inc. Reprinted by permission.

for remuneration. The natural leaders in distress have been holders of specific gifts of the body and spirit; and these gifts have been believed to be supernatural, not accessible to everybody. The concept of 'charisma' is here used in a completely 'value-neutral' sense.

The capacity of the Irish culture hero, Cuchulain, or of the Homeric Achilles for heroic frenzy is a manic seizure, just as is that of the Arabian berserk who bites his shield like a mad dog—biting around until he darts off in raving bloodthirstiness. For a long time it has been maintained that the seizure of the berserk is artificially produced through acute poisoning. In Byzantium, a number of 'blond beasts,' disposed to such seizures, were kept about, just as war elephants were formerly kept. Shamanist ecstasy is linked to constitutional epilepsy, the possession and the testing of which represents charismatic qualification. Hence neither is 'edifying' to our minds. They are just as little edifying to us as is the kind of 'revelation,' for instance, of the Sacred Book of the Mormons, which, at least from an evaluative standpoint, perhaps would have to be called a 'hoax.' But sociology is not concerned with such questions. In the faith of their followers, the chief of the Mormons has proved himself to be charismatically qualified, as have 'heroes' and 'sorcerers.' All of them have practiced their arts and ruled by virtue of this gift (charisma) and, where the idea of God has already been clearly conceived, by virtue of the divine mission lying therein. This holds for doctors and prophets, just as for judges and military leaders, or for leaders of big hunting expeditions.

It is to his credit that Rudolf Sohm brought out the sociological peculiarity of this category of domination-structure for a historically important special case, namely, the historical development of the authority of the early Christian church. Sohm performed this task with logical consistency, and hence, by necessity, he was one-sided from a purely historical point of view. In principle, however, the very same state of affairs recurs universally, although often it is most clearly developed in the field of religion.

In contrast to any kind of bureaucratic organization of offices, the charismatic structure knows nothing of a form or of an ordered procedure of appointment or dismissal. It knows no regulated 'career,' 'advancement,' 'salary,' or regulated and expert training of the holder of charisma or of his aids. It knows no agency of control or appeal, no local bailiwicks or exclusive functional jurisdictions; nor does it embrace permanent institutions like our bureaucratic 'departments,' which are independent of persons and of purely personal charisma.

Charisma knows only inner determination and inner restraint. The holder of charisma seizes the task that is adequate for him and demands obedience and a following by virtue of his mission. His success determines whether he finds them. His charismatic claim breaks down if his mission is not recognized by those to whom he feels he has been sent. If they recognize him, he is their master—so long as he knows how to maintain recognition through 'proving' himself. But he does not derive his 'right' from their will, in the manner of an election. Rather, the reverse holds: it is the *duty* of those to whom he addresses his mission to recognize him as their charismatically qualified leader.

In Chinese theory, the emperor's prerogatives are made dependent upon the recognition of the people. But this does not mean recognition of the sovereignty of the people any more than did the prophet's necessity of getting recognition from the believers in the early Christian community. The Chinese theory, rather, characterizes the charismatic nature of the *monarch's position,* which adheres to his *personal* qualification and to his *proved* worth.

Charisma can be, and of course regularly is, qualitatively particularized. This is an internal rather than an external affair, and results in the qualitative barrier of the charisma holder's mission and power. In meaning and in content the mission may be addressed to a group of men who are delimited locally, ethnically, socially, politically, occupationally, or in some other way. If the mission is thus addressed to a limited group of men, as is the rule, it finds its limits within their circle.

In its economic sub-structure, as in everything else, charismatic domination is the very opposite of bureaucratic domination. If bureaucratic domination depends upon regular income, and hence at least *a potiori* on a money economy and money taxes, charisma lives in, though not off, this world. This has to be properly understood. Frequently charisma quite deliberately shuns the possession of money and of pecuniary income *per se*, as did Saint Francis and many of his like; but this is of course not the rule. Even a pirate genius may exercise a 'charismatic' domination, in the value-neutral sense intended here. Charismatic political heroes seek booty and, above all, gold. But charisma, and this is decisive, always rejects as undignified any pecuniary gain that is methodical and rational. In general, charisma rejects all rational economic conduct.

The sharp contrast between charisma and any 'patriarchal' structure that rests upon the ordered base of the 'household' lies in this rejection of rational economic conduct. In its 'pure' form, charisma is never a source of private gain for its holders in the sense of economic exploitation by the making of a deal. Nor is it a source of income in the form of pecuniary compensation, and just as little does it involve an orderly taxation for the material requirements of its mission. If the mission is one of peace, individual patrons provide the necessary means for charismatic structures; or those to whom the charisma is addressed provide honorific gifts, donations, or other voluntary contributions. In the case of charismatic warrior heroes, booty represents one of the ends as well as the material means of the mission. 'Pure' charisma is contrary to all patriarchal domination (in the sense of the term used here). It is the opposite of all ordered economy. It is the very force that disregards economy. This also holds, indeed precisely, where the charismatic leader is after the acquisition of goods, as is the case with the charismatic warrior hero. Charisma can do this because by its very nature it is not an 'institutional' and permanent structure, but rather, where its 'pure' type is at work, it is the very opposite of the institutionally permanent.

In order to do justice to their mission, the holders of charisma, the master as well as his disciples and followers, must stand outside the ties of this world, outside of routine occupations, as well as outside the routine obligations of family life. The statutes of the Jesuit order preclude the acceptance of church offices; the members of orders are forbidden to own property or, according to the original rule of St. Francis, the order as such is forbidden to do so. The priest and the knight of an order have to live in celibacy, and numerous holders of a prophetic or artistic charisma are actually single. All this is indicative of the unavoidable separation from this world of those who partake ('κλῆρος') of charisma. In these respects, the economic conditions of participation in charisma may have an (apparently) antagonistic appearance, depending upon the type of charisma—artistic or religious, for instance—and the way of life flowing from its meaning. Modern charismatic movements of artistic origin represent 'independents without gainful employment' (in everyday language, rentiers). Normally such persons are the best qualified to follow a charismatic leader. This is just as logically consistent as was the medieval friar's vow of poverty, which demanded the very opposite.

Foundations and Instability of Charismatic Authority

By its very nature, the existence of charismatic authority is specifically unstable. The holder may forego his charisma; he may feel 'forsaken by his God,' as Jesus did on the cross; he may prove to his followers that 'virtue is gone out of him.' It is then that his mission is extinguished, and hope waits and searches for a new holder of charisma. The charismatic holder is deserted by his following, however, (only) because pure charisma does not known any 'legitimacy' other than that flowing from personal strength, that is, one which is constantly being proved. The charismatic hero does not deduce his authority from codes and statutes, as is the case with the jurisdiction of office; nor does he deduce his authority from traditional custom or feudal vows of faith, as is the case with patrimonial power.

The charismatic leader gains and maintains authority solely by proving his strength in life. If he wants to be a prophet, he must perform miracles; if he wants to be a war lord, he must perform heroic deeds. Above all, however, his divine mission must 'prove' itself in that those who faithfully surrender to him must fare well. If they do not fare well, he is obviously not the master sent by the gods.

This very serious meaning of genuine charisma evidently stands in radical contrast to the convenient pretensions of present rulers to a 'divine right of kings,' with its reference to the 'inscrutable' will of the Lord, 'to whom alone the monarch is responsible.' The genuinely charismatic ruler is responsible precisely to those whom he rules. He is responsible for but one thing, that he personally and actually be the God-willed master.

During these last decades we have witnessed how the Chinese monarch impeaches himself before all the people because of his sins and insufficiencies if his administration does not succeed in warding off some distress from the governed, whether it is inundations or unsuccessful wars. Thus does a ruler whose power, even in vestiges and theoretically, is genuinely charismatic deport himself. And if even this penitence does not reconcile the deities, the charismatic emperor faces dispossession and death, which often enough is consummated as a propitiatory sacrifice.

Meng-tse's (Mencius') thesis is that the people's voice is 'God's voice' (according to him the *only* way in which God speaks!) has a very specific meaning: if the people cease to recognize the ruler, it is expressly stated that he simply becomes a private citizen; and if he then wishes to be more, he becomes a usurper deserving of punishment. The state of affairs that corresponds to these phrases, which sound highly revolutionary, recurs under primitive conditions without any such pathos. The charismatic character adheres to almost all primitive authorities with the exception of domestic power in the narrowest sense, and the chieftain is often enough simply deserted if success does not remain faithful to him.

The subjects may extend a more active or passive 'recognition' to the personal mission of the charismatic master. His power rests upon this purely factual recognition and springs from faithful devotion. It is devotion to the extraordinary and unheard-of, to what is strange to all rule and tradition and which therefore is viewed as divine. It is a devotion born of distress and enthusiasm.

Genuine charismatic domination therefore knows of no ab-

stract legal codes and statutes and of no 'formal' way of adjudication. Its 'objective' law emanates concretely from the highly
personal experience of heavenly grace and from the god-like
strength of the hero. Charismatic domination means a rejection
of all ties to any external order in favor of the exclusive glorification of the genuine mentality of the prophet and hero. Hence,
its attitude is revolutionary and transvalues everything; it makes
a sovereign break with all traditional or rational norms: 'It is
written, but I say unto you.'

The specifically charismatic form of settling disputes is by
way of the prophet's revelation, by way of the oracle, or by way
of 'Solomonic' arbitration by a charismatically qualified sage.
This arbitration is determined by means of strictly concrete and
individual evaluations, which, however, claim absolute validity.
Here lies the proper locus of 'Kadi-justice' in the proverbial—
not the historical—sense of the phrase. In its actual historical
appearance the jurisdiction of the Islamic Kadi is, of course,
bound to sacred tradition and is often a highly formalistic
interpretation.

Only where these intellectual tools fail does jurisdiction rise
to an unfettered individual act valuing the particular case; but
then it does indeed. Genuinely charismatic justice always acts in
this manner. In its pure form it is the polar opposite of formal
and traditional bonds, and it is just as free in the face of the
sanctity of tradition as it is in the face of any rationalist deductions
from abstract concepts.

This is not the place to discuss how the reference to the *aegum
et bonum* in the Roman administration of justice and the original
meaning of English 'equity' are related to charismatic justice
in general and to the theocratic Kadi-justice of Islamism in particular.[1] Both the *aegum et bonum* and 'equity' are partly the
products of a strongly rationalized administration of justice and
partly the product of abstract conceptions of natural law. In any
case the *ex bona fide* contains a reference to the 'mores' of
business life and thus retains just as little of a genuine irrational

---

1   Frederick II of Prussia.

justice as does, for instance, the German judge's 'free discretion.'

Any kind of ordeal as a means of evidence is, of course, a derivative of charismatic justice. But the ordeal displaces the personal authority of the holder of charisma by a mechanism of rules for formally ascertaining the divine will. This falls in the sphere of the 'routinization' of charisma, with which we shall deal below.

Charismatic Kingship

In the evolution of political charisma, kingship represents a particularly important case in the historical development of the charismatic legitimization of institutions. The king is everywhere primarily a war lord, and kingship evolves from charismatic heroism.

In the form it displays in the history of civilized peoples, kingship is not the oldest evolutionary form of 'political' domination. By 'political' domination is meant a power that reaches beyond and which is, in principle, distinct from domestic authority. It is distinct because, in the first place, it is not devoted to leading the peaceful struggle of man with nature; it is, rather, devoted to leading in the violent conflict of one human community with another.

The predecessors of kingship were the holders of all those charismatic powers that guaranteed to remedy extraordinary external and internal distress, or guaranteed the success of extraordinary ventures. The chieftain of early history, the predecessor of kingship, is still a dual figure. On the one hand, he is the patriarchal head of the family or sib, and on the other, he is the charismatic leader of the hunt and war, the sorcerer, the rainmaker, the medicine man—and thus the priest and the doctor—and finally, the arbiter. Often, yet not always, such charismatic functions are split into as many special holders of charisma. Rather frequently the chieftain of the hunt and of war stands beside the chieftain of peace, who has essentially economic functions. In contrast to the latter, the chieftain of war acquires his charisma by proving his heroism to a voluntary following in successful raids leading to victory and booty. Even the royal Assyrian inscriptions enumerate booties of the hunt and cedars from Lebanon—dragged along for building purposes—alongside figures on the slain enemies and the size of the walls of conquered cities, which are covered with skins peeled off the enemies.

The charismatic position (among primitives) is thus acquired without regard to position in the sibs or domestic communities and without any rules whatsoever. This dualism of charisma and everyday routine is very frequently found among the American Indians, for instance, among the Confederacy of the Iroquois, as well as in Africa and elsewhere.

Where war and the big game hunt are absent, the charismatic chieftain—the 'war lord' as we wish to call him, in contrast to the chieftain of peace—is absent as well. In peacetime, especially if elemental calamities, particularly drought and diseases, are frequent, a charismatic sorcerer may have an essentially similar power in his hands. He is a priestly lord. The charisma of the war lord may or may not be unstable in nature according to whether or not he proves himself and whether or not there is any need for a war lord. He becomes a permanent figure when warfare becomes a chronic state of affairs. It is a mere terminological question whether one wishes to let kingship, and with it the state, begin only when strangers are affiliated with and integrated into the community as subjects. For our purposes it will be expedient to continue delimiting the term 'state' far more narrowly.

The existence of the war lord as a regular figure certainly does not depend upon a tribal rule over subjects of other tribes or upon individual slaves. His existence depends solely upon a chronic state of war and upon a comprehensive organization set for warfare. On the other hand, the development of kingship into a regular royal administration does emerge only at the stage when a following of royal professional warriors rules over the working or paying masses; at least, that is often the case. The forceful subjection of strange tribes, however, is not an absolutely indispensable link in this development. Internal class stratification may bring about the very same social differentiation: the charismatic following of warriors develops into a ruling caste. But in every case, princely power and those groups having interests vested in it—that is, the war lord's following—strive for legitimacy as soon as the rule has become stable. They crave for a characteristic which would define the charismatically qualified ruler.[2]

2   The manuscript breaks off here (German Editor).

4

MEANING OF DISCIPLINE

The Definition of Discipline

IT IS the fate of charisma, whenever it comes into the permanent institutions of a community, to give way to powers of tradition or of rational socialization. This waning of charisma generally indicates the diminishing importance of individual action. And of all those powers that lessen the importance of individual action, the most irresistible is *rational discipline*.

The force of discipline not only eradicates personal charisma but also stratification by status groups; at least one of its results is the rational transformation of status stratification.

The content of discipline is nothing but the consistently rationalized, methodically trained and exact execution of the received order, in which all personal criticism is unconditionally suspended and the actor is unswervingly and exclusively set for carrying out the command. In addition, this conduct under orders is uniform. Its quality as the communal action of a *mass* organization conditions the specific effects of such uniformity. Those who obey are not necessarily a simultaneously obedient or an especially large mass, nor are they necessarily united in a specific locality. What is decisive for discipline is that the obedience of a plurality of men is rationally uniform.

Discipline as such is certainly not hostile to charisma or to

From *Max Weber: Essays in Sociology*, edited and translated by H. H. Gerth and C. Wright Mills. Copyright 1946 by Oxford University Press, Inc. Reprinted by permission.

status group honor. On the contrary, status groups that are attempting to rule over large territories or large organizations—the Venetian aristocratic counselors, the Spartans, the Jesuits in Paraguay, or a modern officer corps with a prince at its head—can maintain their alertness and their superiority over their subjects only by means of a very strict discipline. This discipline is enforced within their own group, for the blind obedience of subjects can be secured only by training them exclusively for submission under the disciplinary code. The cultivation of a stereotyped prestige and style of life of a status group, only for reasons of discipline, will have a strongly conscious and rationally intended character. This factor effects all culture in any way influenced by these status communities; we shall not discuss these effects here. A charismatic hero may make use of discipline in the same way; indeed, he must do so if he wishes to expand his sphere of domination. Thus Napoleon created a strict disciplinary organization for France, which is still effective today.

Discipline in general, like its most rational offspring, bureaucracy, is impersonal. Unfailingly neutral, it places itself at the disposal of every power that claims its service and knows how to promote it. This does not prevent bureaucracy from being intrinsically alien and opposed to charisma, as well as to honor, especially of a feudal sort. The berserk with maniac seizures of frenzy and the feudal knight who measures swords with an equal adversary in order to gain personal honor are equally alien to discipline. The berserk is alien to it because his action is irrational; the knight because his subjective attitude lacks matter-of-factness. In place of individual hero-ecstasy or piety, of spirited enthusiasm or devotion to a leader as a person, of the cult of 'honor,' or the exercise of personal ability as an 'art'—discipline substitutes habituation to routinized skill. In so far as discipline appeals to firm motives of an 'ethical' character, it presupposes a 'sense of duty' and 'conscientiousness.' ('Men of Conscience' *versus* 'Men of Honor,' in Cromwell's terms.)

The masses are uniformly conditioned and trained for discipline in order that their optimum of physical and psychic power in attack may be rationally calculated. Enthusiasm and unreserved devotion may, of course, have a place in discipline; every modern conduct of war weighs, frequently above everything else, precisely the 'moral' elements of a troop's endurance. Military leadership uses emotional means of all sorts—just as the most sophisticated techniques of religious discipline, the *exercitia spiritualia* of Ignatius Loyola, do in their way. In combat, military leadership seeks to influence followers through 'inspiration' and, even more, to train them in 'emphatic understanding' of the leader's will. The sociologically decisive points, however, are, first, that everything, and especially these 'imponderable' and irrational emotional factors, are rationally calculated—in principle, at least, in the same manner as one calculates the yields of coal and iron deposits. Secondly, devotion, in its purposefulness and according to its normal content, is of an objective character. It is devotion to a common 'cause,' to a rationally intended 'success'; it does not mean devotion to a person as such—however 'personally' tinged it may be in the concrete instance of a fascinating leader.

The case is different only when the prerogatives of a slaveholder create a situation of discipline—on a plantation or in a slave army of the ancient Orient, on galleys manned by slaves or among prisoners in Antiquity and the Middle Ages. Indeed, the individual cannot escape from such a mechanized organization, for routinized training puts him in his place and compels him to 'travel along.' Those who are enlisted in the ranks are forcibly integrated into the whole. This integration is a strong element in the efficacy of all discipline, and especially in every war conducted in a disciplined fashion. It is the only efficacious element and—as *caput mortuum*—it always remains after the 'ethical' qualities of duty and conscientiousness have failed.

The Origins of Discipline in War

The conflict between discipline and individual charisma has been full of vicissitudes. It has its classic seat in the development of the structure of warfare, in which sphere the conflict is, of course, to some extent determined by the technique of warfare. The kind of weapons—pike, sword, bow—are not necessarily decisive; for all of them allow disciplined as well as individual combat. At the beginning of the known history of the Near East and of the Occident, however, the importation of the horse and probably, to some uncertain degree, the beginning of the predominance of iron for tools have played parts which have been epoch-making in every way.

The horse brought the war chariot and with it the hero driving into combat and possibly fighting from his chariot. The hero has been dominant in the warfare of the Oriental, Indian, and ancient Chinese kings, as well as throughout Occidental societies, including the Celtic. In Ireland 'hero combat' prevailed until late times. Horseback riding came after the war chariot, but persisted longer. From such horseback riding the 'knight' emerged—the Persian, as well as the Thessalian, Athenian, Roman, Celtic, and Germanic. The footman, who certainly played some part earlier in the development of discipline, receded in importance for quite some time.

The substitution of iron side-arms for bronze javelins was probably among the factors that again pushed development in the opposite direction, toward discipline. Yet, just as in the Middle Ages gun powder can scarcely be said to have brought about the transition from undisciplined to disciplined fighting, so iron, as such, did not bring about the change—for long-range and knightly weapons were made of iron.

It was the discipline of the Hellenic and Roman Hoplites[1] which brought about the change. Even Homer, as an oft-quoted passage indicates, knew of the beginnings of discipline with its prohibition of fighting out of line. For Rome, the important turning-point is symbolized by the legend of the execution of the consul's son, who, in accordance with the ancient fashion of heroes, had slain the opposing war lord in individual combat. At first, the well-trained army of the Spartan professional soldier, the holy Lochos[2] of the Boeotians, the well-trained *sarissa*-equipped[3] phalanx of the Macedonians, and then the tactic of the highly trained,

---

[1]   Heavily armed footsoldier.
[2]   A military unit, a company.
[3]   The *sarissa* is a Macedonian pike, some 14 feet long, of further reach than the ordinary Greek spear.

more mobile maniple[4] of the Romans, gained supremacy over the Persian knight, the militias of the Hellenic and Italic citizenry, and the people's armies of the Barbarians. In the early period of the Hellenic Hoplites, incipient attempts were made to exclude long range weapons by 'international law' as unchivalrous, just as during the Middle Ages there were attempts to forbid the crossbow.

The kind of weapon has been the result and not the cause of discipline. Exclusive use of the infantry tactic of close combat during antiquity brought about the decay of cavalry, and in Rome the 'census of knights' became practically equivalent to exemption from military service.

At the close of the Middle Ages it was the massed force of the Swiss, with its parallel and ensuing developments, which first broke the monopoly of knighthood to wage war. And even then, the Swiss still allowed the Halberdiers[5] to break forth from the main force for hero combat, after the main force had advanced in closed formation—the pike-men occupying the outside positions. At first these massed forces of the Swiss only succeeded in dispersing the knights. And in the battles of the sixteenth and seventeenth centuries, cavalry, as such, increasingly disciplined, still played a completely decisive role. Without cavalry it was still impossible to wage offensive wars and actually to overpower the enemy, as the course of the English Civil War demonstrated.

It was discipline and not gun powder which initiated the transformation. The Dutch army under Maurice of the House of Orange was one of the first modern disciplined armies. It was shorn of all status privileges; and thus, for example, the previously effective refusal of the mercenaries to do rampart work (*opera servitia*) became ineffective. Cromwell's victories—despite the fierce bravery of the Cavaliers—were due to sober and rational Puritan discipline. His 'Ironsides'—the 'men of conscience'— trotted forward in firmly closed formation, at the same time calmly firing, and then, thrusting, brought about a successful attack. The

4   A subdivision of Roman legion, numbering either 120 or 60 men.
5   Men equipped with a *halberd*, a long-handled weapon.

major contrast lies in the fact that after the attack they remained in closed formation or immediately re-aligned themselves. It was this disciplined cavalry attack which was technically superior to the Cavaliers' ardor. For it was the habit of the Cavaliers to gallop enthusiastically into the attack and then, without discipline, to disperse, either to plunder the camp of the enemy or prematurely and individually to pursue single opponents in order to capture them for ransom. All successes were forfeited by such habits, as was typically and often the case in Antiquity and the Middle Ages (for example, at Tagliacozzo). Gun powder and all the war techniques associated with it became significant only with the existence of discipline—and to the full extent only with the use of war machinery, which presupposes discipline.

The economic bases upon which army organizations have been founded are not the only agent determining the development of discipline, yet they have been of considerable importance. The discipline of well-trained armies and the major or minor role they have played in warfare reacted still more, and with more lasting effects, upon the political and social order. This influence, however, has been ambiguous. Discipline, as the basis of warfare, gave birth to patriarchal kingship among the Zulus, where the monarch is constitutionally limited by the power of the army leaders (like the Spartan Ephors).[6] Similarly, discipline gave birth to the Hellenic polis with its gymnasiums.

When infantry drill is perfected to the point of virtuosity (Sparta), the polis has an inevitably 'aristocratic' structure. When cities are based upon naval discipline, they have 'democratic' structures (Athens). Discipline gave rise to Swiss 'democracy,' which is quite different in nature. It involved a dominance (in Hellenic terms) over metics as well as territorial helots, during the time when Swiss mercenaries enlisted in foreign armies. The rule of the Roman patriciate, of the Egyptian, Assyrian, and finally of the modern European bureaucratic state organizations —all have their origin in discipline.

War discipline may go hand in hand with totally different

6   Five Spartan magistrates.

economic conditions, as these examples show. However, discipline has always affected the structure of the state, the economy, and possibly the family. For in the past a fully disciplined army has necessarily been a professional army, and therefore the basic problem has always been how to provide for the sustenance of the warriors.

The primeval way of creating trained troops—ever ready to strike, and allowing themselves to be disciplined—was *warrior communism*, which we have already mentioned. It may take the form of the bachelor house as a kind of barracks or casino of the professional warriors; in this form it is spread over the largest part of the earth. Or, it may follow the pattern of the communist community of the Ligurian pirates, or of the Spartan syssitia organized according to the 'picnic' principle; or it may follow Caliph Omar's organization, or the religious knight orders of the Middle Ages. The warrior community may constitute, as we have noticed above, either a completely autonomous society closed against the outside, or, as is the rule, it may be incorporated into a political association whose territory is fixed by boundaries. As a part of such a corporate group, the warrior community may decisively determine its order. Thus, the recruitment of the warrior community is linked to the order of the corporate group. But this linkage is largely relative. Even the Spartans, for example, did not insist upon a strict 'purity of blood.' Military education was decisive for membership in its warrior community.

Under warrior communism, the existence of the warrior is the perfect counterpart to the existence of the monk, whose garrisoned and communist life in the monastery also serves the purpose of disciplining him in the service of his master in the hereafter (and possibly also resulting in service to a this-worldly master). The dissociation from the family and from all private economic interests also occurs outside the celibate knight orders, which were created in direct analogy to the monk orders.

When the institution of the bachelor house is fully developed, familial relations are often completely excluded. The inmates of the house purchase or capture girls, or they claim that the girls of the subject community be at their disposal so long as they have not been sold in marriage. The children of the Ariloi—the ruling estate in Melanesia—are killed. Men can join enduring sexual communities with a separate economy only after having completed their 'service' in the bachelor house—often only at an advanced age. Stratification according to age groups, which with some peoples is also important for the regulation of sexual relationship; the alleged survivals from primitive 'endogenous sexual promiscuity'; the alleged survivals of a supposedly 'primeval right' of all comrades to all girls not yet appropriated by an individual; as well as 'marriage by capture'—allegedly the earliest form of marriage; and, above all, the 'matriarchate'—all of these might be in most cases survivals of such military organizations as we are discussing. These military organizations split the life of the warrior from the household and family, and, under conditions of chronic warfare, such organizations have been widely diffused.

Almost everywhere the communistic warrior community may be the *caput mortuum* of the followers of charismatic war lords. Such a following has usually been societalized into a chronic institution and, once existing in peacetime, has led to the decline of warrior chieftainship. Yet under favorable conditions, the warrior chief may well rise to absolute lordship over the disciplined warrior formations. Accordingly, the *oikos,* as the basis of a military structure, offers an extreme contrast to this communism of warriors who live on accumulated stores, as well as contributions of the women, of those unfit to bear arms, and possibly of serfs. The patrimonial army is sustained and equipped from the stores of a commanding overlord. It was known especially in Egypt, but its fragments are widely dispersed in military organizations of different natures, and they form the bases of princely despotisms.

The reverse phenomenon, the emancipation of the warrior community from the unlimited power of the overlord, as evidenced in Sparta through the institution of the Ephors, has proceeded only so far as the interest in discipline has permitted. In the polis, therefore, the weakening of the king's power—which meant the weakening of discipline—prevailed only in peace and in the homeland (*domi* in contrast to *militiae,* according to the technical terms of Roman administrative law). The Spartan king's prerogatives approached the zero point only in peacetime. In the interests of discipline, the king was omnipotent in the field.

An all-around weakening of discipline usually accompanies any kind of decentralized military establishment—whether it is of prebendal or of feudal type. This weakening of discipline may vary greatly in degree. The well-trained Spartan army, the δκλῆροι[7] of the other Hellenic and Macedonian and of several Oriental military establishments, the Turkish quasi-prebendal fiefs, and finally the feudal fiefs of the Japanese and Occidental Middle Ages—all of these were phases of economic decentralization, usually going hand in hand with the weakening of discipline and the rising importance of individual heroism.

From the disciplinary aspect, just as from the economic, the feudal lord and vassal represents an extreme contrast to the patrimonial or bureaucratic soldier. And the disciplinary aspect is a consequence of the economic aspect. The feudal vassal and lord not only cares for his own equipment and provisions, directs his own baggage-train, but he summons and leads sub-vassals who, in turn, also equip themselves.

Discipline has grown on the basis of an increased concentration of the means of warfare in the hands of the war lord. This has been achieved by having a condottiere recruit mercenary armies, in part or wholly, in the manner of a private capitalist. Such an arrangement was dominant in the late Middle Ages and the beginning of the modern era. It was followed by the raising and equipping of standing armies by means of political authority and a collective economy. We shall not describe here in detail the increasing rationalization of procurement for the armies. It began with Maurice of the House of Orange, proceeded to Wallenstein, Gustav Adolf, Cromwell, the armies of the French, of Frederick the Great, and of Maria Theresa; it passed through a transition from the professional army to the people's army of the French Revolution, and from the disciplining of the people's army by Napoleon into a partly professional army. Finally universal conscription was introduced during the nineteenth century. The whole

7   Military colonies of the city-states.

development meant, in effect, the clearly increasing importance of discipline and, just as clearly, the consistent execution of the economic process through which a public and collective economy was substituted for private capitalism as the basis for military organization.

Whether the exclusive dominance of universal conscription will be the last word in the age of machine warfare remains to be seen. The shooting records of the British navy, for instance, seem to be affected by ensembling gun crews of professional soldiers, which allows for their continuation as a team through the years. The belief in the technical superiority of the professional soldier for certain categories of troops is almost sure to gain in influence, especially if the process of shortening the term of service—stagnating in Europe at the moment—should continue. In several officers' circles, this view is already esoterically held. The introduction of a three-year period of compulsory service by the French army (1913) was motivated here and there by the slogan of 'professional army'—a somewhat inappropriate slogan, since all differentiation of the troops into categories was absent. These still ambiguous possibilities, and also their possible political consequences, are not to be discussed here. In any case, none of them will alter the exclusive importance of mass discipline. What has concerned us here has been to show that the separation of the warrior from the means of warfare, and the concentration of the means of warfare in the hands of the war lord have everywhere been one of the typical bases of mass discipline. And this has been the case whether the process of separation and of concentration was executed in the form of oikos, capitalist enterprise, or bureaucratic organization.

The Discipline of Large-Scale Economic Organizations

The discipline of the army gives birth to all discipline. The large-scale economic organization is the second great agency which trains men for discipline. No direct historical and transitional organizations link the Pharaonic workshops and construction work (however little detail about their organization is known) with the Carthaginian Roman plantation, the mines of the late Middle Ages, the slave plantation of colonial economies, and finally the modern factory. However, all of these have in common the one element of discipline.

The slaves of the ancient plantations slept in barracks, living without family and without property. Only the managers—especially the *villicus*—had individual domiciles, somewhat comparable to the lieutenant's domicile or the residence of a manager of a modern, large-scale agricultural enterprise. The *villicus* alone usually had quasi-property (*peculium*, i.e. originally property in cattle) and quasi-marriage (*contubernium*). In the morning the work-slaves lined up in 'squads' (in *decuriae*) and were led to work by overseers (*monitores*); their personal equipment (to use a barrack term) was stored away and handed out according to need. And hospitals and prison cells were not absent. The discipline of the manor of the Middle Ages and the modern era was considerably less strict because it was traditionally stereotyped, and therefore it somewhat limited the lord's power.

No special proof is necessary to show that military discipline is the ideal model for the modern capitalist factory, as it was for the ancient plantation. In contrast to the plantation, organizational discipline in the factory is founded upon a completely rational basis. With the help of appropriate methods of measurement, the optimum profitability of the individual worker is calculated like that of any material means of production. On the basis of this calculation, the American system of 'scientific management' enjoys the greatest triumphs in the rational conditioning and training of work performances. The final consequences are drawn from the mechanization and discipline of the plant, and the psycho-physical apparatus of man is completely adjusted to the demands of the outer world, the tools, the machines—in short, to an individual 'function.' The individual is shorn of his natural rhythm as determined by the structure of his organism; his psycho-physical apparatus is atuned to a new rhythm through a methodical specialization of separately functioning muscles, and an optimal economy of forces is established corresponding to the conditions of work. This whole process of rationalization, in the factory as elsewhere, and especially in the bureaucratic state machine, parallels the centralization of the material implements of organization in the discretionary power of the overlord.

The ever-widening grasp of discipline irresistibly proceeds with the rationalization of the supply of economic and political demands. This universal phenomenon increasingly restricts the importance of charisma and of individually differentiated conduct.

Discipline and Charisma[8]

Charisma, as a creative power, recedes in the face of domination, which hardens into lasting institutions, and becomes efficacious only in short-lived mass emotions of incalculable effects, as on elections and similar occasions. Nevertheless charisma remains a highly important element of the social structure, although of course in a greatly changed sense.

We must now return to the economic factors, already mentioned above, which predominantly determine the routinization of charisma: the need of social strata, privileged through existing political, social, and economic orders, to have their social and economic positions 'legitimized.' They wish to see their positions transformed from purely factual power relations into a cosmos of acquired rights, and to know that they are thus sanctified. These interests comprise by far the strongest motive for the conservation of charismatic elements of an objectified nature within the structure of domination. Genuine charisma is absolutely opposed to this objectified form. It does not appeal to an enacted or traditional order, nor does it base its claims upon acquired rights. Genuine charisma rests upon the legitimation of personal heroism or personal revelation. Yet precisely this quality of charisma as an extraordinary, supernatural, divine power transforms it, after its routinization, into a suitable source for the legitimate acquisition of sovereign power by the successors of the charismatic hero.

[8]   See also part II, pages 43–77.

Routinized charisma thus continues to work in favor of all those whose power and possession is guaranteed by that sovereign power, and who thus depend upon the continued existence of such power.

The forms in which a ruler's charismatic legitimation may express itself vary according to the relation of the original charismatic powerholder with the supernatural powers. If the ruler's legitimation cannot be determined, according to unambiguous rules, through hereditary charisma, he is in need of legitimation through some other charismatic power. Normally, this can only be hierocratic power. This holds expressly for the sovereign who represents a divine incarnation, and who thus possesses the highest 'personal charisma.' Unless it is supported and proved by personal deeds, his claim of charisma requires the acknowledgment of professional experts in divinity. Incarnated monarchs are indeed exposed to the peculiar process of interment by close court officials and priests, who are materially and ideally interested in legitimacy. This seclusion may proceed to a permanent palace arrest and even to killing upon maturity, lest the god have occasion to compromise divinity or to free himself from tutelage. Yet generally, according to the genuine view as well as in practice, the weight of responsibility which the charismatic ruler must carry before his subjects works very definitely in the direction of the need for his tutelage.

It is because of their high charismatic qualifications that such rulers as the Oriental Caliph, Sultan, and Shah urgently need, even nowadays (1913), a single personality to assume responsibility for governmental actions, especially for failures and unpopular actions. This is the basis for the traditional and specific position of the 'Grand Vizier' in all those realms. The attempt to abolish and replace the office of the Grand Vizier by bureaucratic departments under ministers with the Shah's personal chairmanship failed in Persia during the last generation. This change would have placed the Shah in the role of a leader of the administration, personally responsible for all its abuses and for all the sufferings of the people. This role not only would have continuously jeopardized him, but would have shaken the belief in his very 'charismatic' legitimacy. The office of Grand Vizier with its responsibilities had to be restored in order to protect the Shah and his charisma.

The Grand Vizier is the Oriental counterpart of the position of the responsible prime minister of the Occident, especially in parliamentary states. The formula, *le roi règne mais il ne gouverne pas*, and the theory that, in the interest of the dignity of his position, the king must not 'figure without ministerial decorations,' or, that he must abstain entirely from intervening in the normal administration directed by bureaucratic experts and specialists, or that he must abstain from administration in favor of the political party leaders occupying ministerial positions—all these theories correspond entirely to the enshrinement of the deified, patrimonial sovereign by the experts in tradition and ceremony: priests, court officers, and high dignitaries. In all these cases the sociological nature of charisma plays just as great a part as that of court officials or party leaders and their followings. Despite his lack of parliamentary power, the constitutional monarch is preserved, and above all, his mere existence and his charisma guarantee the *legitimacy* of the existing social and property order, since decisions are carried out 'in his name.' Besides, all those interested in the social order must fear for the belief in 'legality' lest it be shaken by doubts of its legitimacy.

A president elected according to fixed rules can formally legitimize the governmental actions of the respective victorious party as 'lawful,' just as well as a parliamentary monarch. But the monarch, in addition to such legitimation, can perform a function which an elected president can not fulfil: a parliamentary monarch formally delimits the politicians' quest for power, because the highest position in the state is occupied once and for all. From a political point of view this essentially negative function, associated with the mere existence of a king enthroned according to fixed rules, is of the greatest practical importance. Formulated positively it means, for the archetype of the species, that the king cannot gain an actual share in political power by prerogative (kingdom of prerogative). He can share power only by virtue of outstanding personal ability or social influence (kingdom of influence). Yet he is in position to exert this influence in spite of all parliamentary government, as events and personalities of recent times have shown.

'Parliamentary' kingship in England means a selective admission to actual power for that monarch who qualifies as a statesman. But a misstep at home or in foreign affairs, or the raising of pretensions that do not correspond with his personal abilities and prestige, may cost him his crown. Thus English parliamentary kingship is formed in a more genuinely charismatic fashion than kingships on the Continent. On the Continent, mere birth-right equally endows the fool and the political genius with the pretensions of a sovereign.

II. Charisma and Institutionalization
in the Political Sphere

In the following excerpts I shall first present Weber's general analytical approach to the nature of the political action and organization which emphasizes the problem of regulation of allocation of power within any society, and the crucial importance of legitimacy for the continuous maintenance of the political order. As is well known, Weber distinguishes three bases of legitimate authority: the rational, the traditional, and the charismatic. In this context, he emphasizes the importance of charisma as an innovating power in the institutional sphere. Already it can be seen that Weber's definition of charisma stresses the duality of its nature—on the one hand, its tendency to innovation, but, on the other hand, the dependence of the permanence of the innovation on the routinization of charisma.

The first part of this section presents excerpts from Weber's work which emphasize the qualities of charisma and of its routinization within the political sphere. It is here that we find that the most elaborated definition of the term "charisma" appears in Weber's work in connection with the analysis of charismatic authority. But he applies in his work the general characteristics of charisma as defined in this chapter to other social spheres as well.

The second part of this section presents Weber's analysis of the development of political institutions in different types of societies, ranging from primitive societies, through various historical societies, to modern frameworks. Weber's treatment of the subject varies greatly. Some of his writings contain rather broad generalizations about certain types of political action and organization with illustrations from many different societies, whereas others concentrate on the analysis of the development of specific societies at definite historical periods. The selections from *Wirtschaft u. Gesellschaft*, translated in *The Theory of Social and*

Economic Organization and *Essays in Sociology,* analyze the general characteristics of the various political institutions within different types of societies, primitive, historical, and modern. Within this context special excerpts present Weber's classical analysis of bureaucracy.

In other excerpts, *Die Gesammelte Aufsätze zur Religionssoziologie* as translated in *The Religion of China* and *The Religion of India,* Weber analyzes the structure of a given political institution within a given historical society. In these works he describes not only the specific characteristics of a given political institution, but shows how its structure is related to the broader social framework in which it is placed. Throughout these excerpts we find continuous reference to the interplay between the charismatic potentialities inherent in the political field, the ways in which these potentialities become unfolded in different situations, their interplay within the more organizational aspects of political processes, and the changing patterns of the meaning of political participation in different societies. In the last selection presented here, these problems are analyzed in the context of the first attempts in Russia to establish some parliamentary pattern and they may serve as an illustration of Weber's analysis of these unfolding problems in the context of modern societies.

5

THE PURE TYPES OF
LEGITIMATE AUTHORITY

THERE ARE three pure types of legitimate authority. The validity of their claims to legitimacy may be based on:

1. Rational grounds—resting on a belief in the "legality" of patterns of normative rules and the right of those elevated to authority under such rules to issue commands (legal authority).

2. Traditional grounds—resting on an established belief in the sanctity of immemorial traditions and the legitimacy of the status of those exercising authority under them (traditional authority); or finally,

3. Charismatic grounds—resting on devotion to the specific and exceptional sanctity, heroism or exemplary character of an individual person, and of the normative patterns or order revealed or ordained by him (charismatic authority).

In the case of legal authority, obedience is owed to the legally established impersonal order. It extends to the persons exercising the authority of office under it only by virtue of the formal legality of their commands and only within the scope of authority of the office. In the case of traditional authority, obedience is owed to the *person* of the chief who occupies the traditionally sanctioned position of authority and who is (within its sphere) bound by tradition. But here the obligation of obedience is not based on the impersonal order, but is a matter of personal loyalty within the area of accustomed obligations. In the case of charismatic au-

Reprinted with permission of The Macmillan Company from *Theory of Social and Economic Organization* by Max Weber, translated by A. R. Henderson and Talcott Parsons. Copyright 1947 by Talcott Parsons.

thority, it is the charismatically qualified leader as such who is obeyed by virtue of personal trust in him and his revelation, his heroism or his exemplary qualities so far as they fall within the scope of the individual's belief in his charisma.

The usefulness of the above classification can only be judged by its results in promoting systematic analysis. The concept of "charisma" ("the gift of grace") is taken from the vocabulary of early Christianity. For the Christian religious organization Rudolf Sohm, in his *Kirchenrecht,* was the first to clarify the substance of the concept, even though he did not use the same terminology. Others (for instance, Hollin, *Enthusiasmus und Buss-gewalt*) have clarified certain important consequences of it. It is thus nothing new.

The fact that none of these three ideal types, the elucidation of which will occupy the following pages, is usually to be found in historical cases in "pure" form, is naturally not a valid objection to attempting their conceptual formulation in the sharpest possible form. In this respect the present case is no different from many others. Later on the transformation of pure charisma by the process of routinization will be discussed and thereby the relevance of the concept to the understanding of empirical systems of authority considerably increased. But even so it may be said of every empirically historical phenomenon of authority that it is not likely to be "as an open book." Analysis in terms of sociological types has, after all, as compared with purely empirical historical investigation, certain advantages which should not be minimized. That is, it can in the particular case of a concrete form of authority determine what conforms to or approximates such types as "charisma," "hereditary charisma," "the charisma of office," "patriarchy," "bureaucracy," the authority of status groups,[1] and in doing so it can work with relatively unambiguous concepts. But the idea that the whole of concrete historical reality can be exhausted in the conceptual scheme about to be developed is as far from the author's thoughts as anything could be.

[1]   *Ständische.* There is no really acceptable English rendering of this term.—T. PARSONS (see note 30 on p. 121 below).

6

THE NATURE OF CHARISMATIC AUTHORITY AND ITS ROUTINIZATION

Charismatic Authority

THE TERM "charisma" will be applied to a certain quality of an individual personality by virtue of which he is set apart from ordinary men and treated as endowed with supernatural, super-human, or at least specifically exceptional powers or qualities. These are such as are not accessible to the ordinary person, but are regarded as of divine origin or as exemplary, and on the basis of them the individual concerned is treated as a leader. In prim-itive circumstances this peculiar kind of deference is paid to prophets, to people with a reputation for therapeutic or legal wis-dom, to leaders in the hunt, and heroes in war. It is very often thought of as resting on magical powers. How the quality in ques-tion would be ultimately judged from any ethical, aesthetic, or other such point of view is naturally entirely indifferent for pur-poses of definition. What is alone important is how the individual is actually regarded by those subject to charismatic authority, by his "followers" or "disciples."

For present purposes it will be necessary to treat a variety of different types as being endowed with charisma in this sense. It includes the state of a "berserker" whose spells of maniac passion have, apparently wrongly, sometimes been attributed to the use of drugs. In Medieval Byzantium a group of people endowed with

Reprinted with permission of The Macmillan Company from *Theory of Social and Economic Organization* by Max Weber, translated by A. R. Henderson and Talcott Parsons. Copyright 1947 by Talcott Parsons.

this type of charismatic war-like passion were maintained as a kind of weapon. It includes the "shaman," the kind of magician who in the pure type is subject to epileptoid seizures as a means of falling into trances. Another type is that of Joseph Smith, the founder of Mormonism, who, however, cannot be classified in this way with absolute certainty since there is a possibility that he was a very sophisticated type of deliberate swindler. Finally it includes the type of intellectual, such as Kurt Eisner,[1] who is carried away with his own demagogic success. Sociological analysis, which must abstain from value judgments, will treat all these on the same level as the men who, according to conventional judgments are the "greatest" heroes, prophets and saviours.

It is recognition on the part of those subject to authority which is decisive for the validity of charisma. This is freely given and guaranteed by what is held to be a "sign" or proof,[2] originally always a miracle, and consists in devotion to the corresponding revelation, hero worship, or absolute trust in the leader. But where charisma is genuine, it is not this which is the basis of the claim to legitimacy. This basis lies rather in the conception that it is the *duty* of those who have been called to a charismatic mission to recognize its quality and to act accordingly. Psychologically this "recognition" is a matter of complete personal devotion to the possessor of the quality, arising out of enthusiasm, or of despair and hope.

No prophet has ever regarded his quality as dependent on the attitudes of the masses toward him. No elective king or military leader has ever treated those who have resisted him or tried to ignore him otherwise than as delinquent in duty. Failure to take part in a military expedition under such leader, even though recruitment is formally voluntary, has universally been met with disdain.

If proof of his charismatic qualification fails him for long, the leader endowed with charisma tends to think his god or his magical or heroic powers have deserted him. If he is for long unsuc-

---

1   The leader of the communistic experiment in Bavaria in 1919.—
T. PARSONS
2   *Bewährung.*

cessful, above all if his leadership fails to benefit his followers, it is likely that his charismatic authority will disappear. This is the genuine charismatic meaning of the "gift of grace."[3]

Even the old Germanic kings were sometimes rejected with scorn. Similar phenomena are very common among so-called "primitive" peoples. In China the charismatic quality of the monarch, which was transmitted unchanged by heredity, was upheld so rigidly that any misfortune whatever, not only defeats in war, but drought, floods, or astronomical phenomena which were considered unlucky, forced him to do public penance and might even force his abdication. If such things occurred, it was a sign that he did not possess the requisite charismatic virtue, he was thus not a legitimate "Son of Heaven."

The corporate group which is subject to charismatic authority is based on an emotional form of communal relationship.[4] The administrative staff of a charismatic leader does not consist of "officials"; at least its members are not technically trained. It is not chosen on the basis of social privilege nor from the point of view of domestic or personal dependency. It is rather chosen in terms of the charismatic qualities of its members. The prophet has his disciples; the warlord his selected henchmen; the leader, generally, his followers. There is no such thing as "appointment" or "dismissal," no career, no promotion. There is only a "call" at the instance of the leader on the basis of the charismatic qualification of those he summons. There is no hierarchy; the leader merely intervenes in general or in individual cases when he considers the members of his staff inadequate to a task with which they have been entrusted. There is no such thing as a definite sphere of authority and of competence, and no appropriation of official powers on the basis of social privileges. There may, however, be territorial or functional limits to charismatic powers and and to the individual's "mission." There is no such thing as a salary or a benefice. Disciples or followers tend to live primarily in a communistic relationship with their leader on means which

3   *Gottesgnadentum.*
4   Weber uses the term *Gemeinde,* which is not directly translatable.
—T. Parsons

have been provided by voluntary gift. There are no established administrative organs. In their place are agents who have been provided with charismatic authority by their chief or who possess charisma of their own. There is no system of formal rules, of abstract legal principles, and hence no process of judicial decision oriented to them. But equally there is no legal wisdom oriented to judicial precedent. Formally concrete judgments are newly created from case to case and are originally regarded as divine judgments and revelations. From a substantive point of view, every charismatic authority would have to subscribe to the proposition, "It is written . . . , but I say unto you, . . ."[5] The genuine prophet, like the genuine military leader and every true leader in this sense, preaches, creates, or demands *new* obligations. In the pure type of charisma, these are imposed on the authority of revelation by oracles, or of the leader's own will, and are recognized by the members of the religious, military, or party group, because they come from such a source. Recognition is a duty. When such an authority comes into conflict with the competing authority of another who also claims charismatic sanction, the only recourse is to some kind of a contest, by magical means or even an actual physical battle of the leaders. In principle only one side can be in the right in such a conflict; the other must be guilty of a wrong which has to be expiated.

Charismatic authority is thus specifically outside the realm of every-day routine and the profane sphere.[6] In this respect, it is sharply opposed both to rational, and particularly bureaucratic, authority, and to traditional authority, whether in its patriarchal, patrimonial, or any other form. Both rational and traditional authority are specifically forms of every-day routine control of action; while the charismatic type is the direct antithesis of this. Bureaucratic authority is specifically rational in the sense of being bound to intellectually analysable rules; while charismatic authority is specifically irrational in the sense of being foreign to all rules. Traditional authority is bound to the precedents handed down from the past and to this extent is also oriented to rules. Within the sphere of its claims, charismatic authority repudiates the past, and is in this sense a specifically revolutionary force. It recognizes no appropriation of positions of power by virtue of the possession of property, either on the part of a chief or of socially privileged groups. The only basis of legitimacy for it is personal charisma, so long as it is proved; that is, as long as it receives recognition and is able to satisfy the followers or disciples. But this lasts only so long as the belief in its charismatic inspiration remains.

The above is scarcely in need of further discussion. What has been said applies to the position of authority of such elected monarchs as Napoleon, with his use of the plebiscite. It applies to the "rule of genius," which has elevated people of humble origin to thrones and high military commands, just as much as it applies to religious prophets or war heroes.

Pure charisma is specifically foreign to economic considerations. Whenever it appears, it constitutes a "call" in the most emphatic sense of the word, a "mission" or a "spiritual duty." In the pure type, it disdains and repudiates economic exploitation of the gifts of grace as a source of income, though, to be sure, this often remains more an ideal than a fact. It is not that charisma always means the renunciation of property or even of acquisition, as under certain circumstances prophets and their disciples do. The heroic warrior and his followers actively seek "booty"; the elective ruler or the charismatic party leader requires the material means of power. The former in addition requires a brilliant display of his authority to bolster his prestige. What is despised, so long as the genuinely charismatic type is adhered to, is traditional or rational every-day economizing, the attainment of a regular income by continuous economic activity devoted to this end. Support by gifts, sometimes on a grand scale involving foundations, even by bribery and grand-scale honoraria, or by begging, constitute the strictly voluntary type of support. On the other hand, "booty," or coercion, whether by force or by other means, is the other typical form of charismatic provision for needs. From the point of view of rational economic activity, charisma is a typical anti-economic force. It repudiates any sort of involvement in the every-day routine world. It can only tolerate, with an attitude of complete emotional indifference, irregular, unsystematic, acquisitive acts. In that it relieves the recipient of economic concerns, dependence on property income can be the economic basis of a charismatic mode of life for some groups; but that is not usually acceptable for the normal charismatic "revolutionary."

The fact that incumbency of church office has been forbidden to the Jesuits is a rationalized application of this principle of discipleship. The fact that all the "virtuosi" of asceticism, the mendicant orders, and fighters for a faith belong in this category, is quite clear. Almost all prophets have been supported by voluntary gifts. The well-known saying of St. Paul, "If a man does not work, neither shall he eat," was directed against the swarm of charismatic missionaries. It obviously has nothing to do with a positive valuation of economic activity for its own sake, but only lays it down as a duty of each individual somehow to provide for his own support. This because he realized that the purely charismatic parable of the lilies of the field was not capable of literal application, but at best "taking no thought for the morrow" could be hoped for. On the other hand, in such a case as primarily an artistic type of charismatic discipleship, it is conceivable that insulation from economic struggle should mean limitation of those who were really eligible to the "economically independent"; that is, to persons living on income from property. This has been true of the circle of Stefan George, at least in its primary intentions.

In traditionally stereotyped periods, charisma is the greatest revolutionary force. The equally revolutionary force of "reason" works from without by altering the situations of action, and hence its problems, finally in this way changing men's attitudes toward them; or it intellectualizes the individual. Charisma, on the other hand, may involve a subjective or internal reorientation born out of suffering, conflicts, or enthusiasm. It may then result in a radical alteration of the central system of attitudes and directions of action with a completely new orientation of all attitudes toward the different problems and structures of the "world."⁷ In pre-rationalistic periods, tradition and charisma between them have almost exhausted the whole of the orientation of action.

The Routinization of Charisma

In its pure form charismatic authority has a character specifically foreign to every-day routine structures. The social relationships directly involved are strictly personal, based on the validity and practice of charismatic personal qualities. If this is not to remain a purely transitory phenomenon, but to take on the character of a permanent relationship forming a stable community of disciples or a band of followers or a party organization or any sort of political or hierocratic organization, it is necessary for the character of charismatic authority to become radically changed. Indeed, in its pure form charismatic authority may be said to exist only in the process of originating. It cannot remain stable, but becomes either traditionalized or rationalized, or a combination of both.

The following are the principal motives underlying this transformation: (a) The ideal and also the material interests of the followers in the continuation and the continual reactivation of the community, (b) the still stronger ideal and also stronger material interests of the members of the administrative staff, the disciples or other followers of the charismatic leader in continuing their relationship. Not only this, but they have an interest in continuing it in such a way that both from an ideal and a material point of view, their own status is put on a stable every-day basis. This means, above all, making it possible to participate in normal family relationships or at least to enjoy a secure social position in place of the kind of discipleship which is cut off from ordinary worldly connexions, notably in the family and in economic relationships.

⁷   Weber here uses *Welt* in quotation quotation marks, indicating that it refers to its meaning in what is primarily a religious context. It is the sphere of "worldly" things and interests as distinguished from transcendental religious interests.—T. PARSONS

These interests generally become conspicuously evident with the disappearance of the personal charismatic leader and with the problem of succession, which inevitably arises. The way in which this problem is met, if it is met at all and the charismatic group continues to exist, is of crucial importance for the character of the subsequent social relationships. The following are the principal possible types of solution:—

(a) The search for a new charismatic leader on the basis of criteria of the qualities which will fit him for the position of authority. This is to be found in a relatively pure type in the process of choice of a new Dalai Lama. It consists in the search for a child with characteristics which are interpreted to mean that he is a reincarnation of the Buddha. This is very similar to the choice of the new Bull of Apis.

In this case the legitimacy of the new charismatic leader is bound to certain distinguishing characteristics; thus, to rules with respect to which a tradition arises. The result is a process of traditionalization in favour of which the purely personal character of leadership is eliminated.

(b) By revelation manifested in oracles, lots, divine judgments or other techniques of selection. In this case the legitimacy of the new leader is dependent on the legitimacy of the technique of his selection. This involves a form of legalization. It is said that at times the *Schofetim* of Israel had this character. Saul is said to have been chosen by the old war oracle.

(c) By the designation on the part of the original charismatic leader of his own successor and his recognition on the part of the followers. This is a very common form. Originally, the Roman magistracies were filled entirely in this way. The system survived most clearly into later times in the appointment of "dictators" and in the institution of the "interrex." In this case legitimacy is acquired through the act of designation.

(d) Designation of a successor by the charismatically qualified administrative staff and his recognition by the community. In its typical form this process should quite definitely not be interpreted as "election" or "nomination" or anything of the sort. It is not a matter of free selection, but of one which is strictly bound to objective duty. It is not to be determined merely by majority vote, but is a question of arriving at the correct designation, the designation of the right person who is truly endowed with charisma. It is quite possible that the minority and not the majority should be right in such a case. Unanimity is often required. It is obligatory to acknowledge a mistake and persistence in error is a serious offence. Making a wrong choice is a genuine wrong requiring expiation. Originally it was a magical offence.

Nevertheless, in such a case it is easy for legitimacy to take on the character of an acquired right which is justified by standards of the correctness of the process by which the position was acquired, for the most part, by its having been acquired in accordance with certain formalities, such as coronation. This was the original meaning of the coronation of bishops and kings in the Western World by the clergy or the nobility with the "consent" of the community. There are numerous analogous phenomena all over the world. The fact that this is the origin of the modern conception of "election" raises problems which will have to be gone into later.

(e) By the conception that charisma is a quality transmitted by heredity; thus that it is participated in by the kinsmen of its bearer, particularly by his closest relatives. This is the case of hereditary charisma. The order of hereditary succession in such a case need not be the same as that which is in force for appropriated rights, but may differ from it. It is also sometimes necessary to select the proper heir within the kinship group by some of the methods just spoken of; thus in certain Negro states brothers have had to fight for the succession. In China succession had to take place in such a way that the relation of the living group to the ancestral spirits was not disturbed. The rule either of seniority or of designation by the followers has been very common in the Orient. Hence, in the house of Osman, it has been obligatory to eliminate all other possible candidates.

Only in Medieval Europe and in Japan universally, elsewhere only sporadically, has the principle of primogeniture, as governing the inheritance of authority, become clearly established. This has greatly facilitated the consolidation of political groups in that it has eliminated struggle between a plurality of candidates from the same charismatic family.

In the case of hereditary charisma, recognition is no longer paid to the charismatic qualities of the individual, but to the legitimacy of the position he has acquired by hereditary succession. This may lead in the direction either of traditionalization or of legalization. The concept of "divine right" is fundamentally altered and now comes to mean authority by virtue of a personal right which is not dependent on the recognition of those subject to authority. Personal charisma may be totally absent. Hereditary monarchy is a conspicuous illustration. In Asia there have been very numerous hereditary priesthoods; also, frequently, the hereditary charisma of kinship groups has been treated as a criterion of social rank and of eligibility for fiefs and benefices.

(f) The concept that charisma may be transmitted by ritual means from one bearer to another or may be created in a new person. The concept was originally magical. It involves a dissociation of charisma from a particular individual, making it an objective, transferable entity. In particular, it may become the charisma of office. In this case the belief in legitimacy is no longer directed to the individual, but to the acquired qualities and to the effectiveness of the ritual acts. The most important example is the transmission of priestly charisma by anointing, consecration, or the laying on of hands; and of royal authority, by anointing and by coronation. The *character indelibilis* thus acquired means that the charismatic qualities and powers of the office are emancipated from the personal qualities of the priest. For precisely this reason, this has, from the Donatist and the Montanist heresies down to the Puritan revolution, been the subject of continual conflicts. The "hireling" of the Quakers is the preacher endowed with the charisma of office.

Concomitant with the routinization of charisma with a view to insuring adequate succession, go the interests in its routinization on the part of the administrative staff. It is only in the initial stages and so long as the charismatic leader acts in a way which is completely outside every-day social organization, that it is possible for his followers to live communistically in a community of faith and enthusiasm, on gifts, "booty," or sporadic acquisition. Only the members of the small group of enthusiastic disciples and followers are prepared to devote their lives purely idealistically to their call. The great majority of disciples and followers will in the long run "make their living" out of their "calling" in a material sense as well. Indeed, this must be the case if the movement is not to disintegrate.

Hence, the routinization of charisma also takes the form of the appropriation of powers of control and of economic advantages by the followers or disciples, and of regulation of the recruitment of these groups. This process of traditionalization or of legalization, according to whether rational legislation is involved or not, may take any one of a number of typical forms.

The original basis of recruitment is personal charisma. With routinization, the followers or disciples may set up norms for recruitment, in particular involving training or tests of eligibility. Charisma can only be "awakened" and "tested"; it cannot be "learned" or "taught." All types of magical asceticism, as practiced by magicians and heroes, and all novitiates, belong in this category. These are means of closing the group which constitutes the administrative staff.[8]

Only the proved novice is allowed to exercise authority. A genuine charismatic leader is in a position to oppose this type of prerequisite for membership. His successor is not, at least if he is chosen by the administrative staff. This type is illustrated by the magical and warrior asceticism of the "men's house" with initiation ceremonies and age groups. An individual who has not successfully gone through the initiation, remains a "woman"; that is, is excluded from the charismatic group.

It is easy for charismatic norms to be transformed into those defining a traditional social status on a hereditary charismatic basis. If the leader is chosen on a hereditary basis, it is very easy for hereditary charisma to govern the selection of the administrative staff and even, perhaps, those followers without any position of authority. The term "familistic state"[9] will be applied when a political body is organized strictly and completely in terms of this principle of hereditary charisma. In such a case, all appropriation

---

[8]   On the charismatic type of education, see *Theory of Social and Economic Organization*, chap. iv.
[9]   *Geschlechterstaat.*

of governing powers, of fiefs, benefices, and all sorts of economic advantages follow the same pattern. The result is that all powers and advantages of all sorts become traditionalized. The heads of families, who are traditional gerontocrats or patriarchs without personal charismatic legitimacy, regulate the exercise of these powers which cannot be taken away from their family. It is not the type of position he occupies which determines the rank of a man or of his family, but rather the hereditary charismatic rank of his family determines the position he will occupy. Japan, before the development of bureaucracy, was organized in this way. The same was undoubtedly true of China as well where, before the rationalization which took place in the territorial states, authority was in the hands of the "old families." Other types of examples are furnished by the caste system in India, and by Russia before the *Mjestnitschestvo* was introduced. Indeed, all hereditary social classes with established privileges belong in the same category.

The administrative staff may seek and achieve the creation and appropriation of individual positions and the corresponding economic advantages for its members. In that case, according to whether the tendency is to traditionalization or legalization, there will develop (a) benefices, (b) offices, or (c) fiefs. In the first case a praebendal organization will result; in the second, patrimonialism or bureaucracy; in the third, feudalism. These become appropriated in the place of the type of provision from gifts or booty without settled relation to the every-day economic structure.

Case (a), benefices, may consist in rights to the proceeds of begging, to payments in kind, or to the proceeds of money taxes, or finally, to the proceeds of fees. Any one of these may result from the regulation of provision by free gifts or by "booty" in terms of a rational organization of finance. Regularized begging is found in Buddhism; benefices in kind, in the Chinese and Japanese "rice rents"; support by money taxation has been the rule in all the rationalized conquering states. The last case is common everywhere, especially on the part of priests and judges and, in India, even the military authorities.

Case (b), the transformation of the charismatic mission into an office, may have more of a patrimonial or more of a bureaucratic character. The former is much the more common; the latter is found principally in Mediterranean Antiquity and in the modern Western world. Elsewhere it is exceptional.

In case (c), only land may be appropriated as a fief, whereas the position as such retains its originally charismatic character. On the other hand, powers and authority may be fully appropriated as fiefs. It is difficult to distinguish the two cases. It is, however, rare that orientation to the charismatic character of the position disappears entirely; it did not do so in the Middle Ages.

For charisma to be transformed into a permanent routine structure, it is necessary that its anti-economic character should be altered. It must be adapted to some form of fiscal organization to provide for the needs of the group and hence to the economic conditions necessary for raising taxes and contributions. When a charismatic movement develops in the direction of praebendal provision, the "laity" become differentiated from the "clergy"; that is, the participating members of the charismatic administrative staff which has now become routinized. These are the priests of the developing "church." Correspondingly, in a developing political body the vassals, the holders of benefices, or officials are differentiated from the "tax payers." The former, instead of being the "followers" of the leader, become state officials or appointed party officials. This process is very conspicuous in Buddhism and in the Hindu sects. The same is true in all the states resulting from conquest which have become rationalized to form permanent structures; also of parties and other movements which have originally had a purely charismatic character. With the process of routinization the charismatic group tends to develop into one of the forms of every-day authority, particularly the patrimonial form in its decentralized variant or the bureaucratic. Its original peculiarities are apt to be retained in the charismatic standards of honour attendant on the social status acquired by heredity or the holding of office. This applies to all who participate in the process of appropriation, the chief himself and the members of his staff. It is thus a matter of the type of prestige enjoyed by ruling groups. A hereditary monarch by "divine right" is not a simple patrimonial chief, patriarch, or sheik; a vassal is not a mere household retainer or official. Further details must be deferred to the analysis of social stratification.

As a rule the process of routinization is not free of conflict. In the early stages personal claims on the charisma of the chief are not easily forgotten and the conflict between the charisma of office or of hereditary status with personal charisma is a typical process in many historical situations. . . .

The Transformation of Charisma in an Anti-Authoritarian Direction

A charismatic principle which originally was primarily directed to the legitimization of authority may be subject to interpretation or development in an anti-authoritarian direction. This is true because the validity of charismatic authority rests entirely on recognition by those subject to it, conditioned as this is by "proof" of its genuineness. This is true in spite of the fact that this recognition of a charismatically qualified, and hence legitimate, person is treated as a duty. When the organization of the corporate group undergoes a process of progressive rationalization, it is readily possible that, instead of recognition being treated as a consequence of legitimacy, it is treated as the basis of legitimacy. Legitimacy, that is, becomes "democratic." Thus, for instance, designation of a successor by an administrative staff may be treated as "election" in advance; while designation by the predecessor is "nomination"; whereas the recognition by the group becomes the true "election." The leader whose legitimacy rested on his personal charisma then becomes leader by the grace of those who follow him since the latter are formally free to elect and elevate to power as they please and even to depose. For the loss of charisma and its proof involves the loss of genuine legitimacy. The chief now becomes the freely elected leader.

Correspondingly, the recognition of charismatic decrees and judicial decisions on the part of the community shifts to the doctrine that the group has a right to enact, recognize or repeal laws, according to their own free will, both in general and for an individual case. Under genuinely charismatic authority, on the other hand, it is, to be sure, true that conflicts over the correct law may actually be decided by a vote of the group. But this takes place under the pressure of the feeling that there can be only *one* correct decision and it is a matter of duty to arrive at this. The most important transitional type, is the legitimization of authority by plebiscite. The commonest examples are to be found in the party leaders of the modern state. But it is always present in cases where the chief feels himself to be acting on behalf of the masses and where his recognition is based on this. Both the Napoleons are classical examples, in spite of the fact that legitimization by plebiscite took place only after the seizure of power by force. In the case of the second Napoleon, it was confirmed on this basis after a severe loss of prestige. Regardless of how its real value as an expression of the popular will may be regarded, the plebiscite has been formally the specific means of establishing the legitimacy of authority on the basis of the free confidence of those subject to authority, even though it be only formal or possibly a fiction.

Once the elective principle has been applied to the chief by a process of reinterpretation of charisma, it may be extended to the administrative staff. Elective officials whose legitimacy is derived from the confidence of those subject to their authority and to recall if confidence ceases to exist, are typical of certain types of democracies, for instance, the United States. They are not "bureaucratic" types. Because they have an independent source of legitimacy, they are not strongly integrated in a hierarchical order. To a large extent their "promotion" is not influenced by their superiors and, correspondingly, their functions are not controlled. There are analogies in other cases where several charismatic structures, which are qualitatively heterogeneous, exist side by side, as in the relations of the Dalai Lama and the Taschi Lama. An administrative structure organized in this way is, from a technical point of view, a greatly inferior "instrument of precision" as compared with the bureaucratic type consisting of appointed officials.

The use of the plebiscite as a means of legitimizing leadership on a democratic basis is the most conspicuous type in which democracy is combined with an important role of leadership. In its fundamental significance it is a type of charismatic authority in which the authoritarian element is concealed, because the traditional position of the leader is held to be dependent on the will of those over whom he exercises authority and to be legitimized only by this will. In actual fact the leader, in this case the demagogue, is able to influence action by virtue of the devotion and trust his political followers have in him personally. In the first instance his power is only a power over those recruited to his following, but in case, with their aid, he is able to attain positions of wider authority it may extend to the political group as a whole. The type is best illustrated by the "dictators" who have emerged in the revolutions of the ancient world and of modern times. Examples are: the Greek Aisymnetes and the tyrants and demagogues; in Rome the Gracchi and their successors; in the Italian city states the *Capitani del popolo;* and certain types of political leaders in the German cities such as emerged in the democratic dictatorship of Zürich. In modern states the best examples are the dictatorship of Cromwell, and the leaders of the French Revolution and of the First and Second Empire. Wherever attempts have been made to legitimize this kind of exercise of power legitimacy has been sought in recognition by the sovereign people through a plebiscite. The leader's personal administrative staff is recruited in a charismatic form usually from able people of humble origin. In Cromwell's case, religious qualifications were taken into account. In that of Robespierre along with personal dependability also certain "ethical" qualities. Napoleon was concerned only with personal ability and adaptability to the needs of his imperial "rule of genius."

At the height of revolutionary dictatorship the position of a member of the administrative staff tends to be that of a person entrusted with a specific *ad hoc* task subject to recall. This was true of the role of the agents of the "Committee of Public Safety." When a certain kind of communal "dictators" have been swept into power by the reform movements in American cities the tendency has been to grant them freedom to appoint their own staff. Thus both traditional legitimacy and formal legality tend to be equally ignored by the revolutionary dictator. The tendency of patriarchal authorities, in the administration of justice and in their other functions, has been to act in accordance with substantive ideas of justice, with utilitarian considerations and in terms of reasons of state. These tendencies are paralleled by the revolutionary tribunals and by the substantive postulates of justice of the radical democracy of Antiquity and of modern socialism. The process of routinization or revolutionary charisma then brings with it changes similar to those brought about by the corresponding process in other respects. Thus the development of a professional army in England is derived from the principle of free choice in the participation in religious struggles in the days of Cromwell. Similarly, the French system of administration by prefects is derived from the charismatic administration of the revolutionary democratic dictatorship.

The introduction of elected officials always involves a radical alteration in the position of the charismatic leader. He becomes the "servant" of those under his authority. There is no place for such a type in a technically rational bureaucratic organization. He is not appointed by his superiors and the possibility of promotion is not dependent on their judgment. On the contrary, his position is derived from the favour of the persons whose action he controls. Hence he is likely to be little interested in the prompt and strict observance of discipline which would be likely to win the favour of superiors. The tendency is rather for electoral positions to become autocephalous spheres of authority. It is in general not possible to attain a high level of technical administrative efficiency with an elected staff of officials. This is illustrated by a comparison of the elected officials in the individual states in the United States with the appointed officials of the Federal Government. It is similarly shown by comparing the elected communal officials with the administration of the reform mayors with their own appointed staffs. It is necessary to distinguish the type of democracy where positions of authority are legitimized by plebiscite from that which attempts to dispense with leadership altogether. The latter type is characterized by the attempt to reduce to a minimum the control of some men over others.

It is characteristic of the democracy which makes room for leadership[10] that there should in general be a highly emotional type of devotion to and trust in the leader. This accounts for a tendency to favour the type of individual who is most spectacular, who promises the most, or who employs the most effective propaganda measures in the competition for leadership. This is a natural basis for the utopian component which is found in all revolutions. It also indicates the limitations on the level of rationality which, in the modern world, this type of administration can attain. Even in America it has not *always* come up to expectations.

[10]   *Führerdemokratie.*

7

BUREAUCRACY

Characteristics of Bureaucracy

MODERN OFFICIALDOM functions in the following specific manner:

I. There is the principle of fixed and official jurisdictional areas, which are generally ordered by rules, that is, by laws or administrative regulations.

1. The regular activities required for the purposes of the bureaucratically governed structure are distributed in a fixed way as official duties.

2. The authority to give the commands required for the discharge of these duties is distributed in a stable way and is strictly delimited by rules concerning the coercive means, physical, sacerdotal, or otherwise, which may be placed at the disposal of officials.

3. Methodical provision is made for the regular and continuous fulfilment of these duties and for the execution of the corresponding rights; only persons who have the generally regulated qualifications to serve are employed.

In public and lawful government these three elements constitute 'bureaucratic authority.' In private economic domination, they constitute bureaucratic 'management.' Bureaucracy, thus understood, is fully developed in political and ecclesiastical communities only in the modern state, and, in the private economy,

From *Max Weber: Essays in Sociology*, edited and translated by H. H. Gerth and C. Wright Mills. Copyright 1946 by Oxford University Press, Inc. Reprinted by permission.

only in the most advanced institutions of capitalism. Permanent and public office authority, with fixed jurisdiction, is not the historical rule but rather the exception. This is so even in large political structures such as those of the ancient Orient, the Germanic and Mongolian empires of conquest, or of many feudal structures of state. In all these cases, the ruler executes the most important measures through personal trustees, table-companions, or court-servants. Their commissions and authority are not precisely delimited and are temporarily called into being for each case.

II. The principles of office hierarchy and of levels of graded authority mean a firmly ordered system of super- and subordination in which there is a supervision of the lower offices by the higher ones. Such a system offers the governed the possibility of appealing the decision of a lower office to its higher authority, in a definitely regulated manner. With the full development of the bureaucratic type, the office hierarchy is monocratically organized. The principle of hierarchical office authority is found in all bureaucratic structures: in state and ecclesiastical structures as well as in large party organizations and private enterprises. It does not matter for the character of bureaucracy whether its authority is called 'private' or 'public.'

When the principle of jurisdictional 'competency' is fully carried through, hierarchical subordination—at least in public office—does not mean that the 'higher' authority is simply authorized to take over the business of the 'lower.' Indeed, the opposite is the rule. Once established and having fulfilled its task, an office tends to continue in existence and be held by another incumbent.

III. The management of the modern office is based upon written documents ('the files'), which are preserved in their original or draught form. There is, therefore, a staff of subaltern officials and scribes of all sorts. The body of officials actively engaged in a 'public' office, along with the respective apparatus of material implements and the files, make up a 'bureau.' In private enterprise, 'the bureau' is often called 'the office.'

In principle, the modern organization of the civil service separates the bureau from the private domicile of the official, and, in general, bureaucracy segregates official activity as something distinct from the sphere of private life. Public monies and equipment are divorced from the private property of the official. This condition is everywhere the product of a long development. Nowadays, it is found in public as well as in private enterprises; in the latter, the principle extends even to the leading entrepreneur. In principle, the executive office is separated from the household, business from private correspondence, and business assets from private fortunes. The more consistently the modern type of business management has been carried through the more are these separations the case. The beginnings of this process are to be found as early as the Middle Ages.

It is the peculiarity of the modern entrepreneur that he conducts himself as the 'first official' of his enterprise, in the very same way in which the ruler of a specifically modern bureaucratic state spoke of himself as 'the first servant' of the state.[1] The idea that the bureau activities of the state are intrinsically different in character from the management of private economic offices is a continental European notion and, by way of contrast, is totally foreign to the American way.

IV. Office management, at least all specialized office management—and such management is distinctly modern—usually presupposes thorough and expert training. This increasingly holds for the modern executive and employee of private enterprises, in the same manner as it holds for the state official.

V. When the office is fully developed, official activity demands the full working capacity of the official, irrespective of the fact that his obligatory time in the bureau may be firmly delimited. In the normal case, this is only the product of a long development, in the public as well as in the private office. Formerly, in all cases, the normal state of affairs was reversed: official business was discharged as a secondary activity.

VI. The management of the office follows general rules, which are more or less stable, more or less exhaustive, and which can be learned. Knowledge of these rules represents a special technical

---

1   Frederick II of Prussia.

learning which the officials possess. It involves jurisprudence, or administrative or business management.

The reduction of modern office management to rules is deeply embedded in its very nature. The theory of modern public administration, for instance, assumes that the authority to order certain matters by decree—which has been legally granted to public authorities—does not entitle the bureau to regulate the matter by commands given for each case, but only to regulate the matter abstractly. This stands in extreme contrast to the regulation of all relationships through individual privileges and bestowals of favor, which is absolutely dominant in patrimonialism, at least in so far as such relationships are not fixed by sacred tradition.

The Position of the Official

All this results in the following for the internal and external position of the official:

I. Office holding is a 'vocation.' This is shown, first, in the requirement of a firmly prescribed course of training, which demands the entire capacity for work for a long period of time, and in the generally prescribed and special examinations which are prerequisites of employment. Furthermore, the position of the official is in the nature of a duty. This determines the internal structure of his relations, in the following manner: Legally and actually, office holding is not considered a source to be exploited for rents or emoluments, as was normally the case during the Middle Ages and frequently up to the threshold of recent times. Nor is office holding considered a usual exchange of services for equivalents, as is the case with free labor contracts. Entrance into an office, including one in the private economy, is considered an acceptance of a specific obligation of faithful management in return for a secure existence. It is decisive for the specific nature of modern loyalty to an office that, in the pure type, it does not establish a relationship to a *person*, like the vassal's or disciple's faith in feudal or in patrimonial relations of authority. Modern loyalty is devoted to impersonal and functional purposes. Behind the functional purposes, of course, 'ideas of culture-values' usually stand. These are *ersatz* for the earthly or supra-mundane personal master: ideas such as 'state,' 'church,' 'community,' 'party,' or 'enterprise' are thought of as being realized in a community; they provide an ideological halo for the master.

The political official—at least in the fully developed modern state—is not considered the personal servant of a ruler. Today, the bishop, the priest, and the preacher are in fact no longer, as in early Christian times, holders of purely personal charisma. The supra-mundane and sacred values which they offer are given to everybody who seems to be worthy of them and who asks for them. In former times, such leaders acted upon the personal command of their master; in principle, they were responsible only to him. Nowadays, in spite of the partial survival of the old theory, such religious leaders are officials in the service of a functional purpose, which in the present-day 'church' has become routinized and, in turn, ideologically hallowed.

The Leveling of Social Differences

Bureaucratic organization has usually come into power on the basis of a leveling of economic and social differences. This leveling has been at least relative, and has concerned the significance of social and economic differences for the assumption of administrative functions.

Bureaucracy inevitably accompanies modern *mass democracy* in contrast to the democratic self-government of small homogeneous units. This results from the characteristic principle of bureaucracy: the abstract regularity of the execution of authority, which is a result of the demand for 'equality before the law' in the personal and functional sense—hence, of the horror of 'privilege,' and the principled rejection of doing business 'from case to case.' Such regularity also follows from the social preconditions of the origin of bureaucracies. The non-bureaucratic administration of any large social structure rests in some way upon the fact that existing social, material, or honorific preferences and ranks are connected with administrative functions and duties. This usually means that a direct or indirect economic exploitation or a 'social' exploitation of position, which every sort of administrative activity gives to its bearers, is equivalent to the assumption of administrative functions.

Bureaucratization and democratization within the administration of the state therefore signify and increase the cash expenditures of the public treasury. And this is the case in spite of the fact that bureaucratic administration is usually more 'economical' in character than other forms of administration. Until recent times—at least from the point of view of the treasury—the cheapest way of satisfying the need for administration was to leave almost the entire local administration and lower judicature to the landlords of Eastern Prussia. The same fact applies to the administration of sheriffs in England. Mass democracy makes a clean sweep of the feudal, patrimonial, and—at least in intent—the plutocratic privileges in administration. Unavoidably it puts paid professional labor in place of the historically inherited avocational administration by notables.

This not only applies to structures of the state. For it is no accident that in their own organizations, the democratic mass parties have completely broken with traditional notable rule based upon personal relationships and personal esteem. Yet such personal structures frequently continue among the old conservative as well as the old liberal parties. Democratic mass parties are bureaucratically organized under the leadership of party officials, professional party and trade union secretaries, et cetera. In Germany, for instance, this has happened in the Social Democratic party and in the agrarian mass-movement; and in England, for the first time, in the caucus democracy of Gladstone-Chamberlain, which was originally organized in Birmingham and since the 1870's has spread. In the United States, both parties since Jackson's administration have developed bureaucratically. In France, however, attempts to organize disciplined political parties on the basis of an election system that would compel bureaucratic organization have repeatedly failed. The resistance of local circles of notables against the ultimately unavoidable bureaucratization of the parties, which would encompass the entire country and break their influence, could not be overcome. Every advance of the simple election techniques, for ins ance the system of proportional elections, which calculates with fiᵍures, means a strict and inter-local bureaucratic organization of the parties and therewith an increasing domination of party bureaucracy and discipline, as well as the elimination of the local circles of notables—at least this holds for great states.

The progress of bureaucratization in the state administrat.on itself is a parallel phenomenon of democracy, as is quite obvious in France, North America, and now in England. Of course one must always remember that the term 'democratization' can be misleading. The *demos* itself, in the sense of an inarticulate mass, never 'governs' larger associations; rather, it is governed, and its existence only changes the way in which the executive leaders are selected and the measure of influence which the *demos,* or better, which social circles from its midst are able to exert upon the content and the direction of administrative activities by supplementing what is called 'public opinion.' 'Democratization,' in the sense here intended, does not necessarily mean an increasingly active share of the governed in the authority of the social structure. This may be a result of democratization, but it is not necessarily the case.

We must expressly recall at this point that the political concept of democracy, deduced from the 'equal rights' of the governed, includes these postulates: (1) prevention of the development of a closed status group of officials in the interest of a universal accessibility of office, and (2) minimization of the authority of officialdom in the interest of expanding the sphere of influence of 'public opinion' as far as practicable. Hence, wherever possible, political democracy strives to shorten the term of office by election and recall and by not binding the candidate to a special expertness. Thereby democracy inevitably comes into conflict with the bureaucratic tendencies which, by its fight against notable rule, democracy has produced. The generally loose term 'democratization' cannot be used here, in so far as it is understood to mean the minimization of the civil servants' ruling power in favor of the greatest possible 'direct' rule of the *demos*, which in practice means the respective party leaders of the *demos*. The most decisive thing here—indeed it is rather exclusively so—is the *leveling of the governed* in opposition to the ruling and bureaucratically articulated group, which in its turn may occupy a quite autocratic position, both in fact and in form.

In Russia, the destruction of the position of the old landed nobility through the regulation of the Mjeshtshitelstvo (rank order) and the permeation of the old nobility by an office nobility were characteristic transitional phenomena in the development of bureaucracy. In China, the estimation of rank and the qualification for office according to the number of examinations passed mean something similar, but they have had consequences which, in theory at least, are still sharper. In France, the Revolution and still more Bonapartism have made the bureaucracy all-powerful. In the Catholic Church, first the feudal and then all independent local intermediary powers were eliminated. This was begun by Gregory VII and continued through the Council of Trent, the Vatican Council, and it was completed by the edicts of Pius X. The transformation of these local powers into pure functionaries of the central authority were connected with the constant increase in the factual significance of the formally quite dependent chaplains, a process which above all was based on the political party organization of Catholicism. Hence this process meant an advance of bureaucracy and at the same time of 'passive democratization,' as it were, that is, the leveling of the governed. The substitution of the bureaucratic army for the self-equipped army of notables is everywhere a process of 'passive' democratization, in the sense in which every establishment of an absolute military monarchy in the place of a feudal estate or of a republic of notables is. This has held, in principle, even for the development of the state in Egypt in spite of all the peculiarities involved. Under the Roman principate the bureaucratization of the provincial administration in the field of tax collection, for instance, went hand in hand with the elimination of the plutocracy of a capitalist class, which, under the Republic, had been all-powerful. Ancient capitalism itself was finally eliminated with this stroke.

It is obvious that almost always economic conditions of some sort play their part in such 'democratizing' developments. Very

frequently we meet with the influence of an economically determined origin of new classes, whether plutocratic, petty bourgeois,
or proletarian in character. Such classes may call on the aid of,
or they may only call to life or recall to life, a political power, no
matter whether it is of legitimate or of Caesarist stamp. They
may do so in order to attain economic or social advantages by
political assistance. On the other hand, there are equally possible
and historically documented cases in which initiative came 'from
on high' and was of a purely political nature and drew advantages
from political constellations, especially in foreign affairs. Such
leadership exploited economic and social antagonisms as well as
class interests merely as a means for their own purpose of gaining
purely political power. For this reason, political authority has
thrown the antagonistic classes out of their almost always unstable
equilibrium and called their latent interest conflicts into battle.
It seems hardly possible to give a general statement of this.

The extent and direction of the course along which economic
influences have moved, as well as the nature in which political
power relations exert influence, vary widely. In Hellenic Antiquity,
the transition to disciplined combat by Hoplites, and in Athens,
the increasing importance of the navy laid the foundation for the
conquest of political power by the strata on whose shoulders the
military burden rested. In Rome, however, the same development
shook the rule of the office nobility only temporarily and seemingly. Although the modern mass army has everywhere been a
means of breaking the power of notables, by itself it has in no way
served as a leverage for active, but rather for merely passive,
democratization. One contributing factor, however, has been the
fact that the ancient citizen army rested economically upon self-
equipment, whereas the modern army rests upon the bureaucratic
procurement of requirements.

The advance of the bureaucratic structure rests upon 'technical' superiority. This fact leads here, as in the whole field of
technique, to the following: the advance has been realized most
slowly where older structural forms have been technically well
developed and functionally adjusted to the requirements at hand.
This was the case, for instance, in the administration of notables

in England and hence England was the slowest of all countries to succumb to bureaucratization or, indeed, is still only partly in the process of doing so. The same general phenomenon exists when highly developed systems of gaslight or of steam railroads with large and fixed capital offer stronger obstacles to electrification than in completely new areas which are opened up for electrification.

The Permanent Character of the Bureaucratic Machine

Once it is fully established, bureaucracy is among those social structures which are the hardest to destroy. Bureaucracy is *the* means of carrying 'community action' over into rationally ordered 'societal action.' Therefore, as an instrument for 'societalizing' relations of power, bureaucracy has been and is a power instrument of the first order—for the one who controls the bureaucratic apparatus.

Under otherwise equal conditions, a 'societal action,' which is methodically ordered and led, is superior to every resistance of 'mass' or even of 'communal action.' And where the bureaucratization of administration has been completely carried through, a form of power relation is established that is practically unshatterable.

The individual bureaucrat cannot squirm out of the apparatus in which he is harnessed. In contrast to the honorific or avocational 'notable,' the professional bureaucrat is chained to his activity by his entire material and ideal existence. In the great majority of cases, he is only a single cog in an ever-moving mechanism which prescribes to him an essentially fixed route of march. The official is entrusted with specialized tasks and normally the mechanism cannot be put into motion or arrested by him, but only from the very top. The individual bureaucrat is thus forged to the community of all the functionaries who are integrated into the mechanism. They have a common interest in seeing that the mechanism continues its functions and that the societally exercised authority carries on.

The ruled, for their part, cannot dispense with or replace the bureaucratic apparatus of authority once it exists. For this bureaucracy rests upon expert training, a functional specialization of work, and an attitude set for habitual and virtuoso-like mastery of single yet methodically integrated functions. If the official stops working, or if his work is forcefully interrupted, chaos results, and it is difficult to improvise replacements from among the governed who are fit to master such chaos. This holds for public administration as well as for private economic management. More and more the material fate of the masses depends upon the steady and correct functioning of the increasingly bureaucratic organizations of private capitalism. The idea of eliminating these organizations becomes more and more utopian.

The discipline of officialdom refers to the attitude-set of the official for precise obedience within his *habitual* activity, in public as well as in private organizations. This discipline increasingly becomes the basis of all order, however great the practical importance of administration on the basis of the filed documents may be. The naive idea of Bakuninism of destroying the basis of 'acquired rights' and 'domination' by destroying public documents overlooks the settled orientation of *man* for keeping to the habitual rules and regulations that continue to exist independently of the documents. Every reorganization of beaten or dissolved troops, as well as the restoration of administrative orders destroyed by revolt, panic, or other catastrophes, is realized by appealing to the trained orientation of obedient compliance to such orders. Such compliance has been conditioned into the officials, on the one hand, and, on the other hand, into the governed. If such an appeal is successful it brings, as it were, the disturbed mechanism into gear again.

The objective indispensability of the once-existing apparatus, with its peculiar, 'impersonal' character, means that the mechanism—in contrast to feudal orders based upon personal piety—is easily made to work for anybody who knows how to gain control over it. A rationally ordered system of officials continues to function smoothly after the enemy has occupied the area; he merely needs to change the top officials. This body of officials continues to operate because it is to the vital interest of everyone concerned, including above all the enemy.

During the course of his long years in power, Bismarck brought his ministerial colleagues into unconditional bureaucratic dependence by eliminating all independent statesmen. Upon his retirement, he saw to his surprise that they continued to manage their offices unconcerned and undismayed, as if he had not been the master mind and creator of these creatures, but rather as if some single figure had been exchanged for some other figure in the bureaucratic machine. With all the changes of masters in France since the time of the First Empire, the power machine has remained essentially the same. Such a machine makes 'revolution,' in the sense of the forceful creation of entirely new formations of authority, technically more and more impossible, especially when the apparatus controls the modern means of communication (telegraph, et cetera) and also by virtue of its internal rationalized structure. In classic fashion, France has demonstrated how this process has substituted *coups d'état* for 'revolutions': all successful transformations in France have amounted to *coups d'état*.

III. Charisma and Institutionalization
in the Legal System

The legal sphere is of crucial importance to the institutionalization of charisma, especially in macrosocietal terms. Any legal system may be looked upon as composed of a series of small, detailed regulations and injunctions, all of them dealing mainly with the organizational aspects of maintenance of order and of orderly social relations. But the legal system does also embody, in one way or another, the basic conception of cosmic and cultural order that is prevalent in a particular society. Hence any legal system is not only related to the political but also to the religious and cultural spheres. As a result, the legal system is not only prone to be itself susceptible to charismatic innovation, but also, beyond this, it is the natural institutional sphere in which some of the basic charismatic orientations, born in religious or political spheres, and the charismatic extension of substantive rationality becomes fully articulated.

This part is organized in the same way as the previous ones. First is presented Weber's analysis of the legal system, with special emphasis on the function of charismatic activities and orientations in the formation of new laws and in the transformation of existing laws. The second part is an analysis of the development of the legal system from the sacred law throughout the natural law up to the modern rational legal system.

8

FORMAL AND SUBSTANTIVE RATIONALIZATION IN THE LAW—SACRED LAWS

THE CONSIDERATIONS of the last chapter raise the important problem, already touched upon in various places, of the influence of the form of political authority on the formal aspects of the law. A definitive analysis of this problem requires an analysis of the various types of authority which we shall not undertake until later. However, a few general remarks may be made at this point. The older forms of popular justice had originated in conciliatory proceedings between kinship-groups. The primitive formalistic irrationality of these older forms of justice was everywhere cast off under the impact of the authority of princes or magistrates,[1] or, in certain situations, of an organized priesthood. With this impact, the substance of the law, too, was lastingly influenced, although the character of this influence varied with the various types of authority. The more rational the authority exercising the administrative machinery of the princes or hierarchs became, that is, the greater the extent to which administrative "officials" were used in the exercise of the power, the greater was the likelihood that the legal procedure would also become rational[2] both in form and substance. To the extent to which the

From *Max Weber on Law in Economy and Society*, translated from Max Weber, *Wirtschaft und Gesellschaft*, second edition (1925) by Edward Shils and Max Rheinstein. Published 1954 by Harvard University Press, Cambridge, Mass. Reprinted by permission.

1   Imperium, bannus. [Weber's note.]
2   In a variety of senses. [Weber's note.]

rationality of the organization of authority increased, irrational forms of procedure were eliminated and the substantive law was systematized, i.e., the law as a whole was rationalized. This process occurred, for instance, in antiquity in the *jus honorarium* and the praetorian remedies,[3] in the capitularies of the Frankish Kings,[4] in the procedural innovations of the English Kings and Lords Chancellor,[5] or in the inquisitorial procedure of the Catholic Church.[6] However, these rationalizing tendencies were not part of an articulate and unambiguous policy on the part of the wielders of power; they were rather driven in this direction by the needs of their own rational administration, as, for instance, in the case of the administrative machinery of the Papacy, or by powerful interest-groups with whom they were allied and to whom rationality in substantive law and procedure constituted an advantage, as, for instance, to the bourgeois classes of Rome, of the late Middle Ages, or of modern times. Where these interests were absent the secularization of the law and the growth of a specialized, strictly formal mode of juridical thought either remained in an incipient stage or was even positively counteracted. In general terms, this may be attributed to the fact that the rationality of ecclesiastical hierarchies as well as of patrimonial sovereigns is substantive in character,[7] so that their aim is not that of achieving that highest degree of formal juridical precision which would maximize the chances for the correct prediction of legal conse-

---

[3]   *Ius honorarium*—The law created by the praetor in addition to, or in modification of, the *ius civile* as contained in the formal *leges* or in ancient tradition.

[4]   See *Max Weber on Law in Economy and Society*, p. 56.

[5]   Cf. PLUCKNETT, 82 *et seq.*; 2 ASSOCIATION OF AMERICAN LAW SCHOOLS, SELECT ESSAYS IN ANGLO-AMERICAN LEGAL HISTORY (1908) 367.

[6]   Legal procedure, civil or criminal, is said to be inquisitorial when the ascertainment of the facts is regarded primarily as the task of the judge, while in the so-called adversary procedure the true facts are expected to emerge from the allegations and proofs of the parties without the active coöperation of the judge. A shift from the predominantly adversary procedure of the Germanic laws was initiated in the later Middle Ages by the Church, whose model became influential for procedural development through Western Europe.

[7]   Cf. W.u.G. Part II, c. IV, esp. § 10.

quences and for the rational systematization of law and procedure. The aim is rather to find a type of law which is most appropriate to the expediential and ethical goals of the authorities in question. To these carriers of legal development the self-contained and specialized "juridical" treatment of legal questions is an alien idea, and they are not at all interested in any separation of law from ethics. This is particularly true, generally speaking, of theocratically influenced legal systems, which are characterized by a combination of legal rules and ethical demands. Yet in the course of this kind of rationalization of legal thinking on the one hand and of the forms of social relationships on the other, the most diverse consequences could emerge from the non-juridical components of a legal doctrine of priestly make. One of these possible consequences was the separation of *fas*, the religious command, from *jus*, the established law for the settlement of such human conflicts which had no religious relevance.[8] In this situation, it was possible for *jus* to pass through an independent course of development into a rational and formal legal system, in which emphasis might be either upon logical or upon empirical elements. This actually happened both in Rome and in the Middle Ages. We shall discuss later the ways in which the relationship between the religiously fixed and the freely established components of the law were determined in these cases. As we shall see hereafter, it was quite possible, as thinking became increasingly secular, for the sacred law to encounter as a rival, or to be replaced by, a "natural law" which would operate beside the positive law partly as an ideal postulate and partly as a doctrine with varying actual influence upon legislation or legal practice. It was also possible, however, that the religious prescriptions were never differentiated from secular rules and that the characteristically theocratic combination of religious and ritualistic prescriptions with legal rules remained unchanged. In this case, there arose an inextricable conglomeration of ethical and legal duties, moral exhortations and legal commandments without formalized explicitness and the result

8   On the Roman distinction between *ius* and *fas* see JOLOWICZ, *op. cit.* 86 *et seq.*; MITTEIS 22–30 and literature there listed. For a baroque use of the terms, see BLACKSTONE III, 2.

was a specifically nonformal type of law. Just which of these two possibilities actually occurred depended upon the already mentioned characteristics of the religion in question and the principles that governed its relation to the legal system and the state; in part it depended upon the power position of the priesthood vis-à-vis the state; and finally, upon the structure of the state. It was because of their special structure of authority that in almost all the Asiatic civilizations the last mentioned of these courses of development came to emerge and persist.

But although certain features in the logical structure of different legal systems may be similar, they may nevertheless be the result of diverse types of authority. Authoritarian powers, especially those resting on personal loyalty, and more particularly theocracy and patrimonial monarchy, have usually created a nonformal type of law. But a nonformal type of law may also be produced by certain types of democracy. The explanation lies in the fact that not only such power-wielders as hierarchs and despots, and particularly enlightened despots, but also democratic demagogues may refuse to be bound by formal rules, even by those they have made themselves, excepting, however, those norms which they regard as religiously sacred and hence as absolutely binding. They all are confronted by the inevitable conflict between an abstract formalism of legal certainty and their desire to realize substantive goals. Juridical formalism enables the legal system to operate like a technically rational machine. Thus it guarantees to individuals and groups within the system a relative maximum of freedom, and greatly increases for them the possibility of predicting the legal consequences of their actions. Procedure becomes a specific type of pacified contest, bound to fixed and inviolable "rules of the game."

Primitive procedures for adjusting conflicts of interest between kinship groups are characterized by rigorously formalistic rules of evidence. The same is true of judicial procedure in *Dinggenossenschaften*. These rules were at first influenced by magical beliefs which required that the questions of evidence should be asked in the proper way and by the proper party. Even afterwards it took a long time for procedure to develop the idea that a fact, as understood today, could be "established" by a rational procedure, particularly by the examination of witnesses, which is the most important method now, not to speak at all of circumstantial evidence. The compurgators of earlier epochs did not swear that a statement of fact was true but confirmed the rightness of their side by exposing themselves to the divine wrath. We may observe that this practice was not much less realistic than that of our days when a great many people, perhaps a majority, believe their task as witnesses to be simply that of "swearing" as to which party is "in the right." In ancient law, proof was therefore not regarded as a "burden" but rather as a "right" of one or the other of the contending parties, and ancient law was liberal in allowing a party this right. The judge, however, was strictly bound by rules and the traditional methods of proof. The modern theory of as late a period as that of common law procedure[9] is different from ancient procedure only in that it would treat proof as a burden. It, too, binds the judge to the motions of, and the evidence offered by, the parties and, indeed, the same principle applies to the entire conduct of the suit: in accordance with the principle of adversary procedure the judge has to wait for the motions of the parties. Facts which are neither stipulated nor alleged and proved, and facts which remain undisclosed by the recognized methods of proof, be they rational or irrational, do not exist as far as the judge is concerned, who aims at establishing only that relative truth which is attainable within the limits set by the procedural acts of the parties.

Exactly alike in this respect were the oldest clear-cut forms of adjudication, i.e., arbitration and composition between contending kinship groups, with oracle or ordeal constituting the trial procedure. This ancient legal procedure was rigorously formal like all activities oriented towards the invocation of magical or

9   Namely, of continental Europe, i.e., the procedure which was common on the Continent before the reforms introduced by the codification of the nineteenth and twentieth centuries. In this and the following sentences Weber speaks also, however, of the continental procedure of the present day, which, as will appear, is not basically different from Anglo-American procedure.

divine powers; but, by means of the irrational supernatural character of the decisive acts of procedure, it tried to obtain the substantively "right" decision. When, however, the authority of, and the belief in, these irrational powers came to be lost and when they were replaced by rational proof and the logical derivation of decisions, the formalistic adjudication had to become a mere contest between litigants, regulated so as to aim at the relatively optimal chance of finding the truth. The promotion of the progress of the suit is the concern of the parties rather than that of the state. They are not compelled by the judge to do anything they do not wish to do at their own initiative. It is for this very reason that the judge cannot comply with the quest for the optimal realization of substantive demands of a political, ethical or affective character by means of an adjudication which could give effect to considerations of concrete expediency or equity in individual cases. Formal justice guarantees the maximum freedom for the interested parties to represent their formal legal interests. But because of the unequal distribution of economic power, which the system of formal justice legalizes, this very freedom must time and again produce consequences which are contrary to the substantive postulates of religious ethics or of political expediency. Formal justice is thus repugnant to all authoritarian powers, theocratic as well as patriarchic, because it diminishes the dependency of the individual upon the grace and power of the authorities.[10] To democracy, however, it has been repugnant because it decreases the dependency of the legal practice and therewith of the individuals upon the decisions of their fellow citizens.[11] Furthermore, the development of the trial into a peace-

---

[10]   Weber has anticipated the procedural reforms of the modern totalitarian states which have shown marked tendencies to strengthen the inquisitorial at the expense of the adversary principle. Cf. M. Ploscowe, *Purging Italian Criminal Justice of Fascism* (1945), 45 COL. L. REV. 240; BERMAN, JUSTICE IN RUSSIA 207; EBERHARD SCHMIDT, EINFÜHRUNG IN DIE GESCHICHTE DER DEUTSCHEN STRAFRECHTSPFLEGE (1947) 406; also SCHOENKE, ZIVILPROZESSRECHT (6th ed. 1949) 25; H. Schroeder, *Die Herrschaft der Parteien im Zivilprozess* (1943), 16 ANNUARIO DI DIRITTO COMPARATO 168.

[11]   Apparently, Weber is thinking here of the democracy of the Athenian rather than of the modern Western type.

ful contest of conflicting interests can contribute to the further concentration of economic and social power. In all these cases formal justice, due to its necessarily abstract character, infringes upon the ideals of substantive justice. It is precisely this abstract character which constitutes the decisive merit of formal justice to those who wield the economic power at any given time and who are therefore interested in its unhampered operation, and also to those who on ideological grounds attempt to break down authoritarian control or to restrain irrational mass emotions for the purpose of opening up individual opportunities and liberating capacities. To all these groups nonformal justice simply represents the likelihood of absolute arbitrariness and subjectivistic instability. Among those groups who favor formal justice we must include all those political and economic interest groups to whom the stability and predictability of legal procedure are of very great importance, i.e., particularly rational, economic, and political organizations intended to have a permanent character. Above all, those in possession of economic power look upon a formal rational administration of justice as a guarantee of "freedom," a value which is repudiated not only by theocratic or patriarchal-authoritarian groups but, under certain conditions, also by democratic groups. Formal justice and the "freedom" which it guarantees are indeed rejected by all groups ideologically interested in substantive justice. Such groups are better served by khadi-justice than by the formal type. The popular justice of the direct Attic democracy, for example, was decidedly a form of khadi-justice. Modern trial by jury, too, is frequently khadi-justice in actual practice although, perhaps, not according to formal law; even in this highly formalized type of a limited adjudication one can observe a tendency to be bound by formal legal rules only to the extent directly required by procedural technique. Quite generally, in all forms of popular justice decisions are reached on the basis of concrete, ethical, or political considerations or of feelings oriented toward social justice. The latter type of justice prevailed particularly in Athens, but it can be found even today. In this respect, there are similar tendencies displayed by popular democracy on the one hand and the authoritarian power of theocracy or of patriarchal monarchs on the other.

When, for example, French jurors, contrary to formal law, regularly acquit a husband who has killed his wife's paramour caught in the act, they are doing exactly what Frederick the Great did when he dispensed "royal justice" for the benefit of Arnold, the miller.[12]

The distinctive characteristic of a theocratic administration of justice consists entirely in the primacy of concrete ethical considerations; its indifference or aversion to formalism is limited only in so far as the rules of the sacred law are explicitly formulated. But in so far as norms of the latter apply, the theocratic type of law results in the exact opposite, viz., a law which, in order to be adaptable to changing circumstances, develops an extremely formalistic casuistry. Secular, patrimonial-authoritarian administration of justice is much freer than theocratic justice, even where it has to conform with tradition, which usually allows quite a degree of flexibility.

Finally, the administration of justice by honoratiores presents two aspects depending on what legal interests there are involved, those of the honoratiores' own class or those of the class dominated by them. In England, for instance, all cases coming before the central courts were adjudicated in a strictly formalistic way. But

[12]   Famous case in which Frederick tried to intervene in a private lawsuit.

In 1779, upon suit by his landlord, a baron, Arnold, a humble miller, was ejected because of nonpayment of rent. Arnold turned to the king who ordered the court to vacate its judgment and restore Arnold to the possession of the mill. The judges refused to render a decision "which would be against the law." When they continued in their "obstinate" refusal to obey the king's angrily repeated command, he ordered the supreme court to sentence them to jail. When the supreme court judges declared that the law would not permit such a step, they, together with the judges of the lower court, were ordered to be arrested by the king and were sentenced by him to one year's imprisonment, loss of office, and payment of damages to Arnold. It was one of the first acts of government of Frederick's successor, Frederick William II, to comply with the demand of the public to rehabilitate the judges and to indemnify them out of the public treasury. See W. JELLINEK, VERWALTUNGSRECHT 85 and literature cited there; for an account in English, see the translation by I. Husik of R. STAMMLER, THE THEORY OF JUSTICE (1925) 243 *et seq.*

the courts of justices of the peace, which dealt with the daily troubles and misdemeanors of the masses, were informal and representative of khadi-justice to an extent completely unknown on the Continent. Furthermore, the high cost of litigation and legal services amounted for those who could not afford to purchase them to a denial of justice, which was rather similar to that which existed, for other reasons, in the judicial system of the Roman Republic.[13] This denial of justice was in close conformity with the interests of the propertied, especially the capitalistic, classes. But such a dual judicial policy of formal adjudication of disputes within the upper class, combined with arbitrariness or de facto denegation of justice for the economically weak, is not always possible. If it cannot be had, capitalistic interests will fare best under a rigorously formal system of adjudication, which applies in all cases and operates under the adversary system of procedure. In any case adjudication by honoratiores inclines to be essentially empirical, and its procedure is complicated and expensive. It may thus well stand in the way of the interests of the bourgeois classes and it may indeed be said that England achieved capitalistic supremacy among the nations not because but rather in spite of its judicial system. For these very reasons the bourgeois strata have generally tended to be intensely interested in a rational procedural system and therefore in a systematized and unambiguously formal and purposefully constructed substantive law which eliminates both obsolete traditions and arbitrariness and in which rights can have their source exclusively in general objective norms. Such a systematically codified law was thus demanded by the English Puritans,[14] the Roman Plebeians,[15] and the German

---

[13]   Cf. A. MENDELSSOHN-BARTHOLDY, IMPERIUM DES RICHTERS (1908). The allusion points to the early period when Rome was dominated by the patricians, who entirely dominated the administration of justice, until their power was broken in the long struggle of the plebeians. Cf. MOMMSEN, HISTORY OF ROME (Dickson's tr. 1900) 341–369; JOLOWICZ 7–12.

[14]   Cf. I. SANFORD, STUDIES AND ILLUSTRATIONS OF THE GREAT REBELLION (1858); P. A. GOOCH, ENGLISH DEMOCRATIC IDEAS IN THE SEVENTEENTH CENTURY (2nd ed. 1927) 308; HOLDSWORTH 412.

[15]   In their struggle against patrician domination the plebeians

bourgeoisie of the fifteenth century.[16] But in all these cases such a system was still a long way off.

In the administration of justice of the theocratic type, in adjudication by secular honoratiores, in a court system guided by private or officially patented jurisconsults, as well as in that development of law and procedure which is based upon the imperium and the contempt powers of magistrates, princes, or officials holding in their hands the direction of the lawsuit,[17] the view is always

---

achieved one of their most important successes when they compelled the patricians to consent to the appointment of a commission to write down the laws and thus to make their knowledge generally accessible. The product of the commission's work was the law of the Twelve Tables, which is reported by Livy (III, 9 *et seq.*) to have been promulgated in 450/449 B.C. and which for centuries was taken as the basis of the Roman *ius civile*.

16   In the fifteenth and sixteenth centuries the laws were collected and "reformed" in numerous German cities. On these "Stadtrechte," see GIERKE, PRIVATRECHT 63; STOBBE I, 488; II, 3; also BRUNNER, GRUNDZÜGE DER DEUTSCHEN RECHTSGESCHICHTE (5th ed. 1912) 270. On one of the most important city laws of this kind, the Frankfurter Reformation, see COING, DIE REZEPTION DES RÖMISCHEN RECHTS IN FRANKFURT AM MAIN (1939) 141.

17   "Magistrates, princes, or officials holding in their hands the direction of the lawsuit": This clumsy circumlocution had to be chosen to translate the German term, "die die Prozesse instruierenden Magistrate, Fürsten, und Beamte." *Prozessinstruktion* is a term of art of German theory of procedure. It means the role and activity of those persons who keep a lawsuit, civil or criminal, going and direct the course which it has to follow.

In the type of procedure mentioned in the text, the *Prozessinstruktion* is vested in a public officer or potentate who presides over the trial or at least that part of it in which the issues are formulated, but does not himself render the final judgment. The principal illustration is constituted by the role of the Roman *praetor* who presided over the proceedings *in iure*, in which there were formulated, with his active participation, those issues of law or fact or both which had to be decided, *in iudicio*, by the *iudex*, whom the *praetor* would appoint.

Another variety is represented by popular assemblies, especially of the Germanic type, which would be presided over by a prince or his representative or by some other person of authority, while the decision would be made by all, or some, of the members of the assembly. Both the Roman *praetor* and the Germanic prince, etc., had the *Banngewalt*, i.e., the power to subpoena attendance upon penalty of outlawry or forfeiture of property.

strictly adhered to that fundamentally the law has always been what it is and that no more is needed than an interpretation of its ambiguities and its application to particular cases. Nonetheless, as we have seen[18] the emergence of rationally compacted norms is in itself possible even under rather primitive economic conditions, once the hold of magical stereotypization has been broken. The existence of irrational techniques of revelation as the sole means of innovation has often implied a high degree of flexibility in tae norms; their absence, on the other hand, has resulted in a higher degree of stereotypization, because in that event the sacred tradition as such remained the sole holy element and would thus be sublimated by the priests into a system of sacred law.

Sacred law and sacred lawmaking have emerged in rather different ways in different geographical areas and in different branches of the law: their persistence has likewise varied. We shall completely disregard at this point of our analysis the special attention which sacred law pays to all problems of punishment and atonement, a concern originally caused by purely magical norms; nor shall we here consider its interest in political law, or the originally magically conditioned norms which regulated the times and places at which trials were allowed to take place, or the modes of proof. In the main, we shall deal only with "private law" as commonly understood. In this branch of law, the fundamental principles regarding the permissibility and the incidents of marriage, the law of the family, and, closely related to it, that of inheritance, have constituted a major branch of sacred law in China and India as well as in the Roman fas, the Islamic Shariah, and the medieval canon law. The ancient magical prohibitions of incest were early forms of religious regulation of marriage.[19] In addition there was the importance of appropriate sacrifices to the ancestors and other familial sacra, which caused the intrusion of sacred law into the law of the family and inheritance, and in the latter field the Church's interest in revenue and, consequently, in the validity of wills, tended to maintain its control, when, in

[18]   Cf. *supra*, c. V.
[19]   See WESTERMARCK, HISTORY OF HUMAN MARRIAGE c. XIX; FREUD, TOTEM AND TABOO (Brill transl. 1927) c. I; Fortune, R., *Incest*, 7 ENCYC. SOC. SCI. 620 and further literature cited there.

the areas of Christianity, the pagan sacred interests had disappeared.[20] Secular law was liable to come into conflict with the religious norms relating to objects and places dedicated to religious purposes or consecrated for other reasons or magically tabooed. In the sphere of contract, sacred law intervened on purely formal grounds whenever a religious form of promise, especially an oath, had been used, a situation which occurred frequently and in the beginning, we may surmise, regularly.[21] On substantive grounds, sacred law became involved whenever important norms of a religious-ethical character, for instance, the prohibition of usury, entered the picture.[22]

The relations between temporal and sacred law in general can vary considerably, depending upon the particular principles underlying the religious ethics in question. As long as religious ethics remains at the stage of magical or ritualistic formalism, it can, under certain circumstances, become paralyzed and completely ineffective through its own inherent means of refined rationalization of magical casuistry. In the course of the history of the Roman Republic the fas met with just this fate. There was scarcely a single sacred norm for the circumvention of which one could not have invented some appropriate sacred device or form

---

[20]   On the role of the Church in maintaining or reëstablishing the principle of freedom of testation, see POLLOCK AND MAITLAND II, 349; HOLDSWORTH III, 536, 541 et seq.

[21]   Here Weber apparently follows JHERING 263. In contrast MITTEIS 23, n. 2, points to the "well-known" fact "that in Roman private life the promissory oath was hardly used in any situations other than those in which legal coercion was lacking." Explicitly referring to Jhering, Mitteis states that "the idea of a religious component in the secular law of Rome has at one time been badly abused" (op. cit. 24, n. 4). More recently such ideas have been resuscitated, however, even more radically by HAEGER-STROEM, DER RÖMISCHE OBLIGATIONSBEGRIFF (1927), and DAS MAGIS-TRATISCHE IUS IM ZUSUMMENHANG MIT DE RÖM. SAKRALRECHT (1929).

[22]   This latter point will be discussed in connection with the problem of the economic significance of religious ethics. (The reference is to 2 W.U.G., c. IV, § 11, p. 336.) See also WEBER'S PROTESTANT ETHIC AND THE SPIRIT OF CAPITALISM (Parson's transl. 1930) 73 et seq., 201 et seq. and HISTORY, c. XXI 267 et seq.

of evasion.[23] The College of Augurs' power of intervention in cases of defective religious form and evil omina, which meant, practically speaking, a power to rescind the resolutions of the popular assemblies, was never formally abolished in Rome as it had been by Pericles and Ephialtes in the case of the equally sacredly conditioned power of the Athenian Areiopagus.[24] But under the absolute domination of the priesthood by the secular magisterial nobility, this power served political purposes exclusively, and its application, like that of the substantive fas, was rendered practically innocuous by peculiar sacred techniques. Thus, like the Hellenic law of the late period, the thoroughly secularized jus was guaranteed against intrusions from this direction, despite the extraordinarily large role played in Roman life by considerations of ritual obligation. The subordination of the priesthood to the profane power in the ancient polis, certain peculiar characteristics of the Roman Olympus and those modes of their treatment of

[23]   See JHERING I, 325 *et seq.* Recent research has thrown doubt on the correctness of applying the word *fas* to the sacred law of Rome. Cf. the following statement in JÖRS AND KUNKEL 19, n. 2: "In modern literature the distinction between *ius* and *fas* is commonly regarded as equivalent to that between temporal and sacred law. Such use of the terms does not, however, correspond to Roman usage. At first, *fas* meant that sphere which was left free by the Gods. It included quite particularly those aspects of life for which the temporal law could be effective. In an ethically deepened usage, which came to be frequent with the Ciceronian period, *fas* means that which is religiously *permitted* in contrast to *ius*, which means that which is *commanded*. Even in this sense, *fas* does not mean, however, a religiously moral order in contrast to *ius* as a man-made order. Such an idea did not arise before Christianity. Even less does *fas* mean the complex of rules concerning religious rites and similar problems. These rules belong to the *ius*, as *ius sacrum* or *ius pontificium*. The development of the meaning of *fas* is largely paralleled by that of the Greek word "ὅσιον; cf. WILAMOWITZ, PLATON I. 61; LATTE, HEILIGES RECHT 55 n. 16." Cf. also *supra* n. 9.

[24]   On the College of Augurs and its *interventio*, see JHERING I, 329 *et seq.* On the abolition of the Areiopagos, "by a decree which was carried, about B.C. 458 and by which, as Aristotle says, the Areiopagos was 'mutilated' and many of its hereditary rights abolished" (ARIST., POL. ii 9; CIC., DE NAT. DEOR. ii 29; DE REP. i 27), see the article in W. SMITH, DICTIONARY OF GREEK AND ROMAN ANTIQUITIES (1848) 128.

which we have spoken, were the factors by which this line of development was determined in Rome.[25]

[25]   Weber's treatment of the relations between religion and law corresponds to the prevailing opinion, as expressed especially by Mitteis. A much closer relationship and a more far-reaching influence of magico-religious ideas upon the development of Roman law has more recently been maintained by HÄGERSTROM, *op. cit. supra* n. 23; as to further literature on the problem see JÖRS AND KUNKEL 4, n. 3, 393.

9

NATURAL LAW

Natural Law as the Normative Standard of Positive Law

CONCEPTIONS OF the "rightness of the law" are sociologically relevant within a rational positive legal order only in so far as the particular answer to the problem gives rise to practical consequences for the behavior of law makers, legal practitioners, and social groups interested in the law. In other words, they become sociologically relevant only when practical legal life is materially affected by the conviction of the particular "legitimacy" of certain legal maxims, and of the directly binding force of certain principles which are not to be disrupted by any concessions to positive law imposed by mere power. Such a situation has repeatedly existed in the course of history, but quite particularly at the beginning of modern times and during the Revolutionary period, and in America it still exists. The substantive content of such maxims is usually designated as "Natural Law."[1]

From *Max Weber on Law in Economy and Society*, translated from Max Weber, *Wirtschaft und Gesellschaft*, second edition (1925) by Edward Shils and Max Rheinstein. Published 1954 by Harvard University Press, Cambridge, Mass. Reprinted by permission.

[1]   For concise surveys of, and bibliographies on, the various forms of Natural Law concepts and their role and significance, see G. Gurvitch, *Natural Law*, 11 ENCYC. SOC. SCI. 284; STONE 215; I. W. JONES, HISTORICAL INTRODUCTION TO THE THEORY OF LAW (1947); see also C. G. HAINES, REVIVAL OF NATURAL LAW CONCEPTS IN AMERICA (1930) and ROMMEN, NATURAL LAW (1947).

We encountered the *lex naturae* earlier[2] as an essentially Stoic creation which was taken over by *Christianity* for the purpose of constructing a bridge between its own ethics and the norms of the world.[3] It was the law legitimated by God's will for all men of this world of sin and violence, and thus stood in contrast to those of God's commands which were revealed directly to the faithful and are evident only to the elect. But here we must look at the lex naturae from another angle. Natural law is the sum total of all those norms which are valid independently of, and superior to, any positive law and which owe their dignity not to arbitrary enactment but, on the contrary, provide the very legitimation for the binding force of positive law. Natural law has thus been the collective term for those norms which owe their legitimacy not to their origin from a legitimate lawgiver, but to their immanent and teleological qualities. It is the specific and only consistent type of legitimacy of a legal order which can remain, once religious revelation and the authoritarian sacredness of a tradition and its bearers have lost their force. Natural law has thus been the specific form of legitimacy of a revolutionarily created order. The invocation of natural law has repeatedly been the method by which classes in revolt against the existing order have legitimated their aspirations, in so far as they did not, or could not, base their claims upon positive religious norms or revelation. Not every natural law, however, has been "revolutionary" in its intentions in the sense that it would provide the justification for the realization of certain norms by violence or by passive disobedience against an existing order. Indeed, natural law has also served to legitimate authoritarian powers of the most diverse types. A "natural law of the historically real" has been quite influential in opposition to the type of natural law which is based upon or produces abstract norms. A natural law axiom of this

---

2   No such passage can be found.
3   See E. TROELTSCH, THE SOCIAL TEACHINGS OF THE CHRISTIAN CHURCHES (2 vols., tr. by O. Wyon, London, 1931) and Weber's remarks on Troeltsch's paper on *The Stoic-Christian Natural Law* in VERHANDLUNGEN DES DEUTSCHEN SOZIOLOGENTAGS (1910) I, 196, 210, repr. in GES. AUFS. ZUR SOZIOLOGIE UND SOZIALPOLITIK (1924) 462.

provenience can be found, for instance, as the basis of the theory of the historical school concerning the preëminence of "customary law," a concept clearly formulated by this school for the first time.[4] It became quite explicit in the assertion that a legislator "could" not in any legally effective way restrict the sphere of validity of customary law by any enactment or exclude the derogation of the enacted law by custom. It was said to be impossible to forbid historical development to take its course. The same assumption by which enacted law is reduced to the rank of "mere" positive law is contained also in all those half historical and half naturalistic theories of Romanticism which regard the *Volksgeist*[5] as the only natural, and thus the only legitimate, source from which law and culture can emanate, and according to which all "genuine" law must have grown up "organically" and must be based directly upon the sense of justice, in contrast to "artificial," i.e., purposefully enacted, law.[6] The irrationalism of such axioms stands in sharp contrast to the natural law axioms of legal rationalism which alone were able to create norms of a formal type and to which the term "natural law" has a potiori been reserved for that reason.

The Origins of Modern Natural Law

The elaboration of natural law in modern times was in part based on the religious motivation provided by the rationalistic sects;[7] it was also partly derived from the concept of nature of the

4   Cf. *supra*, p. 67.

5   Folk spirit.

6   This attitude is represented by the Historical School, especially the Germanists, among whom Gierke has been particularly prominent (cf. *supra* c. IV, n. 9; c. IX, n. 74). An American representative was James C. Carter, the chief opponent of David Dudley Field's codification plans (see the article on him by Llewellyn in 3 Encyc. Soc. Sci. 243).

7   The role of the "rationalist" Protestant "sects," i.e., the Puritans, Baptists, Quakers, Methodists, etc., in the rise of the spirit of modern capitalism and, in this connection, in the development of formally rational modern law, constitutes one of the central themes in Weber's thought. The problem is treated extensively in the first volume of his Ges. Aufsätze zur Religionssoziologie (Parsons' tr. 1930), where the role of the sects

Renaissance, which everywhere strove to grasp the canon of the ends of "Nature's" will. To some extent, it is derived, too, from the idea, particularly indigenous to England, that every member of the community has certain inherent natural rights. This specifically English concept of "birthright" arose essentially under the influence of the popular conception that certain rights, which had been confirmed in Magna Charta as the special status rights of the barons, were national liberties of all Englishmen as such and that they were thus immune against any interference by the King or any other political authority.[8] But the transition to the conception that every human being as such has certain rights was mainly completed through the rationalistic enlightenment of the seventeenth and eighteenth centuries with the aid, for a time, of powerful religious, particularly Anabaptist, influences.

Transformation of Formal into Substantive Natural Law

The axioms of natural law fall into very different groups, of which we shall consider only those which bear some especially close relation to the economic order. The natural law legitimacy of positive law can be connected either with formal or with substantive conditions. The distinction is not a clear-cut one, because there simply cannot exist a completely formal natural law; the reason is that such a natural law would consist entirely of general legal concepts devoid of any content. Nonetheless, the distinction has great significance. The purest type of the first category is that "natural law" concept which arose in the seventeenth and eigh-

---

is discussed on pp. 207–236 (= Essays 302 *et seq.* and 450–459 [Weber's footnotes contain extensive references to literature]). In W.u.G., sociology of religion is treated in Part II, c. IV (pp. 227–356 and, as to the sects in particular, at pp. 812–817) ; see, furthermore, History (1950 ed.) 365.

[8]   The so-called Whig conception of English history; cf. H. Butterfield, The Englishman and His History (1944). On the real and the imaginary Magna Carta see W. S. McKechnie, *Magna Carta 1215–1915*, Magna Carta Commemoration Essays (1917) I, 18; M. Radin, *The Myth of Magna Carta* (1947) 60 Harv. L. Rev. 1060.

teenth centuries as a result of the already mentioned influences, especially in the form of the "contract theory," and more particularly the individualistic aspects of that theory. All legitimate law rests upon enactment, and all enactment, in turn, rests upon rational agreement. This agreement is either, first, real, i.e., derived from an actual original contract of free individuals, which also regulates the form in which new law is to be enacted in the future; or, second, ideal, in the sense that only that law is legitimate whose content does not contradict the conception of a reasonable order enacted by free agreement. The essential elements in such a natural law are the "freedoms," and above all, "freedom of contract." The voluntary rational contract became one of the universal formal principles of natural law construction, either as the assumed real historical basis of all rational consociations including the state, or, at least, as the regulative standard of evaluation. Like every formal natural law, this type is conceived as a system of rights legitimately acquired by purposive contract, and, as far as economic goods are concerned, it rests upon the basis of a community of economic agreement created by the full development of property. Its essential components are property and the freedom to dispose of property, i.e., property legitimately acquired by free contractual transaction made either as "primeval contract" with the whole world, or with certain other persons. Freedom of competition is implied as a constituent element. Freedom of contract has formal limits only to the extent that contracts, and associational conduct in general, must neither infringe upon the natural law by which they are legitimated nor impair inalienable freedoms. This basic principle applies to both private arrangements of individuals and the official actions of the organs of society meant to be obeyed by its members. Nobody may validly surrender himself into political or private slavery. For the rest, no enactment *can* validly limit the free disposition of the individual over his property and his working power. Thus, for example, every act of social welfare legislation prohibiting certain contents of the free labor contract, is on that account an infringement of freedom of contract. Until quite recently the Supreme Court of the United States has held that any such legislation is invalid on the purely formal ground that it is incompatible with the natural law preambles to the constitutions.[9]

"Nature" and "Reason" are the substantive criteria of what is legitimate from the standpoint of natural law. Both are regarded as the same, and so are the rules that are derived from them, so that general propositions about regularities of factual occurrences and general norms of conduct are held to coincide. The knowledge gained by human "reason" is regarded as identical with the "nature of things" or, as one would say nowadays, the "logic of things." The "ought" is identical with the "is," i.e., that which exists in the universal average. Those norms, which are arrived at by the logical analysis of the concepts of the law and ethics, belong, just as the "laws of nature," to those generally binding rules which "not even God Himself could change," and with which a legal order must not come into conflict. Thus, for instance, the only kind of money which meets the requirements of the "nature of things" and the principle of the legitimacy of vested rights is that which has achieved the position of money through the free exchange of goods, in other words, metallic money.[10] Some fifteenth-century fanatics therefore argued that, according to natural law, the state should rather go to pieces than that the legitimate stability of the law be sullied by the illegitimacy of "artificially" created paper money.[11] The very "concept" of the

[9]   *Sic.* What is meant is obviously the due process clause of the Fourteenth Amendment of the Constitution of the United States.

[10]   See WEBER, HISTORY 236 and literature cited at p. 377; also W.U.G. Part I, c. II, §§ 6, 32–36 (THEORY 173, 280 *et seq.*).

[11]   The source for this statement could not be located. It is difficult to visualize how anyone could have argued against paper money in the fifteenth century. While paper money had been used repeatedly in China at earlier times (cf. Lexis, *Papiergeld,* 6 HANDWÖRTERBUCH DER STAATS- WISSENSCHAFTEN, 3rd ed. 1911, p. 997; WEBER, GES. AUFS. ZUR RELI- GIONSSOZIOLOGIE 286), it was practically unknown in the West before the late seventeenth century. Both Lexis (*loc. cit.*) and W. Lotz (FINANZ- WISSENSCHAFT [2nd ed. 1931] 885) mention the occasional use of leather and similar emergency means of payment; however, "the systematic use for the procurement of public revenue of redeemable promises of payment circulating as currency" is said to be connected with the establishment of the Bank of England in 1694. Before that time manipulations of the

State is said to be abused by an infringement upon the legitimate law.

This formalism of natural law, however, was softened in several ways. First of all, in order to establish relations with the existing order, natural law had to accept legitimate grounds for the acquisition of rights which could not be derived from freedom of contract, especially acquisition through inheritance. There were numerous attempts to base the law of inheritance on natural law.[12] They were mainly of philosophical rather than positively juristic

---

currency were carried on by alteration of the coinage, as it was widely practiced by princes (cf. Palyi, *Coinage*, 3 Encyc. Soc. Sci. 622). In France, for instance, the coinage was altered no less than seventy-one times between 1351 and 1360, resulting in serious unrest and an uprising in Paris under Etienne Marcel (cf. A. Landry, Essay économique sur les mutations des monnaies l'ancienne France [1910]).

The problem of the permissibility of such manipulation was widely discussed in the literature. The legists (see *supra*, p. 181) generally supported the princes, the canonists were more reluctant, and the Aristotelians were critical, occasionally basing their position on natural law arguments. Nicolas Oresmes (c. 1320–1382) denied that the prince had any power of his own to change the coinage but conceded that he might do so with the consent of the Estates General for urgent reasons of the common weal (E. Bridrey, Nicole Oresme [1906]; P. Harsin, *Oresme*, 11 Encyc. Soc. Sci 479; A. E. Monroe, Early Economic Thought [1924] 79). Strong criticism was also voiced by Gabriel Biel (d. in 1495; cf. W. Roscher, Geschichte der Nationalökonomik in Deutschland [1874] 26), Cyriakus Spangenberg (1528–1604; cf. Roscher, *op. cit.* 169), and, particularly, in an anonymous pamphlet, published about 1530, on the occasion of a change in the monetary system of Saxony (W. Lotz, *Die drei Flugschriften über den Münzstreit der sächsischen Albertiner und Ernestiner* [1893], esp. at p. 10). No author could be found, however, who would have radically condemned any currency change under any circumstances. Nor could there be found any writer of the eighteenth or nineteenth century taking the position stated in Weber's text (cf. A. E. Monroe, *op. cit.*; and, by the same author, Monetary Theory before Adam Smith [1923]; Roscher, *op. cit.*).

12   See, for instance, Leibniz, who derives inheritance from the immortality of the soul (Nova Methodus Docendi Discendique Juris, Part II, Sec. 20, 17); his argumentation is also followed by Ahrens (Cours de droit naturel [1838], Part II, Sec. 102). Grotius finds the basis of testate succession in natural freedom and that of interstate succession in its

origin, and so we shall disregard them here. In the last analysis, of course, substantive motives almost always enter the picture, and highly artificial constructions are thus frequent. Many other institutions of the prevailing system, too, could not be legitimated except on practical utilitarian grounds. By "justifying" them, natural law "reason" easily slipped into utilitarian thinking, and this shift expresses itself in the change of meaning of the concept of "reasonableness." In purely formal natural law, the reasonable is that which is derivable from the eternal order of nature and logic, both being readily blended with one another. But from the very beginning, the English concept of "reasonable" contained by implication the meaning of "rational" in the sense of "practically appropriate." From this it could be concluded that what would lead in practice to absurd consequences cannot constitute the law desired by nature and reason. This signified the express introduction of substantive presuppositions into the concept of reason which had in fact always been implicit in it.[13] As a matter of fact, it was with the aid of this shift in the meaning of the term that the Supreme Court of the United States was able to free itself from formal natural law so as to be able to recognize the validity of certain acts of social legislation.[14]

In principle, however, the formal natural law was transformed into a substantive natural law as soon as the legitimacy of an acquired right came to be tied up with the substantive economic

---

implied agreement with the will of the decedent (DE IURE PACIS AC BELLI [1625], II, c. vii; cf. on his theory MAINE 190).

The natural law theories were attacked by Pufendorf, who declared inheritance to be an institution of positive law (DE IURE NATURAE ET GENTIUM [1672], 4.10. 2–6). This opinion was followed by Blackstone (Book II, c. xiv).

13   What Weber has in mind is the shift from natural law thinking to utilitarianism, as expressed by Bentham, John Stuart Mill, and Spencer.

14   See Knoxville Iron Co. v. Harbison (1901) 183 U.S. 13; McLean v. Arkansas (1908) 211 U.S. 539; Erie R.R. v. Williams (1914) 233 U.S. 685:—statutes prescribing the character, methods, and time for payment of wages.

Holden v. Hardy (1898) 169 U.S. 366; Bunting v. Oregon (1917) 243 U.S. 426; Muller v. Oregon (1908) 208 U.S. 412; Riley v. Massachu-

rather than with the formal modes of its acquisition. Lassalle, in his System of Vested Rights,[15] still sought to solve a particular problem in natural law fashion by formal means, in his case by those derived from Hegel's theory of evolution. The inviolability of a right formally and legitimately acquired on the basis of a positive enactment is presupposed, but the natural law limitation of this type of legal positivism becomes evident in connection with the problem of the so-called retroactivity of laws and the related question of the state's duty to pay compensation where a privilege is abolished. The attempted solution, which is of no interest to us here, is of a thoroughly formal and natural law character.

The decisive turn towards substantive natural law is connected primarily with socialist theories of the exclusive legitimacy of the acquisition of wealth by one's own labor. For this view rejects not only all unearned income acquired through the channels of inheritance or by means of a guaranteed monopoly, but also the formal principle of freedom of contract and general recognition of the legitimacy of all rights acquired through the instrumentality of contracting. According to these theories, all appropriations of goods must be tested substantively by the extent to which they rest on labor as their ground of acquisition.

---

setts (1914) 232 U.S. 671; Miller v. Wilson (1915) 236 U.S. 373; Bosley v. McLaughlin (1915) 236 U.S. 385:—statutes fixing hours of labor.

N.Y. Central R.R. Co. v. White (1917) 243 U.S. 188: workmen's compensation laws.

Later decisions, such as Adkins v. Children's Hospital (1923) 261 U.S. 525, in which the rule of reason was temporarily nullified, or the New Deal cases, could, of course, not be considered by Weber, whose manuscript was practically complete around 1920.

For a penetrating survey and analysis, from the continental point of view, of the attitudes of the American judiciary toward social legislation, see ED. LAMBERT, LE GOUVERNEMENT DES JUGES ET LA LUTTE JUDICIAIRE CONTRE LA LÉGISLATION SOCIALE AUX ETATS-UNIS (1921).

15   Ferdinand Lassalle, 1825–1864, German socialist, founder of the General German Workers' Association, the predecessor of the German Social Democratic party. His SYSTEM DER ERWORBENEN RECHTE was published in 1861. On Lassalle see the article by G. Mayer in 9 ENCYC. SOC. SCI. 184.

Class Relations in Natural Law Ideology

Naturally both the formal rationalistic natural law of freedom of contract and the substantive natural law of the exclusive legitimacy of the product of labor have definite class implications. Freedom of contract and all the propositions regarding as legitimate the property derived therefrom obviously belong to the natural law of the groups interested in market transactions, i.e., those interested in the ultimate appropriation of the means of production. Conversely, the doctrine that land is not produced by anybody's labor and that it is thus incapable of being appropriated at all, constitutes a protest against the closedness of the circle of landowners, and thus corresponds with the class situation of a proletarianized peasantry whose restricted opportunities for self-maintenance force them under the yoke of the land monopolists.[16] It is equally clear that such slogans must acquire a particularly dramatic power where the product of agricultural exploitation still depends primarily upon the natural condition of the soil and where the appropriation of the land is not, at least internally, completed; where, furthermore, agriculture is not carried on in rationally organized large-scale enterprises, and where the income of the landlord is either derived entirely from the tenants' rent or is produced through the use of peasant equipment and peasant labor. All these conditions exist in large measure in the area of the "black earth."[17] As regards its positive meaning, this natural law of the small peasantry is ambiguous. It can mean in the first place the right to a share in the land to the extent of one's own labor power (*trudovaya norma*); or, secondly, a right to the ownership of land to the extent of the traditional standard of living (*potrebityelnaya norma*). In conventional terminology

16   On this and the following, see Weber's discussion of the Russian revolution of 1905 in ARCHIV F. SOZIALWISSENSCHAFT (1906), XXII, 234 and XXIII, 165; see also his article on *Russlands Übergang zur Scheindemokratie* (1917) 23 DIE HILFE 272, repr. GESAMMELTE POLITISCHE SCHRIFTEN (1921) 107.

17   Black earth—the fertile regions of the Ukraine and South Russia.

the postulate thus means either the "right to work" or the "right to a minimum standard of living"; thirdly, however, the two may be combined with the demand for the right to the full product of one's labor.

As far as one can judge today, the Russian revolution of the last decade will in all probability have been the last of the world's natural law-oriented agrarian revolutions.[18] It has been bled to death by its own intrinsic contradictions including those between its ideological postulates. Those two natural law positions are not only incompatible with one another, but they are also contradictory to the historical, realistically political and practically economical programs of the peasantry, all of which are again incongruous with the evolutionist-Marxist agrarian programs. The result has been hopeless confusion among the Revolution's own basic dogmas.

Those three "socialist" rights of the individual have also played a role in the ideologies of the industrial proletariat. The first and the second are theoretically possible under handicraft as well as under capitalistic conditions of the working class; the third, however, is possible only under handicraft conditions. Under capitalism the third right of natural law is possible either not at all or only where cost prices are strictly and universally maintained in all exchange transactions. In agriculture, it can be applied only where production is not capitalistic, since capitalism shifts the attribution of the agricultural produce of the soil from the direct place of agricultural production to the shop, where the agricultural implements, artificial fertilizers, etc., are produced; and the same holds true for industry. Quite generally, where the return is determined by the sale of the product in a freely competitive market, the content of the right of the individual to the full value of his product inevitably loses its meaning. There simply is no longer an individual "labor yield," and if the claim

---

18   In the second of the two articles mentioned in n. 23 *supra* Weber, at p. 314, predicted the coming of a new revolution in Russia, which would be oriented toward communism rather than natural law and which would create a state of affairs different from anything that had ever existed before (*etwas wirklich noch nicht Dagewesenes*).

is to make any sense it can be only as the collective claim of all those who find themselves in a common class situation. In practice, this comes down to the demand for a "living wage," i.e., to a special variant of the "right to the standard of living as determined by traditional need." It thus resembles the medieval "just price" as demanded by ecclesiastical ethics,[19] which, in case of doubt, was determined by the test (and occasionally experimentally) of whether or not at the given price the craftsmen in question could maintain the standard of living appropriate to their social status.

The "just price" itself, which was the most important natural law element in canonist economic doctrine, fell prey to the same fate. In the canonistic discussions of the determinants of the "just price" one can observe how this labor value price corresponding to the "subsistence principle" is gradually replaced by the competitive price which becomes the new "natural" price in the same measure as the market community progresses. In the writings of Antonin of Florence[20] the latter had already come to prevail. In the outlook of the Puritans it was, of course, completely dominant. The price which was to be rejected as "unnatural" was now one which did not rest on the competition of the free market, i.e., the price which was influenced by monopolies or other arbitrary human intervention. Throughout the whole puritanically influenced Anglo-Saxon world this principle has had a great influence up to the very present.[21] Because of the fact that the principle derived its dignity from natural law, it remained a far stronger support for the ideal of "free competition" than those purely utilitarian economic theories which were produced on the Continent in the manner of Bastiat.[22] . . .

[19]   On the doctrine of "just price" see W.U.G. 801; cf. also the article by Salin in 8 ENCYC. SOC. SCI. 504.

[20]   St. Antonio, 1389–1459, Florentine churchman and writer on ethics and economics; see the article by B. Jarrett in 2 ENCYC. SOC. SCI. 126.

[21]   Cf. *supra* n. 14.

[22]   Frédéric Bastiat, 1801–1850, French economist and social philosopher; see the article by P. T. Homan in 2 ENCYC. SOC. SCI. 476.

10

MODERN LAW

Specialization in Modern Law

As WE have seen, the specifically modern occidental type of administration of justice has arisen on the basis of rational and systematic legislation. However, its basic formal qualities are by no means unambiguously definable. Indeed, this ambiguity is a direct result of more recent developments.

The ancient principles which were decisive for the interlocking of "right" and law have disappeared, especially the idea that one's right has a "valid" quality only by virtue of one's membership in a group of persons by whom this quality is monopolized. To the past now also belongs the tribal or status-group quality of the sum total of a person's rights and, with it, their "particularity" as it once existed on the basis of free association or of usurped or legalized privilege. Equally gone are the estatist and other special courts and procedures. Yet neither all special and personal law nor all special jurisdictions have disappeared completely. On the contrary, very recent legal developments have brought an increasing specialization within the legal system. Only the principle of demarcation of the various spheres has been characteristically changed. A typical case is that of commercial law, which is, indeed, one of the most important instances of modern specializa-

From *Max Weber on Law in Economy and Society*, translated from Max Weber, *Wirtschaft und Gesellschaft*, second edition (1925) by Edward Shils and Max Rheinstein. Published 1954 by Harvard University Press, Cambridge, Mass. Reprinted by permission.

tion. Under the German Commercial Code this special law applies to certain types of contracts,[1] the most important of which is the contract for acquisition of goods with the intention of profitable resale. This definition of commercial contract is entirely in accordance with a rationalized legal system; the definition does not refer to formal qualities, but to the intended functional meaning of the concrete transaction. On the other hand, commercial law also applies to certain categories of persons whose decisive characteristic consists in the fact that contracts are made by them in the course of their business.[2] What is thus really decisive for the demarcation of the sphere of this type of law is the concept of "enterprise." An enterprise is a commercial enterprise when transactions of such peculiar kind are its constitutive elements. Thus every contract which "belongs" substantively, i.e., in its intention, to a commercial enterprise is under the Commercial Code, even though, when regarded alone and by itself, it does not belong to that category of transactions which are generically defined as commercial and even though, in a particular case, such a contract may happen to be made by a nonmerchant. The application of this body of special law is thus determined either by substantive qualities of an individual transaction, especially its intended meaning, or by the objective association of a trans-

---

1   These transactions, which are enumerated in Sec. 1 of the German Commercial Code of 1861/97, are the following:
     (a) purchase and resale of commodities or securities such as bonds; (b) enterprise by an independent contractor to do work on materials or goods supplied by the other party; (c) underwriting of insurance; (d) banking; (e) transportation of goods or passengers, on land, at sea, and on inland waterways; (f) transactions of factors, brokers, forwarding agents, and warehousemen; (g) transactions of commercial brokers, jobbers, and agents; (h) transactions of publishers, book and art dealers; (i) transactions of printers.
2   The German Commercial Code, in Sec. 2, has the following definition: "Any enterprise which requires an established business because of its size or because of the manner in which it is carried on, is a commercial enterprise, even though it does not fall within any of the categories stated in Sec. 1." Similarly, the French Commercial Code of 1807 states in Art. 1: "Merchants are all those who carry on commercial transactions and make this activity their habit and profession."

action with the rational organization of an enterprise. It is not determined, however, by a person's membership in an estate legally constituted by free agreement or privilege, which was in the past the operative factor for the application of a special law. Commercial law, then, inasmuch as its application is personally delimited, is a class law rather than a status-group law. However, this contrast with the past is but a relative one. Indeed, so far as the law of commerce and the law of other purely economic "occupations" are concerned, the principle of jurisdictional delimitation has always had a purely substantive character, which, while often varying in externals, has essentially been the same throughout. But those particularities in the legal system which constituted a definite status law were more significant both quantitatively and qualitatively. Besides, even the vocational special jurisdictions, so far as their jurisdictions did not depend upon the litigants' membership in a certain corporate body, have usually depended upon mere formal criteria such as acquisition of a license or a privilege. For example, under the new German Commercial Code, a person is characterized as a merchant by the mere fact that he is listed in the register of commercial firms.[3] The personal scope of application of the commercial law is thus determined by a purely formal test, while in other respects its sphere is delimited by the economic purpose which a given transaction purports to achieve. The spheres of the special laws applicable to other occupational groups are also predominantly defined along substantive or functional criteria, and it is only under certain circumstances that applicability is governed by formal tests. Many of these modern special laws are also combined with special courts and procedures of their own.[4]

---

[3]   *Handelsregister* (register of firms): cf. Commercial Code, Secs. 2, 5, 8, *et seq.*

[4]   The most important special law of this kind is the labor law with its special hierarchy of labor courts. There are, furthermore, the administrative tribunals of general administrative jurisdiction and a set of special tribunals dealing respectively with claims arising under the social security laws or the war pensions laws, with tax matters, with certain matters of agricultural administration, etc.

Mainly two causes are responsible for the emergence of these particularistic laws. In the first place, they have been a result of the occupational differentiation and the increasing attention which commercial and industrial pressure groups have obtained for themselves. What they expect from these particularistic arrangements is that their legal affairs will be handled by specialized experts.[5] The second cause, which has played an increasingly important role in most recent times, has been the desire to eliminate the formalities of normal legal procedure for the sake of a settlement that would be both expeditious and better adapted to the concrete case.[6] In practice, this trend signifies a weakening of legal formalism out of considerations of substantive expediency and thus constitutes but one instance among a whole series of similar contemporary phenomena.

The Anti-Formalistic Tendencies of Modern Legal Development

From a theoretical point of view, the general development of law and procedure may be viewed as passing through the following stages: first, charismatic legal revelation through "law prophets"; second, empirical creation and finding of law by legal honoratiores, i.e., law creation through cautelary jurisprudence and adherence to precedent; third, imposition of law by secular or theocratic powers; fourth and finally, systematic elaboration of law and professionalized administration of justice by persons who have received their legal training in a learned and formally logical manner. From this perspective, the formal qualities of the law emerge as follows: arising in primitive legal procedure from a combination of magically conditioned formalism and

---

[5]   Both the commercial and the labor courts are usually organized in panels chosen from those lines of business or industry whose affairs are dealt with by the particular division of the court. Cf. ARBEITSGERICHTS-GESETZ of 23 December, 1926 (R.G. BL. I, 507), Sec. 17.

[6]   In the labor courts representation by attorneys is, as a general rule, not permitted at the trial stage (ARBEITSGERICHTSGESETZ of 23 December, 1926 [R.G. BL. I, 507], Sec. 11).

irrationality conditioned by revelation, they proceed to increasingly specialized juridical and logical rationality and systematization, passing through a stage of theocratically or patrimonially conditioned substantive and informal expediency. Finally, they assume, at least from an external viewpoint, an increasingly logical sublimation and deductive rigor and develop an increasingly rational technique in procedure.

Since we are here only concerned with the most general lines of development, we shall ignore the fact that in historical reality the theoretically constructed stages of rationalization have not everywhere followed in the sequence which we have just outlined, even if we ignore the world outside the Occident. We shall not be troubled either by the multiplicity of causes of the particular type and degree of rationalization that a given law has actually assumed. As our brief sketch has already shown, we shall only recall that the great differences in the line of development have been essentially influenced, first, by the diversity of political power relationships, which, for reasons to be discussed later, have resulted in very different degrees of power of the imperium vis-à-vis the powers of the kinship groups, the folk community, and the estates; second, by the relations between the theocratic and the secular powers; and, third, by the differences in the structure of those legal honoratiores who were significant for the development of a given law and which, too, were largely dependent upon political factors.

Only the Occident has witnessed the fully developed administration of justice of the folk-community (*Dinggenossenschaft*) and the status group stereotyped form of patrimonialism; and only the Occident has witnessed the rise of the rational economic system, whose agents first allied themselves with the princely powers to overcome the estates and then turned against them in revolution; and only the West has known "Natural Law," and with it the complete elimination of the system of personal laws and of the ancient maxim that special law prevails over general law. Nowhere else, finally, has there occurred any phenomenon resembling Roman law and anything like its reception. All these events have to a very large extent been caused by concrete political factors, which have only the remotest analogies elsewhere in the world. For this reason, the stage of decisively shaping law by trained legal specialists has not been fully reached anywhere outside of the Occident. Economic conditions have, as we have seen, everywhere played an important role, but they have nowhere been decisive alone and by themselves. To the extent that they contributed to the formation of the specifically modern features of present-day occidental law, the direction in which they worked has been by and large the following: To those who had interests in the commodity market, the rationalization and systematization of the law in general and, with certain reservations to be stated later, the increasing calculability of the functioning of the legal process in particular, constituted one of the most important conditions for the existence of economic enterprise intended to function with stability and, especially, of capitalistic enterprise, which cannot do without legal security. Special forms of transactions and special procedures, like the bill of·exchange and the special procedure for its speedy collection, serve this need for the purely formal certainty of the guaranty of legal enforcement.

On the other hand, the modern and, to a certain extent, the ancient Roman, legal developments have contained tendencies favorable to the dilution of legal formalism. At a first glance, the displacement of the formally bound law of evidence by the "free evaluation of proof" appears to be of a merely technical character.[7]

[7]   Roman-canonical procedure, as it had come to be adopted generally in the continental courts, was characterized by its system of "formal proof," which was in many respects similar to the law of evidence of Anglo-American procedure. There were rules about exclusion of certain kinds of evidence and, quite particularly, detailed rules about corroboration and about the mechanical ways in which the judge had to evaluate conflicting evidence. The testimony of two credible witnesses constituted full proof (*probatio plena*) ; one credible witness made half proof (*probatio semiplena*), but one doubtful witness (*testis suspectus*) made less than half proof (*probatio semiplena minor*), etc.

This entire system of formal proof was swept away by the procedural reforms of the nineteenth century and replaced by the system of free or rational proof, which did away with most of the exclusionary rules, released the judge from his arithmetical shackles, and authorized him to evaluate the evidence in the light of experience and reason. Cf. ENGELMANN-MILLAR 39.

We have seen that the primitive system of magically bound proof was exploded through the rationalism of either the theocratic or the patrimonial kind, both of which postulated procedures for the disclosure of the real truth. Thus the new system clearly appears as a product of substantive rationalization. Today, however, the scope and limits of the free evaluation of proof are determined primarily by commercial interests, i.e., by economic factors. It is clear that, through the system of free evaluation of proof, a very considerable domain which was once subject to formal juristic thought is being increasingly withdrawn therefrom.[8] But we are here more concerned with the corresponding trends in the sphere of substantive law. One such trend lies in the intrinsic necessities of legal thought. Its growing logical sublimation has meant everywhere the substitution for a dependence on externally tangible formal characteristics of an increasingly logical interpretation of meaning in relation to the legal norms themselves as well as in relation to legal transactions. In the doctrine of the continental "common law" this interpretation claimed that it would give effect to the "real" intentions of the parties; in precisely this manner it introduced an individualizing and relatively substantive factor into legal formalism. This kind of interpretation seeks to construct the relations of the parties to one another from the point of view

8   Together with the rule of stare decisis and, to some extent, the jury system, the fact that the Common Law has preserved a much more formalistic law of evidence is the principal cause why in such fields as torts, damages, interpretation and construction of legal instruments, English and American law have developed so much more numerous and detailed rules of law than the systems of the Civil Law. The comparison, for instance, of the 951 sections of the Restatement of Torts and the 31 sections dealing with torts in the German Civil Code (Secs. 823–853) or the 5 sections of the French Code (Arts. 1382–86) is revealing in this respect, just as is the comparison of the few sections of the German Code dealing with the interpretation of wills (Secs. 2087 *et seq.*) with the elaborate treatment of the topic in American law.

As to the law of evidence itself, compare the ten volumes of Wigmore's treatise (3rd ed. 1940) with the complete absence of books on evidence in Germany or the brief treatment of a few evidentiary problems in the French treatises on private law, for instance, in JOSSERAND'S COURS DE DROIT CIVIL POSITIF FRANÇAIS (1939), where the chapter on "preuves" covers 43 pages.

of the "inner" kernel of their behavior, from the point of view of their mental "attitudes" (such as good faith or malice).[9] Thus it relates legal consequences to informal elements of the situation and this treatment provides a telling parallel to that systematization of religious ethics which we have already considered previously.[10] Much of the system of commodity exchange, in primitive as well as in technically differentiated patterns of trade, is possible only on the basis of far-reaching personal confidence and trust in the loyalty of others. Moreover, as commodity exchange increases in importance, the need in legal practice to guarantee or secure such trustworthy conduct becomes proportionally greater. But in the very nature of the case, we cannot, of course, define with formal certainty the legal tests according to which the new relations of trust and confidence are to be governed. Hence, through such ethical rationalization the courts have been helpful to powerful interests. Also, outside of the sphere of commodity exchange, the rationalization of the law has substituted attitude-evaluation as the significant element for assessment of events according to external criteria. In criminal law, legal rationalization has replaced the purely mechanistic remedy of vengeance by rational "ends of punishment" of an either ethical or utilitarian character, and has thereby introduced increasingly nonformal elements into legal practice. In the sphere of private law the concern for a party's mental attitude has quite generally entailed evaluation by the judge. "Good faith and fair dealing" or the "good" usage of trade or, in other words, ethical categories have become the test of what the parties are entitled to mean by their "intention."[11] Yet, the reference to the "good" usage of trade implies in substance the recognition of such attitudes which are held by the average party

9   Cf. HEDEMANN I, 117.
10   W.U.G., Part II, c. IV, 227–356.
11   For illustrations of this judicial attitude see the case surveys given in connection with Sec. 242 of the German Civil Code (good faith and fair dealing) or Sec. 346 of the Commercial Code ("good" custom of trade) in the annotated editions of these Codes. The dangers of excessive judicial resort to legal provisions referring the judge to such indefinite standards have been pointed out by HEDEMANN, DIE FLUCHT IN DIE GENERALKLAUSELN, EINE GEFAHR FÜR RECHT UND STAAT (1933).

concerned with the case, i.e., a general and purely business criterion of an essentially factual nature, such as the average expectation of the parties in a given transaction. It is this standard which the law has consequently to accept.[12]

Now we have already seen that the expectations of parties will often be disappointed by the results of a strictly professional legal logic.[13] Such disappointments are inevitable indeed where the facts of life are juridically "construed" in order to make them fit the abstract propositions of law and in accordance with the maxim that nothing can exist in the realm of law unless it can be "conceived" by the jurist in conformity with those "principles" which are revealed to him by juristic science. The expectations of the parties are oriented towards the economic and utilitarian meaning of a legal proposition. However, from the point of view of legal logic, this meaning is an "irrational" one. For example, the layman will never understand why it should be impossible under the traditional definition of larceny to commit a larceny of electric power.[14] It is by no means the peculiar foolishness of modern jurisprudence which leads to such conflicts. To a large extent such conflicts rather are the inevitable consequence of the incompatibility that exists between the intrinsic necessities of logically

[12]   The German Supreme Court has consistently maintained, however, that a usage is not to be considered when it is unfair, and especially when it constitutes a gross abuse of a position of economic power; see, for instance, 114 Entscheidungen des Reichsgerichts in Zivilsachen 97; ⌜1922⌝ Juristische Wochenschrift 488; ⌜1932⌝ o.c. 586.

[13]   The possibilities of such discrepancies have been pointed out especially in the writings of Heck and other advocates of the "jurisprudence of interests." See in this respect The Jurisprudence of Interests, vol. II of this 20th Century Legal Philosophy Series.

[14]   Such was the decision of the German Supreme Court in 29 Entscheidungen des Reichsgerichts in Strafsachen 111 and 32 o.c. 165. In Sec. 242 of the German Criminal Code larceny is defined as the unlawful taking of a chattel. Electric power is not a chattel; hence it cannot be the subject matter of larceny. The gap in the law was filled by the enactment of a Special Law Concerning the Unlawful Taking of Electric Power, of 9 April 1900 (R.G. Bl. 1900, 228). The decisions just mentioned have become the stock "horrible" in modern German excoriations of conceptual jurisprudence.

consistent formal legal thinking and the fact that the legally relevant agreements and activities of private parties are aimed at economic results and oriented towards economically determined expectations. It is for this reason that we find the ever-recurrent protests against the professional legal method of thought as such, which are finding support even in the lawyers' own reflections on their work. But a "lawyers' law" has never been and never will be brought into conformity with lay expectation unless it totally renounce that formal character which is immanent in it. This is just as true of the English law which we glorify so much today,[15] as it has been of the ancient Roman jurists or of the methods of modern continental legal thought. Any attempt, like that of Erich Jung,[16] to replace the antiquated "law of nature"[17] by a new "natural law"[18] aiming at "dispute settlement" (Streitschlichtung) in accordance with the average expectations of average parties would thus come up against certain immanent limitations. But, nevertheless, this idea does have some validity in relation to the realities of legal history. The Roman law of the later Republic and the Empire developed a type of commercial ethics that was in fact oriented towards that which is to be expected on the average. Such a view means, of course, that only a small group of clearly corrupt or fraudulent practices would be outlawed, and the law would not go beyond what is regarded as the "ethical minimum."[19] In spite of the bona fides (which a seller had to display), the maxim of caveat emptor remained valid.

New demands for a "social law" to be based upon such emotionally colored ethical postulates as justice or human dignity,

15   In the years preceding the First World War the English administration of justice and, particularly, the creative role and prominent position of the English "judicial kings" (*Richterkönige*) were highly praised and advocated for adoption, particularly by A. MENDELSSOHN BARTHOLDY, IMPERIUM DES RICHTERS (1908), and F. ADICKES, GRUNDLINIEN EINER DURCHGREIFENDEN JUSTIZREFORM (1906).
16   DAS PROBLEM DES NATÜRLICHEN RECHTS (1912).
17   *Naturrecht.* [Weber's note.]
18   *Natürliches Recht* [Weber's note.]
19   Expression of G. JELLINEK, in DIE SOZIAL-ETHISCHE BEDEUTUNG VON RECHT, UNRECHT UND STRAFE (2nd ed. 1908).

and thus directed against the very dominance of a mere business morality have arisen in modern times with the emergence of the modern class problem. They are advocated not only by labor and other interested groups but also by legal ideologists.[20] By these demands legal formalism itself has been challenged. Such a concept as economic duress,[21] or the attempt to treat as immoral, and thus as invalid, a contract because of a gross disproportion between promise and consideration,[22] are derived from norms which, from the legal standpoint, are entirely amorphous and which are neither juristic nor conventional nor traditional in character but ethical and which claim as their legitimation substantive justice rather than formal legality.

Internal professional ideologies of the lawyers themselves have been operative in legal theory and practice along with those influences which have been engendered by both the social demands of democracy and the welfare ideology of monarchical bureaucracy. The status of being confined to the interpretation of statutes and contracts, like a slot machine into which one just drops the facts (plus the fee) in order to have it spew out the decision (plus opinion), appears to the modern lawyer as beneath his dignity; and the more universal the codified formal statute law has become, the more unattractive has this notion come to be. The present demand is for "judicial creativeness," at least where the

20   On Gierke as the leading legal scholar in the movement for law as an expression of "social justice," see G. Böhmer, Grundlagen der bürgerlichen Rechtsordnung (1951) II, 155; see, especially, Gierke's lecture on The Social Task of Private Law (Die soziale Aufgabe des Privatrechts, 1899), repr. E. Wolf, Deutsches Rechtsdenken (1948).

21   On the development of the doctrine of economic duress in positive German law, see J. Dawson, *Economic Duress and the Fair Exchange in French and German Law* (1937), 12 Tulane L. Rev. 42.

22   In Sec. 138 the German Civil Code provides as follows:

"A legal transaction which violates good morals is void.

"Void, in particular, is any transaction in which one party, by exploiting the emergency situation, the imprudence, or the inexperience of another causes such other person to promise or to give to him or to a third person a pecuniary benefit which so transcends the value of his own performance that under the circumstances of the case the relationship between them appears as manifestly disproportionate."

statute is silent. The school of "free law" has undertaken to prove that such silence is the inevitable fate of every statute in view of the irrationality of the facts of life; that in countless instances the application of the statutes as "interpreted" is a delusion, and that the decision is, and ought to be, made in the light of concrete evaluations rather than in accordance with formal norms.[23]

23   The School of Free Law (*Freirecht*) constitutes the German counterpart of American and Scandinavian "realism." The basic theoretical idea of these three schools, viz., that law is not "found" by the judges but "made" by them, was anticipated in 1885 by Oskar Bülow in his GESETZ UND RICHTERAMT. The first attack upon the Pandectist "Konstruktionsjurisprudenz" (conceptual jurisprudence) or, in Weber's terminology, rational formalism, was made in 1848 by v. Kirchmann in his sensational pamphlet ÜBER DIE WERTLOSIGKEIT DER JURISPRUDENZ ALS WISSENSCHAFT. The attack was later joined by no less a scholar than Jhering, who until then had been one of the most prominent expounders of the traditional method, but who now came to emphasize the role of the law as a means to obtain utilitarian ends in a way which would now be called "social engineering" or, in Weber's terms, "substantive rationality" (DER ZWECK IM RECHT, 1877/83; Husik's tr. s.t. LAW AS A MEANS TO AN END, 1913) and to ridicule legal conceptualism in his SCHERZ UND ERNST IN DER JURISPRUDENZ (1855; on Jhering see STONE 299). At the turn of the century the attack was intensified and combined with the postulates that the courts should shake off the technique of conceptual jurisprudence (i.e., in Weber's terminology, the technique of rational formalism), should give up the fiction of the gaplessness of the legal order, should thus treat statutes and codes as ordaining nothing beyond the narrowest meaning of the words of the text, and should fill in the gaps thus created, i.e., in the great mass of problems, in a process of free, "kingly" creativeness. The leaders of this movement were E. Fuchs, a practicing attorney (principal works: DIE GEMEINSCHÄDLICHKEIT DER KONSTRUKTIVEN JURISPRUDENZ ["The Dangers of the Conceptual Jurisprudence to the Common Weal," 1909]; WAS WILL DIE FREIRECHTSSCHULE? ["What Are the Aims of the School of Free Law?" 1929]). Professor H. Kantorowicz (writing under the pen name of Gnaeus Flavius: DER KAMPF UM DIE RECHTSWISSENSCHAFT [1908]; AUS DER VORGESCHICHTE DER FREIRECHTSLEHRE [1925]; see also the article by him and E. Patterson, *Legal Science—a Summary of its Methodology* [1928], 28 COL. L. REV. 679, and *Some Rationalizations about Realism* [1934], 43 YALE L.J., 1240 (where Kantorowicz recedes from some of his earlier theses), and the judge J. G. Gmelin (QUOUSQUE? BEITRAG ZUR SOZIOLOGISCHEN RECHTSFINDUNG [1910, Bruncken's transl. in Modern Legal Philos-

For the case where the statute fails to provide a clear rule, the well-known Article 1 of the Swiss Civil Code orders the judge to decide according to that rule which he himself would promulgate if he were the legislator.[24] This provision, the practical import of

---

ophy Series, IX, SCIENCE OF LEGAL METHOD (1917)]). These passionate radicals were joined by E. Ehrlich, who provided for the new movement a broad historical and sociological basis (FREIE RECHTSFINDUNG UND FREIE REICHTSWISSENSCHAFT [1903, Bruncken's transl. in Modern Legal Philosophy Series, IX, SCIENCE OF LEGAL METHOD (1917), 47]; *Die juristische Logik* [1918], 115 ARCHIV FÜR DIE CIVILISTISCHE PRAXIS, nos. 2 and 3, repr. as a book in 1925; and his GRUNDLEGUNG DER SOZIOLOGIE DES RECHTS [1913], Moll's transl. s.t. FUNDAMENTAL PRINCIPLES OF THE SOCIOLOGY OF LAW [1936]).

The movement stirred up violent discussion (see especially H. REICHEL, GESETZ UND RICHTERSPRUCH [1915]; G. BÖHMER, GRUNDLAGEN DER BÜRGERLICHEN RECHTSORDNUNG [1951], II, 158) and also found some attention in the United States. (See the translations listed above in this note.) Its exaggerations were generally repudiated, however, and actual developments came to be more effectively influenced by the ideas of the so-called school of jurisprudence of interests, whose principal writings are collected in vol. II of this 20th Century Legal Philosophy Series, entitled THE JURISPRUDENCE OF INTERESTS (1948). The method was elaborated primarily by M. Rümelin, P. Heck, and their companions at Tübingen and by R. Müller-Erzbach, who has been working at the elaboration of social and concrete bases for that "balancing of interests" which the method requires (see especially DAS PRIVATE RECHT DER MITGLIEDSCHAFT ALS PRÜFSTEIN EINES KAUSALEN RECHTSDENKENS [1948] and DIE RECHTSWISSENSCHAFT IM UMBAU [1950]). The Jurisprudence of Interests is close to Roscoe Pound's sociological jurisprudence. It aims at replacing the system of formally rational with one of substantively rational concepts, and it has come to establish itself firmly in German legal practice (for a concise survey and evaluation see BÖHMER, *op cit.* 190, and, very brief, W. FRIEDMANN, LEGAL THEORY [2nd ed. 1949] 225; no complete survey is as yet available in English).

The following passages in Weber's text are concerned with the School of Free Law.

24   "The law must be applied in all cases which come within the letter or the spirit of its provisions.

"Where no provision is applicable, the judge shall decide according to the existing customary law and, in default thereof, according to the rule which he would lay down if he had himself to act as legislator.

"Herein he must be guided by tested doctrine and tradition."

which should not be overestimated, however,[25] corresponds formally with the Kantian formula. But in reality a judicial system which would practice such ideals would, in view of the inevitability of value-compromises, very often have to forget about abstract norms and, at least in cases of conflict, would have to admit concrete evaluations, i.e., not only nonformal but irrational lawfinding. Indeed, the doctrine of the inevitability of gaps in the legal order as well as the campaign to recognize as fiction the systematic coherence of the law has been given further impetus by the assertions that the judicial process never consisted, or, at any rate never should consist, in the "application" of general norms to a concrete case, just as no utterance in language should be regarded as an application of the rules of grammar.[26] In this view, the "legal propositions" are regarded as secondary and as being derived by abstraction from the concrete decisions which, as the products of judicial practice, are said to be the real embodiment of the law. Going still farther, one has pointed out the quantitative infrequency of those cases which ever come to trial and judicial decision as against the tremendous mass of rules by which human behavior is actually determined; from this observation one has come derogatively to call "mere rules of decision" those norms which appear in the judicial process, to contrast them with those norms which are factually valid in the course of everyday life and independently of their reaffirmation or declaration in legal procedure, and, ultimately, to establish the postulate that the true foundation of the law is entirely "sociological."[27]

Use has also been made of the historical fact that for long periods, including our own, private parties have to a large extent been advised by professional lawyers and judges who have had technical legal training or that, in other words, all customary law

---

[25] Cf. I. WILLIAMS, THE SOURCES OF LAW IN THE SWISS CIVIL CODE (1923) 34; see also the discussion of this provision and the similarly worded Sec. 1 of the Civil Code of the Russian Federal Soviet Socialist Republic by V. E. Greaves, *Social-economic Purpose of Private Rights* (1934/5, 12 N.Y.U.L.Q. REV. 165, 430).

[26] Cf. H. ISAY, RECHTSNORM UND ENTSCHEIDUNG (1929).

[27] Cf. EHRLICH, esp. chapters 5 and 6.

is in reality lawyers' law. This fact has been associated with the incontrovertible observation that entirely new legal principles are being established not only *praeter legem* but also *contra legem*[28] by judicial practice, for instance, that of the German Supreme Court after the entry into force of the Civil Code. From all these facts the idea was derived that case law is superior to the rational establishment of objective norms and that the expediential balancing of concrete interests is superior to the creation and recognition of "norms" in general.[29] The modern theory of legal sources has thus disintegrated both the half-mystical concept of "customary law," as it had been created by historicism, as well as the equally historicist concept of the "will of the legislator" that could be discovered through the study of the legislative history of an enactment as revealed in committee reports and similar sources. The statute rather than the legislator has been thus proclaimed to be the jurists' main concern. Thus isolated from its background, the "law" is then turned over for elaboration and application to the jurists, among whom the predominant influence is ascribed at one time to the practitioners and at others, for instance, in the reports accompanying certain of the modern codes, to the scholars.[30] In this manner the significance of the legislative

---

[28]   *Praeter legem*—alongside the (statute) law; *contra legem*—in contradiction to the (statute) law.

[29]   So especially LAMBERT, *op. cit.* (1903) ; EHRLICH.

[30]   In the last two sentences of the text three different phenomena are brought together in a way which indicates the possibility that some connecting part has been omitted. The postulate that in statutory interpretation the judge has to look upon the text "objectively" as a self-sufficient entity and that he should not, or that he is not even allowed to, inquire into the intentions of the legislature has not been confined to Germany. It has long been the established method of statutory interpretation in England and for a considerable time it was dominant in the United States. In Germany its principal representatives were A. Wach (HANDBUCH DES ZIVILPROZESSES [1885]) and K. Binding (HANDBUCH DES STRAFRECHTS [1885]) ; see also J. Kohler, *Über die Interpretation von Gesetzen* (1886), 13 GRÜNHUT'S ZEITSCHRIFT 1. The Theory has had some influence on the German courts but could not prevent them in the long run from paying careful attention to parliamentary hearings and other legislative materials.

determination of a legal command is, under certain circumstances, degraded to the role of a mere "symptom" of either the validity of a legal proposition or even of the mere desire of such validity which, however, until it has been accepted in legal practice, is to remain uncertain. But the preference for a case law which remains in contact with legal reality—which means with the reality of the lawyers—to statute law is in turn subverted by the argument that no precedent should be regarded as binding beyond its concrete facts. The way is thus left open to the free balancing of values in each individual case.

In opposition to all such value-irrationalism, there have also arisen attempts to reëstablish an objective standard of values. The more the impression grows that legal orders as such are no more than "technical tools," the more violently will such degradation be rejected by the lawyers. For to place on the same level such merely "technical rules" as a customs tariff and legal norms concerning marriage, parental power, or the incidents of ownership, offends the sentiment of the legal practitioners, and there emerges the nostalgic notion of a transpositive law above that merely technical positive law which is acknowledged to be subject to change. The old natural law, it is true, looks discredited by the criticisms leveled at it from the historical and positivist points of view. As a substitute there are now advanced the religiously inspired natural law of the Catholic scholars,[31] and certain efforts to deduce

---

The idea that statutes ought to be interpreted narrowly so as to leave free reign to free judicial law creation in the interstices constituted one of the postulates of the School of Free Law.

The phrase that the solution of certain problems be left to "legal science and doctrine" recurs constantly in the report (*Motive*) accompanying the Draft of the German Civil Code. The draftsmen used it whenever they felt that too much detail would be detrimental to the purposes of the codification. It is difficult to see what it might have to do with the Free Law tenet stated in the following sentence of the text.

31   Especially VICTOR CATHREIN, RECHT, NATURRECHT UND POSITIVES RECHT (2nd ed. 1909) ; v. HERTLING, RECHT, STAAT UND GESELLSCHAFT (4th ed. 1917) ; MAUSBACH, NATURRECHT UND VÖLKERRECHT (1918) ; more recently H. ROMMEN, DIE EWIGE WIEDERKEHR DES NATURRECHTS (1936; Hanley's transl. s.t. THE NATURAL LAW, 1948), and the survey of the latest Catholic literature by I. Zeiger in (1952) 149 STIMMEN DER ZEIT 468.

objective standards from the "nature" of the law itself. The latter effort has taken two forms. In the a prioristic, neo-Kantian doctrines, the "right law," as the normative system of a "society of free men," is to be both a legislative standard for rational legislation and a source for judicial decisions where the law refers the judge to apparently nonformal criteria.[32] In the empiricist, Comtean, way those "expectations" which private parties are justified to have in view of the average conception existing with regard to the obligations of others, are to serve as the ultimate standard, which is to be superior even to the statute and which is to replace such concepts as equity, etc., which are felt to be too vague.[33]

At this place we cannot undertake a detailed discussion or a full criticism of these tendencies which, as our brief sketch has shown, have produced quite contradictory answers. All these movements are international in scope, but they have been most pronounced in Germany and France.[34] They are agreed only in

[32]   On Neo-Kantianism, see FRIEDMANN, *op. cit.* 91; the principal representative is R. Stammler, whose LEHRE VON DEM RICHTIGEN RECHT (1902) has been translated by Husik s.t. THE THEORY OF JUSTICE (1925). For a trenchant criticism, see E. KAUFMANN, KRITIK DER NEUKANTISCHEN RECHTSPHILOSOPHIE (1921).

[33]   The reference is to the continuation and elaboration of Jhering's ideas through the school of jurisprudence of interests.

[34]   On French legal theory, see vol. VII of the Modern Legal Philosophy Series: MODERN FRENCH LEGAL PHILOSOPHY (1916) containing writings by A. Fouillée, J. Charmont, L. Duguit, and R. Demogue. A comprehensive, critical history is presented by J. BONNECASE, LA PENSÉE JURIDIQUE FRANÇAISE DE 1804 A L'HEURE PRÉSENTE (1933). Cf. also in the 20th Century Legal Philosophy Series, vol. IV, THE LEGAL PHILOSOPHIES OF LASK, RADBRUCH, AND DABIN (1950) 227; and, for latest trends, B. Horváth, *Social Value and Reality in Current French Legal Thought* (1952), 1 AM. J. OF COMPAR. LAW 243.

The principal representatives of the trends mentioned by Weber are François Gény, the founder of the French counterpart to the jurisprudence of interests (MÉTHODE D'INTERPRÉTATION [1899]; cf. his article in Modern Legal Philosophy Series, vol. IX, SCIENCE OF LEGAL METHOD [1917] 498); the sociological jurists Edouard Lambert (*op. cit.*), Léon Duguit (LE DROIT SOCIAL, LE DROIT INDIVIDUEL, ET LA TRANSFORMATION DE L'ÉTAT [1910]; L'ÉTAT, LE DROIT OBJECTIF ET LA LOI POSITIVE [1901]; LES TRANSFORMATIONS GÉNÉRALES DU DROIT PRIVÉ [1912], transl. in Continental Legal History Series, vol. XI, s.t. THE PROGRESS OF CONTINENTAL

their rejection of the once universally accepted and until recently prevalent petitio principii of the consistency and "gaplessness" of the legal order. Moreover, they have directed themselves against very diverse opponents, for instance, in France against the school of the Code-interpreters and in Germany against the methodology of the Pandectists. Depending upon who are the leaders of a particular movement, the results favor either the prestige of "science," i.e., of the legal scholars, or that of the practitioners. As a result of the continuous growth of formal statute law and, especially, of systematic codification, the academic scholars feel themselves to be painfully threatened both in their importance and in their opportunities for unencumbered intellectual activity. The rapid growth of anti-logical as well as the anti-historical movements in Germany can be historically explained by the fear that, following codification, German legal science might have to undergo the same decline which befell French jurisprudence after the enactment of the Napoleonic Code of Prussian jurisprudence after the enactment of the Allgemeine Landrecht. Up to this point these fears are thus the result of an internal constellation of intellectual interests. However, all variants of the developments which have led to the rejection of that purely logical systematization of the law as it had been developed by Pandectist learning, including even the irrational variants, are in their turn products of a self-defeating scientific rationalization of legal thought as well as of its relentless self-criticism. To the extent that they do not themselves have a rationalistic character, they are a flight into the irrational and as such a consequence of the increasing rationalization of legal technique. In that respect they are a parallel to the irrationalization of religion.[35] One must not overlook, however, that the same trends have also been inspired by the desire of the modern lawyers, through the pressure groups in which they

---

LAW IN THE 19TH CENTURY [1918]; LES TRANSFORMATIONS DU DROIT PUBLIC [1913], transl. by Laski s.t. LAW IN THE MODERN STATE [1919]), and RAYMOND SALEILLES (MÉTHODE ET CODIFICATION [1903]; *Le code civil et la méthode historique* in LIVRE DU CENTENAIRE DU CODE CIVIL [1904]).

[35]   Cf. W.U.G. Part II, c. IV, pp. 227 *et seq.*

are so effectively organized, to heighten their feeling of self-importance and to increase their sense of power. This is undoubtedly one of the reasons why in Germany such continuous reference is made to the "distinguished" position of the English judge who is said not to be bound to any rational law. Yet, the differences in the attribution of honorific status on the continent and in England are rather rooted in circumstances which are connected with differences in the general structure of authority.

IV. Charisma and Institutionalization in the Economic Sphere

Weber's analysis of the economic sphere, in those parts of *Wirtschaft u. Gesellschaft* which were translated in the *Theory of Social and Economic Organization,* combines his general analytical approach to the sociological characteristics of the economic sphere and the use of illustrations from different types of social systems—primitive organizations, various types of traditional (historical) economic organizations, and the modern economic institution. Throughout this discussion he analyzes the nature and importance of rationality in the economic sphere, and distinguishes between two types of rationality—formal and substantive. Excerpts in this section present Weber's analysis of different types of capitalism, premodern and modern, and the nature of the latter as a unique social and economic phenomenon. Here also, as in the political sphere, are emphasized the place and problems of the charismatic orientation in its encounter with the organizational exigencies of the economic sphere. They are especially articulated in the analysis of modern capitalism and of its relation to charismatic innovation in the religious sphere.

11

PREMODERN CAPITALISM

Disintegration of the Guilds and Development of the Domestic System

THE DISINTEGRATION of the guilds, which took place after the close of the Middle Ages, proceeded along several lines. 1. Certain craftsmen within the guilds rose to the position of merchant and capitalist-employer of home workers, i.e. of "factor" (*Verleger*). Masters with a considerable invested capital purchased the raw material, turned over the work to their fellow guildsmen who carried on the process of production for them, and sold the finished product. The guild organization struggled against this tendency, but none the less it is the typical course of the English guild development, especially in London. In spite of the desperate resistance of the guild democracies against the "older men," the guilds were transformed into "livery companies," guilds of dealers in which the only full members were those who produced for the market, while those who had sunk to the level of wage workers and home workers for others lost the vote in the guild and hence their share in its control. This revolution first made possible progress in technique whereas the dominance of the guild democracies would have meant its stagnation. In Germany we do not meet with this course of development; here if a craftsman became an employer or factor he changed his guild,

From *General Economic History*, by Max Weber, translated by Frank H. Knight. Published 1961 by Collier Books, New York. Reprinted by permission.

joining that of the shopkeepers, or merchant-tailors or constablers, a guild of upper class importing and exporting merchants.

2. One guild might rise at the expense of another. Just as we find trading masters in many guilds, others changed entirely into mercantile guilds, forcing the members of other guilds into their employ. This was possible where the production process was transversely divided. Examples are found in England—the merchant tailors—and elsewhere. The 14th century especially is filled with struggles of the guilds for independence of other guilds. Frequently both processes run along together; within the individual guild, certain masters rise to the position of traders and at the same time many guilds become organizations of traders. The symptom of this eventuality is regularly the fusion of guilds, which took place in England and France but not in Germany. Its opposite is represented by the splitting of the guilds and the union of the traders, especially common in the 15th and 16th centuries. The dealers within the guilds of walkers, weavers, dyers, etc. form an organization and in common regulate the whole industry. Production processes of diverse character are united on the level of small shop industry.

3. Where the raw material was very costly and its importation demanded considerable capital, the guilds became dependent upon the importers. In Italy, silk gave occasion to this development, in Perugia, for example, and similarly for amber in the north. New raw materials might also provide the impetus. Cotton worked in this way; as soon as it became an article in general demand, putting-out enterprises arose alongside the guilds or through their transformation as in Germany, where the Fuggers took a notable part in the development.

4. The guilds might become dependent upon the exporters. Only in the beginnings of the industry could the household or tribal unit peddle its own products. As soon, on the other hand, as an industry became entirely or strongly based on exportation, the factor-entrepreneur was indispensable; the individual craftsman failed in the face of the requirements of exportation. The merchant, however, possessed not only the necessary capital but also the requisite knowledge of market operations—and treated them as trade secrets.

The textile industry became the main seat of the domestic system; here, its beginnings go back into the early middle ages. From the 11th century on there was a struggle between wool and linen, and in the 17th and 18th centuries between wool and cotton, with the victory of the second in each case. Charlemagne wore nothing but linen, but later, with increasing demilitarization, the demand for wool increased and at the same time with the clearing of forests the fur industry disappeared and furs became constantly dearer. Woolen goods were the principal commodity in the markets of the Middle Ages; they play the leading role everywhere, in France, England and Italy. Wool was always partly worked up in the country, but became the foundation of the greatness and the economic prosperity of the medieval city; at the head of the revolutionary movements in the city of Florence, marched the guilds of the wool workers. Here again we find early traces of the putting-out system. As early as the 13th century independent wool factors worked in Paris for the permanent market of the Champagne fairs. In general we find the system earliest in Flanders, and later in England, where the Flanders woolen industry called forth mass production of wool.

In fact, wool determined the course of English industrial history, in the form of raw wool, partial products and finished goods. As early as the 13th and 14th centuries England exported wool and partial manufactures of wool. Under the initiative of the dyers and made-up clothing interests, the English woolen industry finally became transformed to the basis of exportation of finished products. The peculiar feature of this development is that it resulted in the rise of domestic industry through the rural weavers and the town merchants. The English guilds became predominantly trading guilds, and in the final period of the middle ages attached to themselves rural craftsmen. At this time the garment makers and the dyers were settled in the towns, the weavers in the country. Within the city trading guilds broke out finally the struggle between the dyers and garment makers on the one hand and the exporters on the other. Export capital and merchant-employer capital became separated and fought out their conflicts of interest within the woolen industry under Elizabeth and in the 17th century, while on the other side employer capital had also to contend with the craft guilds; this was the first conflict between industrial and trading capital. This situation, which became characteristic of all the large industries of England, led to the complete exclusion of the English guilds from influence on the development of production.

The further course of events followed different lines in England and France as compared with Germany, in consequence of the difference in the relation between capital and the craft guilds. In England, and especially in France, the transition to the domestic system is the universal phenomenon. Resistance to it ceased automatically without calling forth interference from 'above. As a result, in England after the 14th century, a small master class took the place of the working class. Precisely the opposite happened in Germany. In England, the development just described signified the dissolution of the guild spirit. Where we find amalgamation and fusion of various guilds, the initiative proceeds from the trading class, which was not to be restrained by guild limitations. They united within the guilds and excluded the masters without capital. Thus formally the guilds maintained themselves for a long time; the suffrage of the city of London, which was nothing but an organization of wealthy dignitaries, was a guild survival.

In Germany, the development proceeds in reverse order. Here the guilds more and more became closed groups in consequence of the narrowing of the field of subsistence policy, and political considerations also played a part. In England there was wanting the particularism of the towns, which dominates the whole of German economic history. The German town pursued an independent guild policy as long as it could, even after it was included in the territorial state of a prince. By contrast, the independent economic policy of the towns ceased early in England and France, as their autonomy was cut off. The English towns found the path to progress open because they were represented in Parliament, and in the 14th and 15th centuries—in contrast with later times— the overwhelming majority of the representatives came from urban circles. In the period of the Hundred Years War with France, the Parliament determined English policy and the interests brought together there pursued a rational, unitary industrial policy. In the 16th century a uniform wage was fixed, the adjustment of wages being taken out of the hands of the justices of the peace and given to the central authority; this facilitated entry into the guilds, the symptom of the fact that the capitalistic trading class, who predominated in the guilds and sent their representatives to parliament, were in control of the situation. In Germany, on the other hand, the towns, incorporated in the territorial principalities, controlled the guild policy. It is true that the princes regulated the guilds in the interests of peace and order, but in the large their regulative measures were conservative and carried out in line with the older policy of the guilds. In consequence the guilds maintained their existence in the critical perod of the 16th and 17th centuries; they were able to close their organization, and the stream of the unchained forces of capitalism flowed through England and the Netherlands, less strongly even through France, while Germany remained in the background. Germany was as far from the position of leadership in the early capitalistic movement at the close of the middle ages and the beginning of the modern era as it had been centuries before in the development of feudalism.

A further characteristic divergence is the difference in regard to social stresses. In Germany, from the close of the middle ages on, we find unions, strikes and revolutions among the journeymen. In England and France, these became more and more rare since in those countries the apparent independence of the home-working small masters beckoned to them and they could work immediately for the factor. In Germany, on the contrary, this apparent independence was not available as there was no domestic industry, and the closing of the guilds established a relation of hostility between the masters and the journeymen.

The pre-capitalistic domestic industry of the west did not develop uniformly, or even as a rule, out of the craft organization; this occurred to the smallest extent in Germany and to a much greater extent in England. Rather it quite commonly existed side by side with craft work, in consequence of the substitution of rural craft workers for urban, or of the fact that new branches of industry arose through the introduction of new raw materials, especially cotton. The crafts struggled against the putting-out system as long as they could, and longer in Germany than in England and France.

Typically, the stages in the growth of the domestic system are the following: 1. A purely factual buying monopoly of the factor in relation to the craft worker. This was regularly established through indebtedness; the factor compels the worker to turn over his product to him exclusively, on the ground of his knowledge of the market as merchant. Thus the buying monopoly is connected with a selling monopoly and taking possession of the market by the factor; he alone knowing where the products were finally to stop. 2. Delivery of the raw material to the worker by the factor. This appears frequently, but is not connected with the buying monopoly of the factor from the beginning. The stage was general in Europe but was seldom reached elsewhere. 3. Control of the production process. The factor has an interest in the process because he is responsible for uniformity in the quality of the product. Consequently, the delivery of raw material to the worker is often associated with a delivery of partial products, as in the 19th century the Westphalian linen weavers had to work up a prescribed quantity of warp and yarn. 4. With this was connected not infrequently, but also not quite commonly, the provision of the tools by the factor; this practice obtained in England from the 16th century on, while on the continent it spread more slowly. In general the relation was confined to the textile industry; there were orders on a large scale for looms for the clothiers who turned them over to the weavers for a rental. Thus the worker was entirely separated from the means of production, and at the same time the entrepreneur strove to monopolize for himself the disposal of the product. 5. Sometimes the factor took the step of combining several stages in the production process; this also was not very common, and was most likely to occur in the textile industry. He bought the raw material and put it out to the individual workman, in whose hands the product remained until it was finished. When this stage was reached the craft worker again had a master, in quite the same sense as the craftsman on an estate, except that in contrast with the latter he received a money wage and an entrepreneur producing for the market took the place of the aristocratic household.

The ability of the putting out system to maintain itself so long rested on the unimportance of fixed capital. In weaving, this consisted only of the loom; in spinning, prior to the invention of mechanical spinning machines, it was still more insignificant. The capital remained in the possession of the independent worker, and its constituent parts were decentralized, not concentrated as in a modern factory, and hence without special importance. Although the domestic system was spread widely over the earth, yet this last stage, the provision of the tools and the detailed direction of production in its various stages by the factor, was reached comparatively seldom outside the western world. As far as can be learned, no trace whatever of the system survived from antiquity, but in China and India it was present. Where it dominated, craftsmen might none the less in form continue to exist. Even the guild with journeymen and apprentices might remain, though divested of its original significance. It became either a guild of home workers— not a modern labor organization but at most a forerunner of such —or within the guild there might be a differentiation between wage workers and masters.

In the form of capitalistic control of unfree labor power, we find house industry spread over the world, as manorial, monastic and temple industry. As a free system it is found in connection with the industrial work of peasants; the cultivator gradually becomes a home worker producing for the market. In Russia especially, industrial development took this course. The "kustar" originally brought only the surplus production of the peasant household to market, or peddled it through third parties. Here we have a rural industry which does not take its course toward tribal industry but goes over into the domestic system. Quite the same thing is found in the east and in Asia in the east, it is true, strongly modified by the bazaar system, in which the work place of the craftsman is separate from his dwelling and closely connected with a general centralized market place in order, as far as possible, to guard against dependence on the merchant; to a certain extent this represents an intensification of the medieval guild system.

Dependence of urban as well as rural craft workers upon an

employer (factor or "putter out") is met with. China especially affords an example, though the clan retails the products of its members and the connection with clan industry obstructed the development of domestic industry. In India the castes stood in the way of the complete subjugation of the craftsman by the merchant. Down to recent times the merchant was unable to obtain possession of the means of production to the extent we find true elsewhere, because these were hereditary in the caste. None the less, the domestic system in a primitive form developed here. The last and essential reason for its retarded development in these countries as compared with Europe is found in the presence of unfree workers and the magical traditionalism of China and India. . . . To sum up, it must be held at present, first, that the factory did not develop out of hand work or at the expense of the latter but to begin with alongside of and in addition to it. It seized upon new forms of production or new products, as for example cotton, porcelain, colored brocade, substitute goods, or products which were not made by the craft guilds, and with which the factories could compete with the latter. The extensive inroads by the factories in the sphere of guild work really belongs to the 19th century at the earliest, just as in the 18th century, especially in the English textile industry, progress was made at the expense of the domestic system. None the less the guilds combated the factories and closed workshops growing out of them, especially on grounds of principle; they felt themselves threatened by the new method of production.

As little as out of craft work did the factories develop out of the domestic system, rather they grew up alongside the latter. As between the domestic system and the factory the volume of fixed capital was decisive. Where fixed capital was not necessary the domestic system has endured down to the present; where it was necessary, factories arose, though not out of the domestic system; an originally feudal or communal establishment would be taken over by an entrepreneur and used for the production of goods for the market under private initiative.

Finally, it is to be observed that the modern factory was not in the first instance called into being by machines but rather there is a correlation between the two. Machine industry made use originally of animal power; even Arkwright's first spinning machines in 1768 were driven by horses. The specialization of work and labor discipline within the workshop, however, formed a predisposing condition, even an impetus toward the increased application and improvement of machines. Premiums were offered for the construction of the new engines. Their principle—the lifting of water by fire—arose in the mining industry and rested upon the application of steam as a motive force. Economically, the significance of the machines lay in the introduction of systematic calculation.

The consequences which accompanied the introduction of the modern factory are extraordinarily far reaching, both for the entrepreneur and for the worker. Even before the application of machinery, workshop industry meant the employment of the worker in a place which was separate both from the dwelling of the consumer and from his own. There has always been concentration of work in some form or other. In antiquity it was the Pharaoh or the territorial lord who had products made to supply his political or large-household needs. Now, however, the proprietor of the workshop became the master of the workman, an entrepreneur producing for the market. The concentration of workers within the shop was at the beginning of the modern era partly compulsory; the poor and homeless and criminals were pressed into factories, and in the mines of Newcastle the laborers wore iron collars down into the 18th century. But in the 18th century itself the labor contract everywhere took the place of unfree work. It meant a saving in capital, since the capital requirement for purchasing the slaves disappeared; also a shifting of the capital risk onto the worker, since his death had previously meant a capital loss for the master. Again, it removed responsibility for the reproduction of the working class, whereas slave manned industry was wrecked on the question of the family life and reproduction of the slaves. It made possible the rational division of labor on the basis of technical efficiency alone, and although precedents existed, still freedom of contract first made concentration of labor in the shop the general rule. Finally, it created the possibility of exact calculation, which again could only be carried out in connection with a combination of workshop and free worker.

In spite of all these conditions favoring its development, the workshop industry was and remained in the early period insecure; in various places it disappeared again, as in Italy, and especially in Spain, where a famous painting of Velasquez portrays it to us although later it is absent. Down into the first half of the 18th century it did not form an unreplaceable, necessary, or indispensable part of the provision for the general needs. One thing is always certain; before the age of machinery, workshop industry with free labor was nowhere else developed to the extent that it was in the western world at the beginning of the modern era. The reasons for the fact that elsewhere the development did not take the same course will be explained in what follows.

India once possessed a highly developed industrial technique, but here the caste stood in the way of development of the occidental workshop, the castes being "impure" to one another. It is true that the caste ritual of India did not go to the extent of forbidding members of different castes to work together in the same shop; there was a saying—"the workshop is pure." However, if the workshop system could not here develop into the factory, the exclusiveness of the caste is certainly in part responsible. Such a workshop must have appeared extraordinarily anomalous. Down into the 19th century, all attempts to introduce factory organization even in the jute industry, encountered great difficulties. Even after the rigor of caste law had decayed, the lack of labor discipline in the people stood in the way. Every caste had a different ritual and different rest pauses, and demanded different holidays.

In China, the cohesion of the clans in villages was extraordinarily strong. Workshop industry is there communal clan economy. Beyond this, China developed only the domestic system. Centralized establishments were founded only by the emperor and great feudal lords, especially in the manufacture of porcelain by servile hand workers for the requirements of the maker and only to a limited extent for the market, and generally on an unvarying scale of operation.

For antiquity, the political uncertainty of slave capital is characteristic. The slave ergasterion was known, but it was a difficult and risky enterprise. The lord preferred to utilize the slave as a source of rent rather than as labor power. On scrutinizing the slave property of antiquity, one observes that slaves of the most diverse types were intermingled to such a degree that a modern shop industry could produce nothing by their use. However, this is not so incomprehensible; today one invests his wealth in assorted securities, and in antiquity the owner of men was compelled to acquire the most diverse sorts of hand workers in order to distribute his risk. The final result, however, was that the possession of slaves militated against the establishment of large scale industry.

In the early middle ages, unfree labor was lacking or became notably more scarce; new supplies did indeed come on the market, but not in considerable volume. In addition there was an extraordinary dearth of capital, and money wealth could not be converted into capital. Finally, there were extensive independent opportunities for peasants and industrially trained free workers, on grounds opposite to the condition of antiquity; that is, the free worker had a chance, thanks to the continual colonization in the east of Europe, of securing a position and finding protection against his erstwhile master. Consequently, it was hardly possible in the early middle ages to establish large workshop industries. A further influence was the increasing strength of social bonds due to industrial law, especially guild law. But even if these obstacles had not existed, a sufficiently extended market for the product would not have been at hand. Even where large establishments had originally existed, we find them in a state of retrogression, like the rural large industries in the Carolingian period. There were also beginnings of industrial shop labor within the royal *fisci* and the monasteries, but these also decayed. Everywhere work shop industry remained still more sporadic than at the beginning of the modern era, when at best it could reach its full development only as a royal establishment or on the basis of royal privileges. In every case a specific workshop technique was wanting; this first arose gradually in the 16th and 17th centuries and first definitely with the mechanization of the production process. The impulse to this mechanization came, however, from mining.

12

MODERN CAPITALISM

The Meaning and Presuppositions of Modern Capitalism

CAPITALISM IS PRESENT wherever the industrial provision for the needs of a human group is carried out by the method of enterprise, irrespective of what need is involved. More specifically, a rational capitalistic establishment is one with capital accounting, that is, an establishment which determines its income yielding power by calculation according to the methods of modern book-keeping and the striking of a balance. The device of the balance was first insisted upon by the Dutch theorist Simon Stevin in the year 1698.

It goes without saying that an individual economy may be conducted along capitalistic lines to the most widely varying extent; parts of the economic provision may be organized capitalistically and other parts on the handicraft or the manorial pattern. Thus at a very early time the city of Genoa had a part of its political needs, namely those for the prosecution of war, provided in capitalistic fashion, through stock companies. In the Roman empire, the supply of the population of the capital city with grain was carried out by officials, who however for this purpose, besides control over their subalterns, had the right to command the services of transport organizations; thus the leiturgical or forced contribution type of organization was combined with administration

From *General Economic History*, by Max Weber, translated by Frank H. Knight. Published 1961 by Collier Books, New York. Reprinted by permission.

of public resources. Today, in contrast with the greater part of the past, our everyday needs are supplied capitalistically, our political needs however through compulsory contributions, that is, by the performance of political duties of citizenship such as the obligation to military service, jury duty, etc. A whole epoch can be designated as typically capitalistic only as the provision for wants is capitalistically organized to such a predominant degree that if we imagine this form of organization taken away the whole economic system must collapse.

While capitalism of various forms is met with in all periods of history, the provision of the everyday wants by capitalistic methods is characteristic of the occident alone and even here has been the inevitable method only since the middle of the 19th century. Such capitalistic beginnings as are found in earlier centuries were merely anticipatory, and even the somewhat capitalistic establishments of the 16th century may be removed in thought from the economic life of the time without introducing any overwhelming change.

The most general presupposition for the existence of this present-day capitalism is that of rational capital accounting as the norm for all large industrial undertakings which are concerned with provision for everyday wants. Such accounting involves, again, first, the appropriation of all physical means of production —land, apparatus, machinery, tools, etc. as disposable property of autonomous private industrial enterprises. This is a phenomenon known only to our time, when the army alone forms a universal exception to it. In the second place, it involves freedom of the market, that is, the absence of irrational limitations on trading in the market. Such limitations might be of a class character, if a certain mode of life were prescribed for a certain class or consumption were standardized along class lines, or if class monopoly existed, as for example if the townsman were not allowed to own an estate or the knight or peasant to carry on industry; in such cases neither a free labor market nor a commodity market exists. Third, capitalistic accounting presupposes rational technology, that is, one reduced to calculation to the largest possible degree, which implies mechanization. This applies to both production and commerce, the outlays for preparing as well as moving goods.

The fourth characteristic is that of calculable law. The capitalistic form of industrial organization, if it is to operate rationally, must be able to depend upon calculable adjudication and administration. Neither in the age of the Greek city-state (polis) nor in the patrimonial state of Asia nor in western countries down to the Stuarts was this condition fulfilled. The royal "cheap justice" with its remissions by royal grace introduced continual disturbances into the calculations of economic life. The proposition that the Bank of England was suited only to a republic, not to a monarchy, was related in this way to the conditions of the time. The fifth feature is free labor. Persons must be present who are not only legally in the position, but are also economically compelled, to sell their labor on the market without restriction. It is in contradiction to the essence of capitalism, and the development of capitalism is impossible, if such a propertyless stratum is absent, a class compelled to sell its labor services to live; and it is likewise impossible if only unfree labor is at hand. Rational capitalistic calculation is possible only on the basis of free labor; only where in consequence of the existence of workers who in the formal sense voluntarily, but actually under the compulsion of the whip of hunger, offer themselves, the costs of products may be unambiguously determined by agreement in advance. The sixth and final condition is the commercialization of economic life. By this we mean the general use of commercial instruments to represent share rights in enterprise, and also in property ownership.

To sum up, it must be possible to conduct the provision for needs exclusively on the basis of market opportunities and the calculation of net income. The addition of this commercialization to the other characteristics of capitalism involves intensification of the significance of another factor not yet mentioned, namely speculation. Speculation reaches its full significance only from the moment when property takes on the form of negotiable paper.

The External Facts in the Evolution of Capitalism

Commercialization involves, in the first place, the appearance of paper representing shares in enterprise, and, in the second place, paper representing rights to income, especially in the form of state bonds and mortgage indebtedness. This development has taken place only in the modern western world. Forerunners are indeed found in antiquity in the share-commandite companies of the Roman *publicani,* who divided the gains with the public through such share paper. But this is an isolated phenomenon and without importance for the provision for needs in Roman life; if it had been wanting entirely, the picture presented by the economic life of Rome would not have been changed.

In modern economic life the issue of credit instruments is a means for the rational assembly of capital. Under this head belongs especially the stock company. This represents a culmination of two different lines of development. In the first place, share capital may be brought together for the purpose of anticipating revenues. The political authority wishes to secure command over a definite capital sum or to know upon what income it may reckon; hence it sells or leases its revenues to a stock company. The Bank of St. George in Genoa is the most outstanding example of such financial operations, and along the same line are the income certificates of the German cities and treasury notes (*Rentenmeister-briefe*) especially in Flanders. The significance of this system is that in place of the original condition under which unusual state requirements were covered by compulsory law, usually without interest and frequently never repaid, loans come to be floated which appeal to the voluntary economic interests of the participants. The conduct of war by the state becomes a business operation of the possessing classes. War loans bearing a high interest rate were unknown in antiquity; if the subjects were not in a position to supply the necessary means the state must turn to a foreign financier whose advances were secured by a claim against the spoils of war. If the war terminated unfortunately his money was lost. The securing of money for state purposes, and especially for war purposes, by appeal to the universal economic interest, is a creation of the middle ages, especially of the cities.

Another and economically more important form of association is that for the purpose of financing commercial enterprise—although the evolution toward the form of association most familiar today in the industrial field, the stock company, went forward very gradually from this beginning. Two types of such organizations are to be distinguished; first, large enterprises of an inter-regional character which exceeded the resources of a single commercial house, and second, inter-regional colonial undertakings.

For inter-regional enterprises which could not be financed by individual entrepreneurs, finance groups was typical, especially in the operations of the cities in the 15th and 16th centuries. In part the cities themselves carried on inter-regional trade, but for economic history the other case is more important, in which the city went before the public and invited share participation in the commercial enterprise which it organized. This was done on a considerable scale. When the city appealed to the public, compulsion was exercised on the company thus formed to admit any citizen; hence the amount of share capital was unlimited. Frequently the capital first collected was insufficient and an additional contribution was demanded, where today the liability of the share holder is limited to his share. The city frequently set a maximum limit to the individual contribution so that the entire citizenship might participate. This was often done by arranging the citizens in groups according to the taxes paid or their wealth and reserving a definite fraction of the capital for each class. In contrast with the modern stock company the investment was often rescindable, while the share of the individual was not freely transferable. Hence the whole enterprise represented a stock company only in an embryonic sense. Official supervision was exercised over the conduct of operations.

In this form the so-called "regulated" company was common, especially in the iron trade as in Steier, and it was occasionally used in the cloth trade, as in Iglau. A consequence of the structure of the organizations just described was the absence of fixed capital and, as in the case of the workers' association, the absence of capital accounting in the modern sense. Share holders included not only merchants, but princes, professors, courtiers, and in general the public in the strict sense, which participated gladly and to great profit. The distribution of the dividends was carried out in a completely irrational way, according to the gross income alone, without reserves of any kind. All that was necessary was the removal of the official control and the modern stock company was at hand.

The great colonization companies formed another preliminary stage in the development of the modern stock company. The most significant of these were the Dutch and English East India companies, which were not stock companies in the modern sense. On account of the jealousy of the citizens of the provinces of the country the Dutch East India Company raised its capital by distributing the shares among them, not permitting all the stock to be bought up by any single city. The government, that is the federation, participated in the administration, especially because it reserved the right to use the ships and cannon of the company for its own needs. Modern capital accounting was absent as was free transferability of shares, although relatively extensive dealings in the latter soon took place. It was these great successful companies which made the device of share capital generally known and popular; from them it was taken over by all the continental states of Europe. Stock companies created by the state, and granted privileges for the purpose, came to regulate the conditions of participation in business enterprise in general, while the state itself in a supervisory capacity was involved in the most remote details of business activity. Not until the 18th century did the annual balance and inventory become established customs, and it required many terrible bankruptcies to force their acceptance.

Alongside the financing of state needs through stock companies stands direct financing by measures of the state itself. This begins with compulsory loans against a pledge of resources and the issue of certificates of indebtedness against anticipated revenues. The cities of the middle ages secured extraordinary income by bonds, pledging their fixed property and taxing power. These annuities may be regarded as the forerunners of the modern consols, yet only within limitations; for to a large extent the income ran for the life of the purchaser, and they were tied up with other considerations. In addition to these devices the necessity of raising money gave rise to various expedients down to the 17th century. The emperor Leopold I attempted to raise a "cavalier loan," sending mounted messengers around to the nobility to solicit subscriptions; but in general he received for answer the injunction to turn to those who had the money.

If one desires to understand the financial operations of a German city as late as the close of the middle ages, one must bear in mind that there was at that time no such thing as an orderly budget. The city, like the territorial lord, lived from week to week as is done today in a small household. Expenditures were readjusted momentarily as income fluctuated. The device of tax farming was of assistance in overcoming the difficulty of management without a budget. It gave the administration some security as to the sums which it might expect each year, and assisted it in planning its expenditures. Hence the tax farm operated as an outstanding instrument of financial rationalization, and was called into use by the European states occasionally at first and then permanently. It also made possible the discounting of public revenues for war purposes, and in this connection achieved especial significance. Rational administration of taxation was an accomplishment of the Italian cities in the period after the loss of their freedom. The Italian nobility is the first political power to order its finances in accordance with the principle of mercantile bookkeeping obtaining at the time, although this did not then include double entry. From the Italian cities the system spread abroad and came into German territory through Burgundy, France, and the Hapsburg states. It was especially the tax payers who clamored to have the finances put in order.

A second point of departure for rational forms of administration was the English exchequer system, of which the word "check" is a last survival and reminder. This was a sort of checker board device by means of which the payments due the state were computed, in the absence of the necessary facility in operating with figures. Regularly, however, the finances were not conducted through setting up a budget in which all receipts and disbursements were included, but a special-fund system was used. That is, certain receipts were designated and raised for the purpose of specified expenditures only. The reason for this procedure is found in the conflicts between the princely power and the citizens. The latter mistrusted the princes and thought this the only way to protect themselves against having the taxes squandered for the personal ends of the ruler.

In the 16th and 17th centuries an additional force working for the rationalization of the financial operations of rulers appeared in the monopoly policy of the princes. In part they assumed commercial monopolies themselves and in part they granted monopolistic concessions, involving of course the payment of notable sums to the political authority. An example is the exploitation of the quicksilver mines of Idria, in the Austrian province of Carniola, which were of great importance on account of the process of amalgamating silver. These mines were the subject of protracted bargaining between the two lines of the Hapsburgs and yielded notable revenues to both the German and the Spanish houses. The first example of this policy of monopoly concession was the attempt of the Emperor Frederick II to establish a grain monopoly for Sicily. The policy was most extensively employed in England and was developed in an especially systematic manner by the Stuarts, and there also it first broke down, under the protests of Parliament. Each new industry and establishment of the Stuart period was for this purpose bound up with a royal concession and granted a monopoly. The king secured important revenues from the privileges, which provided him with the resources for his struggle against Parliament. But these industrial monopolies established for fiscal purposes broke down almost without exception after the triumph of Parliament. This in itself proves how incorrect it is to regard, as some writers have done, modern western capitalism as an outgrowth of the monopolistic policies of princes.[1]

The Economic Policy of the Rational State

For the state to have an economic policy worthy of the name, that is one which is continuous and consistent, is an institu-

---

[1]   See, for example, H. Levy, *Economic Liberalism* (London, 1913).

tion of exclusively modern origin. The first system which it brought forth is mercantilism, so-called. Before the development of mercantilism there were two widespread commercial policies, namely, the dominance of fiscal interests and of welfare interests, the last in the sense of the customary standard of living.

In the east it was essentially ritualistic considerations, including caste and clan organizations, which prevented the development of a deliberate economic policy. In China, the political system had undergone extraordinary changes. The country had an epoch of highly developed foreign trade, extending as far as India. Later, however, the Chinese economic policy turned to external exclusiveness to the extent that the entire import and export business was in the hands of only 13 firms and was concentrated in the single port of Canton. Internally, the policy was dominated by religious considerations; only on occasion of natural catastrophes were abuses inquired into. At all times the question of co-operation of the provinces determined the viewpoint, and a leading problem was set by the question whether the needs of the state should be provided by taxation or through compulsory services.

In Japan, the feudal organization led to the same consequences and resulted in complete exclusiveness as regards the outer world. The object was here the stabilization of class relations; it was feared that foreign trade would disturb conditions as to the distribution of property. In Korea, ritualistic grounds determined the exclusive policy. If foreigners, that is profane persons, were to come into the country the wrath of the spirits was to be feared. In the Indian middle ages we find Greek and Roman merchants, as well as Roman soldiers, and also the immigration of Jews with grants of privileges to them; but these germs were unable to develop, for later everything was again stereotyped by the caste system, which made a planned economic policy impossible. An additional consideration was that Hinduism strongly condemned traveling abroad; one who went abroad had on his return to be re-admitted to his caste.

In the occident down to the 14th century a planned economic policy had a chance to develop only in connection with the towns. It is true that there were beginnings of an economic policy on the part of the princes; in the Carolingian period we find price fixing and public concern for welfare expressed in various directions. But most of this remained on paper only, and with the exception of the coinage reform and the system of weights and measures of Charlemagne, everything disappeared without leaving a trace in the succeeding period. A commercial policy which would have been gladly adopted in relation to the orient was rendered impossible by the absence of shipping.

When the state under its prince gave up the fight, the church interested itself in economic life, endeavoring to impose upon economic dealings a minimum of legal honesty and churchly ethics. One of its most important measures was the support of the public peace, which it attempted to enforce first on certain days and finally as a general principle. In addition, the great ecclesiastical property communities, especially the monasteries, supported a very rational economic life, which cannot be called capitalistic economy but which was the most rational in existence. Later these endeavors more and more fell into discredit as the church revived its old ascetic ideals and adapted them to the times. Among the emperors again are found a few beginnings of commercial policy under Frederick Barbarossa, including price fixing and a customs treaty with England designed to favor German merchants. Frederick II established the public peace but in general pursued a purely fiscal policy favoring merely the rich merchants; to them he granted privileges, especially customs exemptions.

The single measure of economic policy on the part of the German kings was the conflict over the Rhine tolls, which however was futile in the main, in view of the great number of petty lords along the river. Aside from this there was no planned economic policy. Measures which give the impression of such a policy, such as the embargo of the emperor Sigmund against Venice, or the occasional closing of the Rhine in the struggle with Cologne, are purely political in character. The customs policy was in the hands of the territorial princes, and even here with few exceptions a consistent effort to encourage industry is wanting. Their dominant objectives were, first, to favor local as against distant trade, especially to promote interchange of goods between the towns and the surrounding country; export duties were always to be maintained higher than import duties. Second, to favor local merchants in the customs. Road tolls were differentiated, the prince endeavoring to favor his own roads in order the more conveniently to exploit them as a source of revenue; to this end they even went to the length of requiring the use of certain roads, and systematized the law of the staple. Finally, the city merchants were given privileges; Louis the Rich of Bavaria prided himself on suppressing the rural merchants.

Protective duties are unknown, with few exceptions, of which the Tirolese duties on wine, directed against the competition of imports from Italy, are an example. The customs policy as a whole is dominated by the fiscal point of view and that of maintaining the traditional standard of living. The same applies to the customs treaties, which go back to the 13th century. The technique of the customs fluctuated. The original custom was an ad-valorem duty of one-sixtieth the value; in the 14th century this was increased to a one-twelfth, in view of the fact that the duty was made to function also as an excise. The place of our modern measures of economic policy, such as protective tariffs, was taken by direct prohibitions against trade, which were very frequently suspended when the standard of living of domestic craftsmen, or later of employing factors, was to be protected. Sometimes wholesale trade was allowed and retail trade was prohibited. The first trace of a rational economic policy on the part of the prince appears in the 14th century in England. This was mercantilism, so-called since Adam Smith.

Mercantilism

The essence of mercantilism consists in carrying the point of view of capitalistic industry into politics; the state is handled as if it consisted exclusively of capitalistic entrepreneurs. External economic policy rests on the principle of taking every advantage of the opponent, importing at the lowest price and selling much higher. The purpose is to strengthen the hand of the government in its external relations. Hence mercantilism signifies the development of the state as a political power, which is to be done directly by increasing the tax paying power of the population.

A presupposition of the mercantilistic policy was the inclusion of as many sources of money income as possible within the country in question. It is, to be sure, an error to hold that the mercantilistic thinkers and statesmen confused ownership of the precious metals with national wealth. They knew well enough that the source of this wealth is the tax paying power, and all that they did in the way of retaining in the country the money which threatened to disappear through the commerce was done exclusively with a view to increasing this taxable capacity. A second point in the program of mercantilism, in obvious immediate connection with the power-seeking policy characteristic of the system, was to promote the largest possible increase in the population; in order to sustain the increased numbers, the endeavor was to secure to the greatest extent external markets; this applied especially to those products in which a maximum quantity of domestic labor was embodied, hence finished manufactures rather than raw materials. Finally, trade was to be carried on as far as possible by the merchants of the country, in order that its earnings should all accrue to the taxable capacity. On the side of theory, the system was supported by the doctrine of the balance of trade, which taught that the country would be impoverished if the value of imports exceeded that of exports; this theory was first developed in England in the 16th century.

England is distinctively the original home of Mercantilism. The first traces of the application of mercantilistic principles are found there in the year 1381. Under the weak king Richard II, a money stringency arose and Parliament appointed an investigating commission which for the first time dealt with the balance of trade concept in all its essential features. For the time being it produced only emergency measures, including prohibitions of importation and stimulation of exportation, but without giving to English policy a truly mercantilistic character. The real turning point is generally dated from 1440. At that time, in one of the numerous Statutes of Employment, which were passed for the correction of alleged abuses, two propositions were laid down which indeed had been applied before, but only in an incidental way. The first was that foreign merchants who brought goods to England must convert all the money which they received into English goods; the second that English merchants who had dealings abroad must bring back to England at least a part of their proceeds in cash. On the basis of these two propositions developed gradually the whole system of mercantilism down to the Navigation Act of 1651, with its elimination of the foreign shipping.

Mercantilism in the sense of a league between the state and the capitalistic interest had appeared under two aspects. One was that of class monopoly, which appears in its typical form in the policy of the Stuarts and the Anglican church—especially that of Bishop Laud who was later beheaded. This system looked toward a class organization of the whole population in the Christian socialist sense, a stabilization of the classes with a view to establishing social relations based on Christian love. In the sharpest contrast with Puritanism, which saw every poor person as work-shy or as a criminal, its attitude toward the poor was friendly. In practice, the mercantilism of the Stuarts was primarily oriented along fiscal lines; new industries were allowed to import only on the basis of a royal monopoly concession and were to be kept under the permanent control of the king with a view to fiscal exploitation. Similar, although not so consistent, was the policy of Colbert in France. He aimed at an artificial promotion of industries, supported by monopolies; this view he shared with the Huguenots, on whose persecution he looked with disfavor. In England the royal and Anglican policy was broken down by the Puritans under the Long Parliament. Their struggle with the king was pursued for decades under the war cry "down with the monopolies" which were granted in part to foreigners and in part to courtiers, while the colonies were placed in the hands of royal favorites. The small entrepreneur class which in the meantime had grown up, especially within the guilds though in part outside of them, enlisted against the royal monopoly policy, and the Long Parliament deprived monopolists of the suffrage. The extraordinary obstinacy with which the economic spirit of the English people has striven against trusts and monopolies is expressed in these Puritan struggles.

The second form of mercantilism may be called national; it limited itself to the protection of industries actually in existence, in contrast with the attempt to establish industries through monopolies. Hardly one of the industries created by mercantilism survived the mercantilistic period; the economic creations of the Stuarts disappeared along with those of the western continental states and those of Russia later. It follows that the capitalistic development was not an outgrowth of national mercantilism; rather capitalism developed at first in England alongside the fiscal monopoly policy. The course of events was that a stratum of entrepreneurs which had developed in independence of the political administration secured the systematic support of Parliament in the 18th century, after the collapse of the fiscal monopoly policy of the Stuarts. Here for the last time irrational and rational capitalism faced each other in conflict, that is, capitalism in the field of fiscal and colonial privileges and public monopolies, and capitalism oriented in relation to market opportunities which were developed from within by business interests themselves on the basis of saleable services.

The point of collision of the two types was at the Bank of England. The bank was founded by Paterson, a Scotchman, a capitalist adventurer of the type called forth by the Stuarts' policy of granting monopolies. But Puritan business men also belonged to the bank. The last time the bank turned aside in the direction of speculative capitalism was in connection with the South Sea Company. Aside from this venture we can trace step by step the process by which the influence of Paterson and his kind lost ground in favor of the rationalistic type of bank members who were all directly or indirectly of Puritan origin or influenced by Puritanism.

Mercantilism also played the role familiar in economic history. In England it finally disappeared when free trade was established, an achievement of the Puritan dissenters Cobden and Bright and their league with the industrial interests, which were now in a position to dispense with mercantilistic support.

The Evolution of the Capitalistic Spirit

Traditional obstructions are not overcome by the economic impulse alone. The notion that our rationalistic and capitalistic age is characterized by a stronger economic interest than other periods is childish; the moving spirits of modern capitalism are not possessed of a stronger economic impulse than, for example, an oriental trader. The unchaining of the economic interest merely as such has produced only irrational results; such men as Cortez and Pizarro, who were perhaps its strongest embodiment, were far from having an idea of a rationalistic economic life. If the economic impulse in itself is universal, it is an interesting question as to the relations under which it becomes rationalized and rationally tempered in such fashion as to produce rational institutions of the character of capitalistic enterprise.

Originally, two opposite attitudes toward the pursuit of gain exist in combination. Internally, there is attachment to tradition and to the pietistic relations of fellow members of tribe, clan, and house-community, with the exclusion of the unrestricted quest of gain within the circle of those bound together by religious ties; externally, there is absolutely unrestricted play of the gain spirit in economic relations, every foreigner being originally an enemy in relation to whom no ethical restrictions apply; that is, the ethics of internal and external relations are categorically distinct. The course of development involves on the one hand the bringing in of calculation into the traditional brotherhood, displacing the old religious relationship. As soon as accountability is established within the family community, and economic relations are no longer strictly communistic, there is an end of the naive piety and its repression of the economic impulse. This side of the development is especially characteristic in the west. At the same time there is a tempering of the unrestricted quest of gain with the adoption of the economic principle into the internal economy. The result is a regulated economic life with the economic impulse functioning within bounds.

In detail, the course of development has been varied. In India, the restrictions upon gain-seeking apply only to the two uppermost strata, the Brahmins and the Rajputs. A member of these castes is forbidden to practice certain callings. A Brahmin may conduct an eating house, as he alone has clean hands; but he, like the Rajput, would be unclassed if he were to lend money for interest. The latter, however, is permitted to the mercantile castes, and within it we find a degree of unscrupulousness in trade which is unmatched anywhere in the world. Finally, antiquity had only legal limitations on interest, and the proposition *caveat emptor* characterizes Roman economic ethics. Nevertheless no modern capitalism developed there.

The final result is the peculiar fact that the germs of modern capitalism must be sought in a region where officially a theory was dominant which was distinct from that of the east and of classical antiquity and in principle strongly hostile to capitalism. The *ethos* of the classical economic morality is summed up in the old judgment passed on the merchant, which was probably taken from primitive Arianism: *homo mercator vix aut numquam potest Deo placere;* he may conduct himself without sin but cannot be pleasing to God. This proposition was valid down to the 15th century, and the first attempt to modify it slowly matured in Florence under pressure of the shift in economic relations.

The typical antipathy of Catholic ethics, and following that the Lutheran, to every capitalistic tendency, rests essentially on the repugnance of the impersonality of relations within a capitalist economy. It is this fact of impersonal relations which places certain human affairs outside the church and its influence, and prevents the latter from penetrating them and transforming them along ethical lines. The relations between master and slave could be subjected to immediate ethical regulation; but the relations between the mortgage creditor and the property which was pledged for the debt, or between an endorser and the bill of exchange, would at least be exceedingly difficult if not impossible to moralize. The final consequence of the resulting position assumed by the church was that medieval economic ethics excluded higgling, overpricing and free competition, and were based on the principle of just price and the assurance to everyone of a chance to live.

For the breaking up of this circle of ideas the Jews cannot be made responsible as Sombart does.[2] The position of the Jews during the middle ages may be compared sociologically with that of an Indian caste in a world otherwise free from castes; they were an outcast people. However, there is the distinction that according to the promise of the Indian religion the caste system is valid for eternity. The individual may in the course of time reach heaven through a course of reincarnations, the time depending upon his deserts; but this is possible only within the caste system. The caste organization is eternal, and one who attempted to leave it would be accursed and condemned to pass in hell into the bowels of a dog. The Jewish promise, on the contrary, points toward a reversal of caste relations in the future world as compared with this. In the present world the Jews are stamped as an outcast people, either as punishment for the sins of their fathers, as Deutero-Isaiah holds, or for the salvation of the world, which is the presupposition of the mission of Jesus of Nazareth; from this position they are to be released by a social revolution. In the middle ages the Jews were a guest-people standing outside of political society; they could not be received into any town citizenship group because they could not participate in the communion of the Lord's Supper, and hence could not belong to the *coniuratio*.

The Jews were not the only guest people; besides them the Caursines, for example, occupied a similar position. These were Christian merchants who dealt in money and in consequence were, like the Jews, under the protection of the princes and on consideration of a payment enjoyed the privilege of carrying on monetary dealings. What distinguished the Jews in a striking way from the Christian guest-peoples was the impossibility in their case of entering into *commercium* and *conubium* with the Christians. Originally the Christians did not hesitate to accept Jewish hospitality, in contrast with the Jews themselves who feared that their ritual-

2   W. Sombart, *The Jews and Modern Capitalism* (London, 1913).

istic prescriptions as to food would not be observed by their hosts. On the occasion of the first outbreak of medieval anti-semitism the faithful were warned by the synods not to conduct themselves unworthily and hence not to accept entertainment from the Jews who on their side despised the hospitality of the Christians. Marriage with Christians was strictly impossible, going back to Ezra and Nehemiah.

A further ground for the outcast position of the Jews arose from the fact that Jewish craftsmen existed; in Syria there had even been a Jewish knightly class, though only exceptionally Jewish peasants, for the conduct of agriculture was not to be reconciled with the requirements of the ritual. Ritualistic considerations were responsible for the concentration of Jewish economic life in monetary dealings. Jewish piety set a premium on the knowledge of the law and continuous study was very much easier to combine with exchange dealings than with other occupations. In addition, the prohibitions against usury on the part of the church condemned exchange dealings, yet the trade was indispensable and the Jews were not subject to the ecclesiastical law.

Finally, Judaism had maintained the originally universal dualism of internal and external moral attitudes, under which it was permissible to accept interest from foreigners who did not belong to the brotherhood or established association. Out of this dualism followed the sanctioning of other irrational economic affairs, especially tax farming and political financing of all sorts. In the course of the centuries the Jews acquired a special skill in these matters which made them useful and in demand. But all this was pariah capitalism, not rational capitalism such as originated in the west. In consequence, hardly a Jew is found among the creators of the modern economic situation, the large entrepreneurs; this type was Christian and only conceivable in the field of Christianity. The Jewish manufacturer, on the contrary, is a modern phenomenon. If for no other reason, it was impossible for the Jews to have a part in the establishment of rational capitalism because they were outside the craft organizations. But even alongside the guilds they could hardly maintain themselves, even where, as in Poland, they had command over a numerous prole-

tariat which they might have organized in the capacity of entrepreneurs in domestic industry or as manufacturers. After all, the
genuine Jewish ethic is specifically traditionalism, as the Talmud
shows. The horror of the pious Jew in the face of any innovation
is quite as great as that of an individual among any primitive
people with institutions fixed by the belief in magic.

However, Judaism was none the less of notable significance
for modern rational capitalism, insofar as it transmitted to Christianity the latter's hostility to magic. Apart from Judaism and
Christianity, and two or three oriental sects (one of which is in
Japan), there is no religion with the character of outspoken
hostility to magic. Probably this hostility arose through the
circumstance that what the Israelites found in Canaan was the
magic of the agricultural god Baal, while Jahveh was a god of
volcanoes, earthquakes, and pestilences.The hostility between the
two priesthoods and the victory of the priests of Jahveh discredited
the fertility magic of the priests of Baal and stigmatized it with
a character of decadence and godlessness. Since Judaism made
Christianity possible and gave it the character of a religion essentially free from magic, it rendered an important service from the
point of view of economic history. For the dominance of magic
outside the sphere in which Christianity has prevailed is one of
the most serious obstructions to the rationalization of economic
life. Magic involves a stereotyping of technology and economic
relations. When attempts were made in China to inaugurate the
building of railroads and factories a conflict with geomancy
ensued. The latter demanded that in the location of structures on
certain mountains, forests, rivers, and cemetery hills, foresight
should be exercised in order not to disturb the rest of the spirits.[3]

Similar is the relation to capitalism of the castes in India.

---

3   As soon as the Mandarins realized the chances for gain open to
them these difficulties suddenly ceased to be insuperable. Today they are
the leading stockholders in the railways. In the long run, no religious—
ethical conviction is capable of barring the way to the entry of capitalism,
when it stands in full armor before the gate, but the fact that it is able to
leap over magical barriers does not prove that genuine capitalism could
have originated in circumstances where magic played such a role.

Every new technical process which an Indian employs signifies for him first of all that he leaves his caste and falls into another, necessarily lower. Since he believes in the transmigration of souls, the immediate significance of this is that his chance of purification is put off until another re-birth. He will hardly consent to such a change. An additional fact is that every caste makes every other impure. In consequence, workmen who dare not accept a vessel filled with water from each other's hands, cannot be employed together in the same factory room. Not until the present time, after the possession of the country by the English for almost a century, could this obstacle be overcome. Obviously, capitalism could not develop in an economic group thus bound hand and foot by magical beliefs.

In all times there has been but one means of breaking down the power of magic and establishing a rational conduct of life; this means is great rational prophecy. Not every prophecy by any means destroys the power of magic; but it is possible for a prophet who furnishes credentials in the shape of miracles and otherwise, to break down the traditional sacred rules. Prophecies have released the world from magic and in doing so have created the basis for our modern science and technology, and for capitalism. In China such prophecy has been wanting. What prophecy there was has come from the outside as in the case of Lao-Tse and Taoism. India, however, produced a religion of salvation; in contrast with China it has known great prophetic missions. But they were prophecies by example; that is, the typical Hindu prophet, such as Buddha, lives before the world the life which leads to salvation, but does not regard himself as one sent from God to insist upon the obligation to lead it; he takes the position that whoever wishes salvation, as an end freely chosen, should lead the life. However, one may reject salvation, as it is not the destiny of everyone to enter at death into Nirvana, and only philosophers in the strictest sense are prepared by hatred of this world to adopt the stoical resolution and withdraw from life.

The result was that Hindu prophecy was of immediate significance for the intellectual classes. These became forest dwellers and poor monks. For the masses, however, the significance of the founding of a Buddhistic sect was quite different, namely the opportunity of praying to the saints. There came to be holy men who were believed to work miracles, who must be well fed so that they would repay this good deed by guaranteeing a better reincarnation or through granting wealth, long life, and the like, that is, this world's goods. Hence Buddhism in its pure form was restricted to a thin stratum of monks. The laity found no ethical precepts according to which life should be molded; Buddhism indeed had its decalogue, but in distinction from that of the Jews it gave no binding commands but only recommendations. The most important act of service was and remained the physical maintenance of the monks. Such a religious spirit could never be in a position to displace magic but at best could only put another magic in its place.

In contrast with the ascetic religion of salvation of India and its defective action upon the masses, are Judaism and Christianity, which from the beginning have been plebeian religions and have deliberately remained such. The struggle of the ancient church against the Gnostics was nothing else than a struggle against the aristocracy of the intellectuals, such as is common to ascetic religions, with the object of preventing their seizing of leadership in the church. This struggle was crucial for the success of Christianity among the masses, and hence for the fact that magic was suppressed among the general population to the greatest possible extent. True, it has not been possible even down to today to overcome it entirely, but it was reduced to the character of something unholy, something diabolic.

The germ of this development as regards magic is found far back in ancient Jewish ethics, which is much concerned with views such as we also meet with in the proverbs and the so-called prophetic texts of the Egyptians. But the most important prescriptions of Egyptian ethics were futile when by laying a scarab on the region of the heart one could prepare the dead man to successfully conceal the sins committed, deceive the judge of the dead, and thus get into paradise. The Jewish ethics knows no such sophisticated subterfuges and as little does Christianity. In the Eucharist the latter has indeed sublimated magic into the form of a sacrament, but it gave its adherents no such means for evading the final judgment as were contained in Egyptian religion. If one wishes to study at all the influence of a religion on life one must distinguish between its official teachings and this sort of actual procedure upon which in reality, perhaps against its own will, it places a premium, in this world or the next.

It is also necessary to distinguish between the virtuoso religion of adepts and the religion of the masses. Virtuoso religion is significant for everyday life only as a pattern; its claims are of the highest, but they fail to determine everyday ethics. The relation between the two is different in different religions. In Catholicism, they are brought into harmonious union insofar as the claims of the religious virtuoso are held up alongside the duties of the laymen as *consilia evangelica*. The really complete Christian is the monk; but his mode of life is not required of everyone, although some of his virtues in a qualified form are held up as ideals. The advantage of this combination was that ethics was not split asunder as in Buddhism. After all the distinction between monk ethics and mass ethics meant that the most worthy individuals in the religious sense withdrew from the world and established a separate community.

Christianity was not alone in this phenomenon, which rather recurs frequently in the history of religions, as is shown by the powerful influence in asceticism, which signifies the carrying out of a definite, methodical conduct of life. Asceticism has always worked in this sense. The enormous achievements possible to such an ascetically determined methodical conduct of life are demonstrated by the example of Tibet. The country seems condemned by nature to be an eternal desert; but a community celibate ascetics has carried out colossal construction works in Lhassa and saturated the country with the religious doctrines of Buddhism. An analogous phenomenon is present in the middle ages in the west. In that epoch the monk is the first human being who lives rationally, who works methodically and by rational means toward a goal, namely the future life. Only for him did the clock strike, only for him were the hours of the day divided—for prayer. The economic life of the monastic communities was also rational. The monks in part furnished the officialdom for the early middle ages; the power of the doges of Venice collapsed when the investiture struggle deprived them of the possibility of employing churchmen for oversea enterprises.

But the rational mode of life remained restricted to the monastic circles. The Franciscan movement indeed attempted through the institution of the tertiaries to extend it to the laity, but the institution of the confessional was a barrier to such an extension. The church domesticated medieval Europe by means of its system of confession and penance, but for the men of the middle ages the possibility of unburdening themselves through the channel of the confessional, when they had rendered themselves liable to punishment, meant a release from the consciousness of sin which the teachings of the church had called into being. The unity and strength of the methodical conduct of life were thus in fact broken up. In its knowledge of human nature the church did not reckon with the fact that the individual is a closed unitary ethical personality, but steadfastly held to the view that in spite of the warnings of the confessional and of penances, however strong, he would again fall away morally; that is, it shed its grace on the just and the unjust.

The Reformation made a decisive break with this system. The dropping of the *concilia evangelica* by the Lutheran Reformation meant the disappearance of the dualistic ethics, of the distinction between a universally binding morality and a specifically advantageous code for virtuosi. The other-worldly asceticism came to an end. The stern religious characters who had previously gone into monasteries had now to practice their religion in the life of the world. For such an asceticism within the world the ascetic dogmas of protestantism created an adequate ethics. Celibacy was not required, marriage being viewed simply as an institution for the rational bringing up of children. Poverty was not required, but the pursuit of riches must not lead one astray into reckless enjoyment. Thus Sebastian Franck was correct in summing up the spirit of the Reformation in the words, "you think you have escaped from the monastery, but everyone must now be a monk throughout his life."

The wide significance of this transformation of the ascetic

ideal can be followed down to the present in the classical lands of protestant ascetic religiosity. It is especially discernible in the import of the religious denominations in America. Although state and church are separated, still, as late as fifteen or twenty years ago no banker or physician took up a residence or established connections without being asked to what religious community he belonged, and his prospects were good or bad according to the character of his answer. Acceptance into a sect was conditioned upon a strict inquiry into one's ethical conduct. Membership in a sect which did not recognize the Jewish distinction between internal and external moral codes guaranteed one's business honor and reliability and this in turn guaranteed success. Hence the principle "honesty is the best policy" and hence among Quakers, Baptists, and Methodists the ceaseless repetition of the proposition based on experience that God would take care of his own. "The Godless cannot trust each other across the road; they turn to us when they want to do business; piety is the surest road to wealth." This is by no means "cant," but a combination of religiosity with consequences which were originally unknown to it and which were never intended.

It is true that the acquisition of wealth, attributed to piety, led to a dilemma, in all respects similar to that into which the medieval monasteries constantly fell; the religious guild led to wealth, wealth to fall from grace, and this again to the necessity of re-constitution. Calvinism sought to avoid this difficulty through the idea that man was only an administrator of what God had given him; it condemned enjoyment, yet permitted no flight from the world but rather regarded working together, with its rational discipline, as the religious task of the individual. Out of this system of thought came our word "calling," which is known only to the languages influenced by the Protestant translations of the Bible. It expresses the value placed upon rational activity carried on according to the rational capitalistic principle, as the fulfill-ment of a God-given task. Here lay also in the last analysis the basis of the contrast between the Puritans and the Stuarts. The ideas of both were capitalistically directed; but in a characteristic way the Jew was for the Puritan the embodiment of everything repugnant because he devoted himself to irrational and illegal occupations such as war loans, tax farming, and leasing of offices, in the fashion of the court favorite.

This development of the concept of the calling quickly gave to the modern entrepreneur a fabulously clear conscience— and also industrious workers; he gave to his employees as the wages of their ascetic devotion to the calling and of co-operation in his ruthless exploitation of them through capitalism the prospect of eternal salvation, which in an age when ecclesiastical discipline took control of the whole of life to an extent inconceivable to us now, represented a reality quite different from any it has today. The Catholic and Lutheran churches also recognized and practiced ecclesiastical discipline. But in the Protestant ascetic communities admission to the Lord's Supper was conditioned on ethical fitness, which again was identified with business honor, while into the content of one's faith no one inquired. Such a powerful, unconsciously refined organization for the production of capitalistic individuals has never existed in any other church or religion, and in comparison with it what the Renaissance did for capitalism shrinks into insignificance. Its practitioners occupied themselves with technical problems and were experimenters of the first rank. From art and mining experimentation was taken over into science.

The world-view of the Renaissance, however, determined the policy of rulers in a large measure, though it did not transform the soul of man as did the innovations of the Reformation. Almost all the great scientific discoveries of the 16th and even the beginning of the 17th century were made against the background of Catholicism. Copernicus was a Catholic, while Luther and Melanchthon repudiated his discoveries. Scientific progress and Protestantism must not all be unquestioningly identified. The Catholic church has indeed occasionally obstructed scientific progress; but the ascetic sects of Protestantism have also been disposed to have nothing to do with science, except in a situation where material requirements of everyday life were involved. On the other hand it is its specific contribution to have placed science in the service of technology and economics.

The religious root of modern economic humanity is dead;

today the concept of the calling is a *caput mortuum* in the world. Ascetic religiosity has been displaced by a pessimistic though by no means ascetic view of the world, such as that portrayed in Mandeville's Fable of the Bees, which teaches that private vices may under certain conditions be for the good of the public. With the complete disappearance of all the remains of the original enormous religious pathos of the sects, the optimism of the Enlightenment which believed in the harmony of interests, appeared as the heir of Protestant asceticism in the field of economic ideas; it guided the hands of the princes, statesmen, and writers of the later 18th and early 19th century. Economic ethics arose against the background of the ascetic ideal; now it has been stripped of its religious import. It was possible for the working class to accept its lot as long as the promise of eternal happiness could be held out to it. When this consolation fell away it was inevitable that those strains and stresses should appear in economic society which since then have grown so rapidly. This point had been reached at the end of the early period of capitalism, at the beginning of the age of iron, in the 19th century.

V. Charisma and Institutionalization in the Sphere of Social Stratification

Although problems of stratification were central in Weber's work, he usually dealt with these problems in connection with the political and economic spheres. The central concepts around which his analysis of stratification focuses are status, honor, and estates. In these concepts, especially in that of honor, the charismatic quality of participation in special-status groups is especially emphasized.

Weber's analysis of "status," which he elaborates as the basis of social stratification, opens this part. The second part of this section describes a specific historical system of stratification, that of India. At the end of this chapter is Weber's major criteria of stratification in modern society, as well as an illustrative analysis of one type of a relatively modern estate group, the Prussian Junkers.

13

WEBER'S BASIC CONCEPTS
OF STRATIFICATION

Economically Determined Power and the Social Order

LAW EXISTS when there is a probability that an order will be upheld by a specific staff of men who will use physical or psychical compulsion with the intention of obtaining conformity with the order, or of inflicting sanctions for infringement of it. The structure of every legal order directly influences the distribution of power, economic or otherwise, within its respective community. This is true of all legal orders and not only that of the state. In general, we understand by 'power' the chance of a man or of a number of men to realize their own will in a communal action even against the resistance of others who are participating in the action.

'Economically conditioned' power is not, of course, identical with 'power' as such. On the contrary, the emergence of economic power may be the consequence of power existing on other grounds. Man does not strive for power only in order to enrich himself economically. Power, including economic power, may be valued 'for its own sake.' Very frequently the striving for power is also conditioned by the social 'honor' it entails. Not all power, however, entails social honor: The typical American Boss, as well as the typical big speculator, deliberately relinquishes social honor.

From *Max Weber: Essays in Sociology*, edited and translated by H. H. Gerth and C. Wright Mills. Copyright 1946 by Oxford University Press, Inc. Reprinted by permission.

Quite generally, 'mere economic' power, and especially 'naked' money power, is by no means a recognized basis of social honor. Nor is power the only basis of social honor. Indeed, social honor, or prestige, may even be the basis of political or economic power, and very frequently has been. Power, as well as honor, may be guaranteed by the legal order, but, at least normally, it is not their primary source. The legal order is rather an additional factor that enhances the chance to hold power or honor; but it cannot always secure them.

The way in which social honor is distributed in a community between typical groups participating in this distribution we may call the 'social order.' The social order and the economic order are, of course, similarly related to the 'legal order.' However, the social and the economic order are not identical. The economic order is for us merely the way in which economic goods and services are distributed and used. The social order is of course conditioned by the economic order to a high degree, and in its turn reacts upon it.

Now: 'classes,' 'status groups,' and 'parties' are phenomena of the distribution of power within a community.

Determination of Class-Situation by Market-Situation

In our terminology, 'classes' are not communities; they merely represent possible, and frequent, bases for communal action. We may speak of a 'class' when (1) a number of people have in common a specific causal component of their life chances, in so far as (2) this component is represented exclusively by economic interests in the possession of goods and opportunities for income, and (3) is represented under the conditions of the commodity or labor markets. [These points refer to 'class situation,' which we may express more briefly as the typical chance for a supply of goods, external living conditions, and personal life experiences, in so far as this chance is determined by the amount and kind of power, or lack of such, to dispose of goods or skills for the sake of income in a given economic order. The term 'class' refers to any group of people that is found in the same class situation.]

It is the most elemental economic fact that the way in which the disposition over material property is distributed among a plurality of people, meeting competitively in the market for the purpose of exchange, in itself creates specific life chances. According to the law of marginal utility this mode of distribution excludes the non-owners from competing for highly valued goods; it favors the owners and, in fact, gives to them a monopoly to acquire such goods. Other things being equal, this mode of distribution monopolizes the opportunities for profitable deals for all those who, provided with goods, do not necessarily have to exchange them. It increases, at least generally, their power in price wars with those who, being propertyless, have nothing to offer but their services in native form or goods in a form constituted through their own labor, and who above all are compelled to get rid of these products in order barely to subsist. This mode of distribution gives to the propertied a monopoly on the possibility of transferring property from the sphere of use as a 'fortune,' to the sphere of 'capital goods'; that is, it gives them the entrepreneurial function and all chances to share directly or indirectly in returns on capital. All this holds true within the area in which pure market conditions prevail. 'Property' and 'lack of property' are, therefore, the basic categories of all class situations. It does not matter whether these two categories become effective in price wars or in competitive struggles.

Within these categories, however, class situations are further differentiated: on the one hand, according to the kind of property that is usable for returns; and, on the other hand, according to the kind of services that can be offered in the market. Ownership of domestic buildings; productive establishments; warehouses; stores; agriculturally usable land, large and small holdings—quantitative differences with possible qualitative consequences; ownership of mines; cattle; men (slaves); disposition over mobile instruments of production, or capital goods of all sorts, especially money or objects that can be exchanged for money easily and at any time; disposition over products of one's own labor or of

others' labor differing according to their various distances from
consumability; disposition over transferable monopolies of any
kind—all these distinctions differentiate the class situations of
the propertied just as does the 'meaning' which they can and do
give to the utilization of property, especially to property which
has money equivalence. Accordingly, the propertied, for instance,
may belong to the class of rentiers or to the class of entrepreneurs.

Those who have no property but who offer services are differentiated just as much according to their kinds of services as
according to the way in which they make use of these services, in
a continuous or discontinuous relation to a recipient. But always
this is the generic connotation of the concept of class: that the
kind of chance in the *market* is the decisive moment which presents
a common condition for the individual's fate. 'Class situation' is,
in this sense, ultimately 'market situation.' The effect of naked
possession *per se,* which among cattle breeders gives the non-
owning slave or serf into the power of the cattle owner, is only
a forerunner of real 'class' formation. However, in the cattle
loan and in the naked severity of the law of debts in such communities, for the first time mere 'possession' as such emerges as
decisive for the fate of the individual. This is very much in contrast
to the agricultural communities based on labor. The creditor-
debtor relation becomes the basis of 'class situations' only in those
cities where a 'credit market,' however primitive, with rates of
interest increasing according to the extent of dearth and a factual
monopolization of credits, is developed by a plutocracy. Therewith
'class struggles' begin.

Those men whose fate is not determined by the chance of using
goods or services for themselves on the market, e.g. slaves, are
not, however, a 'class' in the technical sense of the term. They are,
rather, a 'status group.'

Communal Action Flowing from Class Interest

According to our terminology, the factor that creates 'class'
is unambiguously economic interest, and indeed, only those interests involved in the existence of the 'market.' Nevertheless, the

concept of 'class-interest' is an ambiguous one: even as an empirical concept it is ambiguous as soon as one understands by it something other than the factual direction of interests following with a certain probability from the class situation for a certain 'average' of those people subjected to the class situation. The class situation and other circumstances remaining the same, the direction in which the individual worker, for instance, is likely to pursue his interests may vary widely, according to whether he is constitutionally qualified for the task at hand to a high, to an average, or to a low degree. In the same way, the direction of interests may vary according to whether or not a *communal* action of a larger or smaller portion of those commonly affected by the 'class situation,' or even an association among them, e.g. a 'trade union,' has grown out of the class situation from which the individual may or may not expect promising results. [Communal action refers to that action which is oriented to the feeling of the actors that they belong together. Societal action, on the other hand, is oriented to a rationally motivated adjustment of interests.] The rise of societal or even of communal action from a common class situation is by no means a universal phenomenon.

The class situation may be restricted in its effects to the generation of essentially *similar* reactions, that is to say, within our terminology, of 'mass actions.' However, it may not have even this result. Furthermore, often merely an amorphous communal action emerges. For example, the 'murmuring' of the workers known in ancient oriental ethics: the moral disapproval of the work-master's conduct, which in its practical significance was probably equivalent to an increasingly typical phenomenon of precisely the latest industrial development, namely, the 'slow down' (the deliberate limiting of work effort) of laborers by virtue of tacit agreement. The degree in which 'communal action' and possibly 'societal action,' emerges from the 'mass actions' of the members of a class is linked to general cultural conditions, especially to those of an intellectual sort. It is also linked to the extent of the contrasts that have already evolved, and is especially linked to the *transparency* of the connections between the causes and the consequences of the 'class situation.' For however different life chances may be, this fact in itself, according to all experience, by no means gives birth to 'class action' (communal action by the members of a class). The fact of being conditioned and the results of the class situation must be distinctly recognizable. For only then the contrast of life chances can be felt not as an absolutely given fact to be accepted, but as a resultant from either (1) the given distribution of property, or (2) the structure of the concrete economic order. It is only then that people may react against the class structure not only through acts of an intermittent and irrational protest, but in the form of rational association. There have been 'class situations' of the first category (1), of a specifically naked and transparent sort, in the urban centers of Antiquity and during the Middle Ages; especially then, when great fortunes were accumulated by factually monopolized trading in industrial products of these localities or in foodstuffs. Furthermore, under certain circumstances, in the rural economy of the most diverse periods, when agriculture was increasingly exploited in a profit-making manner. The most important historical example of the second category (2) is the class situation of the modern 'proletariat.'

Types of 'Class Struggle'

Thus every class may be the carrier of any one of the possibly innumerable forms of 'class action,' but this is not necessarily so. In any case, a class does not in itself constitute a community. To treat 'class' conceptually as having the same value as 'community' leads to distortion. That men in the same class situation regularly react in mass actions to such tangible situations as economic ones in the direction of those interests that are most adequate to their average number is an important and after all simple fact for the understanding of historical events. Above all, this fact must not lead to that kind of pseudo-scientific operation with the concepts of 'class' and 'class interests' so frequently found these days, and which has found its most classic expression in the statement of a talented author, that the individual may be in error concerning his interests but that the 'class' is 'infallible' about its interests. Yet, if classes as such are not communities, nevertheless class situations emerge only on the basis of communalization. The communal action that brings forth class situations, however, is not basically action between members of the identical class; it is an action between members of different classes. Communal actions that directly determine the class situation of the worker and the entrepreneur are: the labor market, the commodities market, and the capitalistic enterprise. But, in its turn, the existence of a capitalistic enterprise presupposes that a very specific communal action exists and that it is specifically structured to protect the possession of goods *per se,* and especially the power of individuals to dispose, in principle freely, over the means of production. The existence of a capitalistic enterprise is preconditioned by a specific kind of 'legal order.' Each kind of class situation, and above all when it rests upon the power of property *per se,* will become most clearly efficacious when all other determinants of reciprocal relations are, as far as possible, eliminated in their significance. It is in this way that the utilization of the power of property in the market obtains its most sovereign importance.

Now 'status groups' hinder the strict carrying through of the sheer market principle. In the present context they are of interest to us only from this one point of view. Before we briefly consider them, note that not much of a general nature can be said about the more specific kinds of antagonism between 'classes' (in our meaning of the term). The great shift, which has been going on continuously in the past, and up to our times, may be summarized, although at the cost of some precision: the struggle in which class situations are effective has progressively shifted from consumption credit toward, first, competitive struggles in the commodity market and, then, toward price wars on the labor market. The 'class struggles' of antiquity—to the extent that they were genuine class struggles and not struggles between status groups—were initially carried on by indebted peasants, and perhaps also by artisans threatened by debt bondage and struggling against urban creditors. For debt bondage is the normal result of the differentiation of wealth in commercial cities, especially in seaport cities. A similar situation has existed among cattle breeders. Debt relationships as such produced class action up to the time of Cataline. Along with this, and with an increase in provision of grain for the city by transporting it from the outside, the struggle over the means of sustenance emerged. It centered in the first place around the provision of bread and the determination of the price of bread. It lasted throughout antiquity and the entire Middle Ages. The propertyless as such flocked together against those who actually and supposedly were interested in the dearth of bread. This fight spread until it involved all those commodities essential to the way of life and to handicraft production. There were only incipient discussions of wage disputes in antiquity and in the Middle Ages. But they have been slowly increasing up into modern times. In the earlier periods they were completely secondary to slave rebellions as well as to fights in the commodity market.

The propertyless of antiquity and of the Middle Ages protested against monopolies, pre-emption, forestalling, and the withholding of goods from the market in order to raise prices. Today the central issue is the determination of the price of labor.

This transition is represented by the fight for access to the market and for the determination of the price of products. Such fights went on between merchants and workers in the putting-out system of domestic handicraft during the transition to modern times. Since it is quite a general phenomenon we must mention here that the class antagonisms that are conditioned through the market situation are usually most bitter between those who actually and directly participate as opponents in price wars. It is not the rentier, the share-holder, and the banker who suffer the ill will of the worker, but almost exclusively the manufacturer and the business executives who are the direct opponents of workers in price wars. This is so in spite of the fact that it is precisely the cash boxes of the rentier, the share-holder, and the banker into which the more or less 'unearned' gains flow, rather than into the pockets of the manufacturers or of the business executives. This simple state of affairs has very frequently been decisive for the role the class situation has played in the formation of political parties. For example, it has made possible the varieties of patriarchal socialism and the frequent attempts—formerly, at least—

of threatened status groups to form alliances with the proletariat against the 'bourgeoisie.'

Status Honor

In contrast to classes, *status groups* are normally communities. They are, however, often of an amorphous kind. In contrast to the purely economically determined 'class situation' we wish to designate as 'status situation' every typical component of the life fate of men that is determined by a specific, positive or negative, social estimation of *honor*. This honor may be connected with any quality shared by a plurality, and, of course, it can be knit to a class situation: class distinctions are linked in the most varied ways with status distinctions. Property as such is not always recognized as a status qualification, but in the long run it is, and with extraordinary regularity. In the subsistence economy of the organized neighborhood, very often the richest man is simply the chieftain. However, this often means only an honorific preference. For example, in the so-called pure modern 'democracy,' that is, one devoid of any expressly ordered status privileges for individuals, it may be that only the families coming under approximately the same tax class dance with one another. This example is reported of certain smaller Swiss cities. But status honor need not necessarily be linked with a 'class situation.' On the contrary, it normally stands in sharp opposition to the pretensions of sheer property.

Both propertied and propertyless people can belong to the same status group, and frequently they do with very tangible consequences. This 'equality' of social esteem may, however, in the long run become quite precarious. The 'equality' of status among the American 'gentlemen,' for instance, is expressed by the fact that outside the subordination determined by the different functions of 'business,' it would be considered strictly repugnant— wherever the old tradition still prevails—if even the richest 'chief,' while playing billiards or cards in his club in the evening, would not treat his 'clerk' as in every sense fully his equal in birthright. It would be repugnant if the American 'chief' would bestow upon his 'clerk' the condescending 'benevolence' marking a distinction of 'position,' which the German chief can never dissever from his attitude. This is one of the most important reasons why in America the German 'clubby-ness' has never been able to attain the attraction that the American clubs have.

Guarantees of Status Stratification

In content, status honor is normally expressed by the fact that above all else a specific *style of life* can be expected from all those who wish to belong to the circle. Linked with this expectation are restrictions on 'social' intercourse (that is, intercourse which is not subservient to economic or any other business's 'functional' purposes). These restrictions may confine normal marriages to within the status circle and may lead to complete endogamous closure. As soon as there is not a mere individual and socially irrelevant imitation of another style of life, but an agreed-upon communal action of this closing character, the 'status' development is under way.

In its characteristic form, stratification by 'status groups' on the basis of conventional styles of life evolves at the present time in the United States out of the traditional democracy. For example, only the resident of a certain street ('the street') is considered as belonging to 'society,' is qualified for social intercourse, and is visited and invited. Above all, this differentiation evolves in such a way as to make for strict submission to the fashion that is dominant at a given time in society. This submission to fashion also exists among men in America to a degree unknown in Germany. Such submission is considered to be an indication of the fact that a given man *pretends* to qualify as a gentleman. This submission decides, at least *prima facie*, that he will be treated as such. And this recognition becomes just as important for his employment chances in 'swank' establishments, and above all, for social intercourse and marriage with 'esteemed' families, as the qualification for dueling among Germans in the Kaiser's day. As for the rest: certain families resident for a long time, and, of course, correspondingly wealthy, e.g. 'F. F. V.,' i.e. First Families of Virginia,' or the actual or alleged descendants of the 'Indian Princess' Pocahontas, of the Pilgrim fathers, or of the Knickerbockers, the members of almost inaccessible sects and all sorts of circles setting themselves apart by means of any other characteristics and badges . . . all these elements usurp 'status' honor. The development of status is essentially a question of stratification resting upon usurpation. Such usurpation is the normal origin of almost all status honor. But the road from this purely conventional situation to legal privilege, positive or negative, is easily traveled as soon as a certain stratification of the social order has in fact been 'lived in' and has achieved stability by virtue of a stable distribution of economic power.

'Ethnic' Segregation and 'Caste'

Where the consequences have been realized to their full extent, the status group evolves into a closed 'caste.' Status distinctions are then guaranteed not merely by conventions and laws, but also by *rituals*. This occurs in such a way that every physical contact with a member of any caste that is considered to be 'lower' by the members of a 'higher' caste is considered as making for a ritualistic impurity and to be a stigma which must be expiated by a religious act. Individual castes develop quite distinct cults and gods.

In general, however, the status structure reaches such extreme consequences only where there are underlying differences which are held to be 'ethnic.' The 'caste' is, indeed, the normal form in which ethnic communities usually live side by side in a 'societalized' manner. These ethnic communities believe in blood relationship and exclude exogamous marriage and social intercourse. Such a caste situation is part of the phenomenon of 'pariah' peoples and is found all over the world. These people form communities, acquire specific occupational traditions of handicrafts or of other arts, and cultivate a belief in their ethnic community. They live in a 'diaspora' strictly segregated from all personal intercourse, except that of an unavoidable sort, and their situation is legally precarious. Yet, by virtue of their economic indispensability, they are tolerated, indeed, frequently privileged, and they live in interspersed political communities. The Jews are the most impressive historical example.

A 'status' segregation grown into a 'caste' differs in its structure from a mere 'ethnic' segregation: the caste structure transforms the horizontal and unconnected coexistences of ethnically segregated groups into a vertical social system of super- and subordination. Correctly formulated: a comprehensive societalization integrates the ethnically divided communities into specific political and communal action. In their consequences they differ precisely in this way: ethnic coexistences condition a mutual repulsion and disdain but allow each ethnic community to consider its own honor as the highest one; the caste structure brings about a social subordination and an acknowledgment of 'more honor' in favor of the privileged caste and status groups. This is due to the fact that in the caste structure ethnic distinctions as such have become 'functional' distinctions within the political societalization (warriors, priests, artisans that are politically important for war and for building, and so on). But even pariah people who are most despised are usually apt to continue cultivating in some manner that which is equally peculiar to ethnic and to status communities: the belief in their own specific 'honor.' This is the case with the Jews.

Only with the negatively privileged status groups does the 'sense of dignity' take a specific deviation. A sense of dignity is the precipitation in individuals of social honor and of conventional demands which a positively privileged status group raises for the deportment of its members. The sense of dignity that characterizes positively privileged status groups is naturally related to their 'being' which does not transcend itself, that is, it is to their 'beauty and excellence' ($\kappa\alpha\lambda o\text{-}\kappa\dot\alpha\gamma\alpha\vartheta\iota\alpha$). Their kingdom is 'of this world.' They live for the present and by exploiting their great past. The sense of dignity of the negatively privileged strata naturally refers to a future lying beyond the present, whether it is of this life or of another. In other words, it must be nurtured by the belief in a providential 'mission' and by a belief in a specific honor before God. The 'chosen people's' dignity is nurtured by a belief either that in the beyond 'the last will be the first,' or that in this life a Messiah will appear to bring forth into the light of the world which has cast them out the hidden honor of the pariah people. This simple state of affairs, and not the 'resentment' which is so strongly emphasized in Nietzsche's much admired construction in the *Genealogy of Morals*, is the source of the religiosity cultivated by pariah status groups. In passing, we may note that resentment may be accurately applied only to a limited extent; for one of Nietzsche's main examples, Buddhism, it is not at all applicable.

Incidentally, the development of status groups from ethnic segregations is by no means the normal phenomenon. On the contrary, since objective 'racial differences' are by no means basic to every subjective sentiment of an ethnic community, the ultimately racial foundation of status structure is rightly and absolutely a question of the concrete individual case. Very frequently a status group is instrumental in the production of a thoroughbred anthropological type. Certainly a status group is to a high degree effective in producing extreme types, for they select personally qualified individuals (e.g. the Knighthood selects those who are fit for warfare, physically and psychically). But selection is far from being the only, or the predominant, way in which status groups are formed: Political membership or class situation has at all times been at least as frequently decisive. And today the class situation is by far the predominant factor, for of course the possibility of a style of life expected for members of a status group is usually conditioned economically.

Status Privileges

For all practical purposes, stratification by status goes hand in hand with a monopolization of ideal and material goods or opportunities, in a manner we have come to know as typical. Besides the specific status honor, which always rests upon distance and exclusiveness, we find all sorts of material monopolies. Such honorific preferences may consist of the privilege of wearing special costumes, of eating special dishes taboo to others, of carrying arms—which is most obvious in its consequences—the right to pursue certain non-professional dilettante artistic practices, e.g. to play certain musical instruments. Of course, material monopolies provide the most effective motives for the exclusiveness of a status group; although, in themselves, they are rarely sufficient, almost always they come into play to some extent. Within a status circle there is the question of intermarriage: the interest of the families in the monopolization of potential bridegrooms is at least of equal importance and is parallel to the interest in the monopolization of daughters. The daughters of the circle must be provided for. With an increased inclosure of the status group, the conventional preferential opportunities for special employment grow into a legal monopoly of special offices for the members. Certain goods become objects for monopolization by status groups. In the typical fashion these include 'entailed estates' and frequently also the possessions of serfs or bondsmen and, finally, special trades. This monopolization occurs positively when the status group is exclusively entitled to own and to manage them; and negatively when, in order to maintain its specific way of life, the status group must *not* own and manage them.

The decisive role of a 'style of life' in status 'honor' means that status groups are the specific bearers of all 'conventions.' In whatever way it may be manifest, all 'stylization' of life either originates in status groups or is at least conserved by them. Even if the principles of status conventions differ greatly, they reveal certain typical traits, especially among those strata which are most privileged. Quite generally, among privileged status groups there is a status disqualification that operates against the performance of common physical labor. This disqualification is now 'setting in' in America against the old tradition of esteem for labor. Very frequently every rational economic pursuit, and especially 'entrepreneurial activity,' is looked upon as a disqualification of status. Artistic and literary activity is also considered as degrading work as soon as it is exploited for income, or at least when it is connected with hard physical exertion. An example is the sculptor working like a mason in his dusty smock as over against the painter in his salon-like 'studio' and those forms of musical practice that are acceptable to the status group.

14

CASTE STRATIFICATION—
THE CASE OF INDIA

Caste Criteria

THE BRITISH census experts rightly distinguish two basic types of castes: tribal and professional. Our previous discussion of the former may now be supplemented. In all probability a multitude of castes developed historically from Hinduized tribal and guest peoples. It is principally these which make the picture of the caste rank order so irrational. For, other things being equal, a tribe which at the time of its Hinduization was settled on its own land achieved and maintained higher rank than pure pariah tribes which have been Hinduized. Moreover, a tribe which supplied mercenaries and soldiers of fortune fared still better. How then are we to recognize "tribal castes"?

A tribal caste is often identifiable by the form of its name. Yet, in the course of Hinduization quite a few tribes have assumed professional names. There are other criteria: subcastes frequently state a common ancestor; true upper castes usually have ancestral subcaste figures. There are frequently survivals of totem organization. Former tribal deities may be retained and, above all, tribal priests may serve as caste priests. Finally, members may be recruited from definite territories. Both the last named criteria are important only when taken in combination with one or other

From *The Religion of India: The Sociology of Hinduism and Buddhism,* by Max Weber, translated and edited by Hans H. Gerth and Don Martindale. Published 1958 by The Free Press, Glencoe, Ill. Reprinted by permission.

of the preceding criteria, for there are professional castes with strictly local recruitment and their own priests.

The endogamy of a tribal caste is often the less strict the closer it is to tribal status; it is also less exclusive toward caste outsiders. Generally pure-professional castes are most inflexible in these respects, which proves that ritualistic caste exclusiveness, though partly determined thereby, is no mere religious projection of ethnic strangeness.

The tribal caste is most clearly recognizable when one or several of a plurality of castes of the same profession retain a tribal name in addition to the usual professional caste name. The extent to which the castes were originally tribal castes is not determinable. The lowest castes may indeed have developed largely out of guest and pariah tribes. However, this is certainly not true of all of them. Relatively few of the more esteemed handicrafts, particularly the free and liturgical crafts of the cities and the ancient merchant castes, could have had this origin. Probably most of them developed out of economic specialization—from the differentiation of properties and skills. The peculiarity of Indian development which requires explanation is this: Why did it result in caste formation?

Apart from the reception of tribes caste formation could be modified only by caste schism.

Caste Schism

Caste schism is always expressed by the complete or partial denial of connubium and commensalism. This may, in the first place, result from residential mobility of caste members. Migrant members were suspect of having offended against ritual caste duties. At very least, their correctness could not be controlled. The nomadism of cattle-breeders contributed to their loss of rank. Inasmuch as only Indian land, and that only insofar as proper caste order is established on it, can be holy land, strict orthodoxy views as doubtful any change of residence even within India since it takes the immigrant into a different ritualistic environment.

Only in cases of absolute necessity was travel considered correct. Internal migration in India, therefore, even at present, is far below what might be expected in view of the great transformation of economic conditions. More than nine-tenths of the people live in their native districts. As a rule only ancient village exogamy leads to settlement in another village. Permanent settlement of caste members in other places regularly results in the split up into new subcastes, for the residentially stable members refuse to consider the descendants of migrants as their peers.

As the Hindu system spread eastward from the upper Ganges, new subcastes of the old were formed which, other things being equal, ranked below those of the west.

A second reason for caste schism was the renunciation by some members of various former ritual duties or, the reverse of this, the assumption by some of new ritual duties. Both the renunciation of old rituals or the assumption of new ones could have a variety of causes. (1) Membership in a sect could absolve some ritual prescriptions or impose new ones. This is not very frequent. (2) Differentiation within a caste could lead the propertied members to assume the ritual obligations of higher castes, or to claim higher rank than formerly. To realize such aspirations one had first to break away from intermarriage and commensalism with former caste members. Today simple property differentiation quite often is made the occasion for splitting the community. (3) Occupational changes could lead to schism. According to rigid traditionalistic observance, not only change of occupation but a mere change of work technique may be sufficient reason for the followers of tradition to consider the community as broken. While such consequences do not always occur in fact, it is, perhaps, the most frequent and, in practice, the most important occasion for caste schism. Finally, (4) the disintegration of the ritualistic tradition among some of the members may lead the orthodox ones to cancel communal relations with them.

Today new castes may originate also from ritually illicit inter-caste cohabitation. As is known, classical theory explained all impure castes in terms of caste mixture—the explanation, of course, is quite unhistorical. Still, there are some instances of caste origin from caste mixture, hence from concubinage.

Finally, schisms may simply result from the failure to settle all sorts of internal disputes. This is strongly disapproved of as a reason for caste fission and is usually concealed by alleging ritual offences on the part of the opponent.

Of greatest interest to us are the economic reasons for caste and subcaste origin: property differentiation, occupational mobility, technological change. We may be certain that property differentiation—occupational mobility was legitimate only by way of emergency pursuits—resulted in caste schism far less frequently under the national dynasties than it does at present. For the Brahmans, whose power then was incomparably greater, upheld the caste order as established and habitual. If the stability of the caste order could not hinder property differentiation, it could at least block technological change and occupational mobility, which from the point of view of caste were objectionable and ritually dangerous. Today, the very fact that new skills and techniques actually lead to the formation of new castes or subcastes strongly handicaps innovation. It sustains tradition no matter how often the all-powerful development of imported capitalism overrides it. . . .

Economically, the traditionalism of the professional castes rests not only upon a mutual segregation of the various branches of production, but also, and today very often, upon the protection of the livelihood of caste members against mutual competition. The artisan belonging to the ancient "village staff" who was settled on garden land or who received a fixed income was absolutely protected in this respect. However, the principle of patronage protection, the guarantee of the *jajmani* relation, went much further and still is strictly enforced by numerous occupational castes. We learned of the principle in connection with the Brahmans, and the meaning of the word *jajmani* ("sacrifice giver") suggests that the concept originated in the conditions of the Brahman caste. It could, perhaps, best be rendered by "personal diocese." The status etiquette of the Brahmans secures their dioceses among some other castes. They are by the caste organization and indeed —as always in India—hereditary (clan charismatic). . . .

The Social Rank Order of the Castes in General

When the Census of India (1901) attempted to list by rank contemporary Hindu castes in the presidencies—two to three thousand or even more, according to the method of counting used —certain groups of castes were established which are distinguishable from one another according to the following criteria:

First come the Brahmans, and following them, a series of castes which, claim rightly or wrongly, to belong to the two other "twice-born" castes of classical theory: the Kshatriya and the Vaishya. In order to signify this, they claim the right to wear the "holy belt." This is a right which some of them have only recently rediscovered and which, in the view of the Brahman castes, who are seniors in rank, would certainly belong only to some members of the twice-born castes. But as soon as the right of a caste to wear the holy belt is acknowledged, this caste is unconditionally recognized as being absolutely ritually "clean." From such a caste the high-caste Brahmans accept food of every kind.

Throughout the system, a third group of castes follows. They are counted among the Satsudra, the "clean Shudra" of classical doctrine. In Northern and Central India they are the Jalacharaniya, that is, castes who may give water to a Brahman and from whose *lota* (water bottle) the Brahman accepts water. Close to them are castes, in Northern and Central India, whose water a Brahman would not always accept (that is, acceptance or nonacceptance would possibly depend on the Brahman's rank) or whose water he would never accept (Jalabyabaharya). The high-caste barber does not serve them unconditionally (no pedicure), and the laundryman does not wash their laundry. But they are not considered absolutely "unclean" ritually. They are the Shudra in the usual sense in which the classical teachings refer to them. Finally, there are castes who are considered unclean. All temples are closed to them, and no Brahman and no barber will serve them. They must live outside the village district, and they infect either by touch or, in Southern India, even by their presence at a distance (up to sixty-four feet with the Paraiyans). All these restrictions are related to those castes which, according to the classical doctrine, originated from ritually forbidden sexual intercourse between members of different castes.

Even though this grouping of castes is not equally true throughout India (indeed there are striking exceptions), nevertheless, on the whole, it can be quite well sustained. Within these groupings one could proceed with further gradations of caste rank, but such gradations would present extremely varied characteristics: among the upper castes the criterion would be the correctness of life practices with regard to sib organization, endogamy, child marriage, widow celibacy, cremation of the dead, ancestral sacrifice, foods and drinks, and social intercourse with unclean castes. Among the lower caste one would have to differentiate according to the rank of the Brahmans who are still ready to serve them or who will no longer do so, and according to whether or not castes other than Brahmans accept water from them. In all these cases, it is by no means rare that castes of lower rank raise stricter demands than castes who otherwise are considered to have a higher standing. The extraordinary variety of such rules of rank order forbids here any closer treatment. The acceptance or avoidance of meat, at least of beef, is decisive for caste rank, and is therefore a symptom of it, but an uncertain one. The kinds of occupation and income, which entail the most far-reaching consequences for connubium, commensalism, and ritual rank, are decisive in the case of all castes. We shall speak of this later.

Who arbitrated such rank contests? And who made decisions on matters related to rank? It was stated above that, in general, the Brahmans to this day, are theoretically, the final authorities on questions of rank. Official banquets requiring the attendance of Brahmans always necessitated correct decisions about rank questions. The Brahmans in the past, as now, were in no position to settle the problems alone. As far as we can determine, in the period before the foreign conquests rank questions were always decided by the king or his official advisor on ritualistic matters. Such a chief of protocol was either a Brahman or an official who, as a rule, sought the legal advice of a Brahman. We know, however, of many cases in which Indian kings personally degraded single castes in due form or expelled individuals, including Brahmans from their castes. The person concerned often experienced this as an unjust infringement upon his well-established rights. Degraded castes often continued to contest such decisions for centuries; the Brahmans, however, usually took it.

Moreover, the king advised by Brahmans who had immigrated at his request, had authority to make decisions concerning the original or renewed ordering of caste ranks throughout large territories as, for instance, East-Bengal under the Sena-dynasty. The king was able, too, to make decisions about single caste duties. Under the last great all-Indian rule of the Mahrattas at the turn of the eighteenth century, the legal opinions of Brahmans about questions of single caste duties were submitted to the Peshwa, a descendant of a Brahman family, who obviously gave his *exequatur* after substantive discussion of the controversial issues. The abolition of this support of the Brahmans by the secular arm today —except in the remaining Hindu vassal states where residues survive—is said to have caused the diminished compliance with the decisions of the Brahmans. In short, religious and secular power coöperated in the interest of the legitimate order.

The position of the king allowed him to select the most pliable of the Brahmans. Under the circumstances, not the king's power, but that of the Brahmans and the castes, is astounding. Brahmanical and caste power resulted from the inviolability of all sacred law which was believed to ward off evil enchantment. In problematic caste situations Indian kings followed the unconditional and magically sanctioned principle "Prerogative breaks the common law"; the caste, on the other hand, was sustained only by its economic importance. The royal judge was bound by the traditional customs of the single caste; jury members for the particular caste had to be admitted to court trials, and castes were brought before the royal judge only by organs of the single caste which normally had jurisdiction over caste affairs. Even today single caste organs settle caste problems: they excommunicate, impose fines or amends, settle disputes, and, in relative independence, develop through their judicial practices the norms for newly emerging legal questions. We cannot, therefore, avoid a survey of the problems of caste jurisdiction, practice, and organization.

With this in mind, it is necessary to examine the principles which determine the structure and boundary lines of the various caste types, a question hitherto touched only tangentially.

The Brahmans and the Castes

In classical Hindu times as well as today, the position of the Brahman can be understood only in connection with caste; without an understanding of this it is quite impossible to understand Hinduism. Perhaps the most important gap in the ancient Veda is its lack of any reference to caste. The Veda refers to the four later caste names in only one place, which is considered a very late passage; nowhere does it refer to the substantive content of the caste order with the meaning it later assumed and which is characteristic only of Hinduism.[1]

Caste, that is, the ritual rights and duties it gives and imposes, and the position of the Brahmans, is the fundamental institution of Hinduism. Before everything else, without caste there is no Hindu. But the position of the Hindu with regard to the authority of the Brahman may vary extraordinarily, from unconditional submission to the contesting of his authority. Some castes do contest the authority of the Brahman, but in practice, this means merely that the Brahman is disdainfully rejected as a priest, that his judgment in controversial questions of ritual is not recognized as authoritative, and that his advice is never sought. Upon first sight, this seems to contradict the fact that "castes" and "Brahmans" belong together in Hinduism. But as a matter of fact, if the caste is absolutely essential for each Hindu, the reverse, at least nowadays, does not hold, namely, that every caste be a Hindu caste. There are also castes among the Mohammedans of India, taken over from the Hindus. And castes are also found among the Bud-

---

[1]   The specialists see in the *Purisha Sukto* of the Rig Veda the "Magna Charta of the Caste System." It is the latest product of the Vedic period. We shall discuss the *Atharva-Veda* later.

dhists. Even the Indian Christians have not quite been able to withhold themselves from practical recognition of the castes. These non-Hindu castes have lacked the tremendous emphasis that the Hindu doctrine of salvation placed upon the caste, as we shall see later, and they have lacked a further characteristic, namely, the determination of the social rank of the castes by the social distance from other Hindu castes, and therewith, ultimately, from the Brahman. This is decisive for the connection between Hindu castes and the Brahman; however intensely a Hindu caste may reject him as a priest, as a doctrinal and ritual authority, and in every other respect, the objective situation remains inescapable; in the last analysis, a rank position is determined by the nature of its positive or negative relation to the Brahman.

"Caste" is, and remains essentially social rank, and the central position of the Brahmans in Hinduism rests primarily upon the fact that social rank is determined with reference to Brahmans. In order to understand this, we shall turn to the present condition of the Hindu castes, as described in the excellent scientific Census Reports. We shall also consider briefly the classical theories of caste contained in the ancient books of law and other sources.

Today the Hindu caste order is profoundly shaken. Especially in the district of Calcutta, old Europe's major gateway to India, many norms have practically lost their force. The railroads, the taverns, the changing occupational stratification, the concentration of labor through imported industry, colleges, etc., have all contributed their part. The "commuters to London," that is, those who studied in Europe and maintained voluntary social intercourse with Europeans, were outcasts up to the last generation; but more and more this pattern is disappearing. And it has been impossible to introduce caste coaches on the railroads in the fashion of the American railroad cars or station waiting rooms which segregate "white" from "colored" in the southern states. All caste relations have been shaken, and the stratum of intellectuals bred by the English are here, as elsewhere, bearers of a specific nationalism. They will greatly strengthen this slow and irresistible process. For the time being, however, the caste structure still stands quite firmly.

First we must ask: with what concepts shall we define a "caste"? (The term is of Portuguese derivation. The ancient Indian name is *varna*, "color.") Let us ask it in the negative: What is not a caste? Or, what traits of other associations, really or apparently related to caste, are lacking in caste? What, for instance, is the difference between caste and tribe?

Caste and Tribe

As long as a tribe has not become wholly a guest or a pariah people, it usually has a fixed tribal territory. A genuine caste never has a fixed territory. To a very considerable extent, the caste members live in the country, segregated in villages. Usually in each village there is, or was, only one caste with full title to the soil. But dependent village artisans and laborers also live with this caste. In any case, the caste does not form a local, territorial, corporate body, for this would contradict its nature. A tribe is, or at least originally was, bound together by obligatory blood revenge, mediated directly or indirectly through the sib. A caste never has anything to do with such blood revenge.

Originally, a tribe normally comprised many, often almost all, of the possible pursuits necessary for the gaining of subsistence. A caste may comprise people who follow very different pursuits; at least this is the case today, and for certain upper castes this has been the case since very early times. Yet so long as the caste has not lost its character, the kinds of pursuits admissible without loss of caste are always, in some way, quite strictly limited. Even today "caste" and "way of earning a living" are so firmly linked that often a change of occupation is correlated with a division of caste. This is not the case for a "tribe."

Normally a tribe comprises people of every social rank. A caste may well be divided into subcastes with extraordinarily different social ranks. Today this is usually the case; one caste frequently contains several hundred subcastes. In such cases, these subcastes may be related to one another exactly, or almost exactly, as are different castes. If this is the case, the subcastes, in reality, are castes; the caste name common to all of them has merely historical significance, or almost so, and serves to support the social pretensions of degraded subcastes towards third castes. Hence, by its very nature, caste is inseparably bound up with social ranks within a larger community.

It is decisive for a tribe that it is originally and normally a political association. The tribe is either an independent association, as is always originally the case, or the association is part of a tribal league; or, it may constitute a *phyle,* that is, part of a political association commissioned with certain political tasks and having certain rights: franchise, holding quotas of the political offices, and the right of assuming its share or turn of political, fiscal, and liturgical obligations. A caste is never a political association, even if political associations in individual cases have burdened castes with liturgies, as may have happened repeatedly during the Indian Middle Ages (Bengal). In this case, castes are in the same position as merchant and craft guilds, sibs, and all sorts of associations. By its very nature the caste is always a purely social and possibly occupational association, which forms part of and stands within a social community. But the caste is not necessarily, and by no means regularly, an association forming part of only one political association; rather it may reach beyond, or it may fall short of, the boundaries of any one political association. There are castes diffused over all of India. Of the present Hindu castes (the chief ones), one may say that twenty-five are diffused throughout most of the regions of India. . . .

With regard to the substance of its social norms, a tribe usually differs from a caste in that the exogamy of the totem or of the villages co-exist with the exogamy of the sibs. Endogamy has existed only under certain conditions, but by no means always, for the tribe as a whole. Rules of endogamy, however, always form the essential basis of a caste. Dietary rules and rules of commensality are always characteristic of the caste but are by no means characteristic of the tribe.

We have already observed that when a tribe loses its foothold in its territory it becomes a guest or a pariah people. It may then approximate caste to the point of being actually indistinguishable from it. The Banjaras, for instance, are partly organized as castes in the Central Provinces. In Mysore, however, they are organized as an (Animist) tribe. In both cases they make their living in the same way. Similar instances frequently occur. The differences that remain will be discussed when we determine the positive characteristics of caste. In contrast to the tribe, a caste is usually related intimately to special ways of earning a living, on the one hand, and, on the other, to social rank. Now the question arises, how is caste related to the occupational associations (merchant and craft guilds) and how is it related to status groups? Let us begin with the former. . . .

Caste and Sib

There remains to be examined still another important peculiarity of Indian society which is intimately interrelated with the caste system. Not only the formation of castes but the heightened significance of the sib belongs to the fundamental traits of Indian society. The Hindu social order, to a larger extent than anywhere else in the world, is organized in terms of the principle of *clan charisma*. "Charisma" means that an extraordinary, at least not generally available, quality adheres to a person. Originally charisma was thought of as a magical quality. "Clan charisma" means that this extraordinary quality adheres to sib members per se and not, as originally, to a single person.

We are familar with residues of this sociologically important phenomenon of clan charisma particularly in the hereditary "divine right of kings" of our dynasties. To a lesser degree the legend of the "blue blood" of a nobility, whatever its specific origin, belongs to the same sociological type. Clan charisma is one of the ways personal charisma may be "routinized" (i.e., made a part of everyday social experience).

In contrast to the hereditary chieftain in times of peace who, among some tribes, could also be a woman, the warrior king and his men were heroes whose successes had proven their purely personal and magical qualities. The authority of the war leader, like that of the sorcerer, rested upon strictly personal charisma. The successor also originally claimed his rank by virtue of personal charisma. (The problem, of course, is that more than one "successor" may raise such claims.) The unavoidable demand for law and order in the question of successorship forces the followers to consider different possibilities: either the designation of the qualified successor by the leader; or the selection of a new leader by his disciples, followers, or officials. The progressive regulation of these originally spontaneous and nonprocedural questions may lead to the development of elective bodies of officials in the manner of "princes," "electors," and "cardinals."

In India a suggestive belief won out: that charisma is a quality attached to the sib per se, that the qualified successor or successors should be sought within the sib. This led to the *inheritance* of charisma, which originally had nothing to do with heredity. The wider the spheres to which magical belief applied, the more consistently developed such beliefs became, the wider, in turn, the possible field of application of clan charisma. Not only heroic and magico-cultic abilities, but any form of authority, came to be viewed as determined and bound by clan charisma. Special talents, not only artistic but craft talent as well, fell within the sphere of clan charisma.

In India the development of the principle of clan charisma far surpassed what is usual elsewhere in the world. This did not occur all at once; clan charisma was in conflict with ancient genuine charismatism which continued to uphold only the personal endowment of the single individual, as well as with the pedagogy of status cultivation.

Even in the Indian Middle Ages, many formalities in the apprenticeship to and practice of handicraft show strong traces of the principle of personal charisma. These are evident in the magical elements of the novitiate and the assumption by the apprentice of journeyman status. However, since, originally, occupational differentiation was largely interethnic and the practitioners of many trades were members of pariah tribes, there were strong forces for the development of charismatic clan magic.

The strongest expression of clan charisma was in the sphere of authority. In India the hereditary transmission of authority, i.e., on the basis of family ties, was normal. The further back one traces the more universal the institution of the hereditary village-headship is found to be. Merchant and craft guilds and castes had hereditary elders; anything else was normally out of the question. So self-evident was priestly, royal, and knightly office charisma that free appointment of successors to office by patrimonial rulers, like the free choice of urban occupations, occurred only during upheavals of the tradition or at the frontiers of social organization before the social order was stabilized.

The exceptional quality of the sib was (note!) realized "in principle." Not only could knightly or priestly sibs prove to be barren of magical qualities and thus lose them as an individual does, but a *homo novus* could prove his possession of charisma and thereby legitimatize his sib as charismatic. Thus, charismatic clan authority could be quite unstable in the single case.

In the study of W. Hopkins of present-day Ahmadbad, the Nayar Sheth—the counterpart of the medieval Lord Mayor of the Occident—was the elder of the richest Jain family of the city. He and the Vishnuite Sheth of the clothiers' guild, who was also hereditary, jointly determined public opinion on all social, i.e., ritualistic and proprietary questions of the city. The other hereditary Sheths were less influential beyond their guilds and castes. However, at the time Hopkins made his study a rich manufacturer outside all guilds had successfully entered the competition.

If a son was notoriously unfit his influence waned—be it the son of a craft, guild or caste elder or the son of a priest mystagogue or artist. His prestige was channelized either to a more adequate member of the particular sib or to a member (usually the elder) of the next richest sib. Not new wealth alone, but great wealth combined with personal charisma legitimatized its possessor and his sib in social situations where status conditions were still or once again fluid. Although in single cases charismatic clan authority was quite unstable, everyday life always forced compliance with sib authority once it was established. The sib always reaped the benefits of individually established charisma.

The economic effects of sib integration through magical and animistic beliefs in China was described in a previous work.[2] In

2   Cf. Max Weber, *The Religion of China*, Trans. by H. H. Gerth (Glencoe: The Free Press, 1951), Chapter VII and VIII.

China the charismatic glorification of the sib, countered by the examination system of patrimonial dominion, had economic consequences similar to those in India. In India, the caste organization and extensive caste autonomy and the autonomy of the guild, which was still greater because it was ritually unfettered, placed the development of commercial law almost completely in the hands of the respective interest groups. The unusual importance of trade in India would lead one to believe that a rational law of trade, trading companies, and enterprise might well have developed.

However, if one looks at the legal literature of the Indian Middle Ages one is astonished by its poverty. While partially formalistic, Indian justice and the law of evidence were basically irrational and magical. Much of it was formless in principle, because of hierocratic influence. Ritually relevant questions could only be decided by ordeals. In other questions the general moral code, unique elements of the particular case, tradition (particularly), and a few supplementary royal edicts were employed as legal sources.

Yet, in contrast to China, a formal trial procedure developed with regulated summons (*in jus vocatio,* under the Mahratts summons were served by clerks of the court). The debt-liability of heirs existed but was limited after generations. However, the collection of debts, although debt bondage was known, remained somewhat in the magical stage or in that of a modified billet system. At least as a norm, joint liability of partners was lacking. In general, the right of association appeared only late in Indian development and then only in connection with the right of religious fraternities. The law of corporations remained inconsequential. All sorts of corporations and joint property relationships received mixed treatment. There was a ruling on profit sharing which, incidentally, extended also to artisans coöperating under a foreman, hence in an *ergasterion.* Above all, however, the principle, recognized also in China, that one should grant unconditional credit and pawn objects only among personally close members of the phratry, among relatives and friends, held also in India. Debts under other circumstances were recognized only under provision of guarantors or witnessed promissory notes.

The details of later legal practice, to be sure, were adequate to implement trading needs but they hardly promoted trade on its own. The quite considerable capitalistic development which occurred in the face of such legal conditions can be explained only in terms of the power of guilds. They knew how to pursue their interests by use of boycott, force, and expert arbitration. However, in general, under conditions such as those described, the sib fetters of credit relationships had to remain the normal state of affairs.

The principle of clan charisma also had far-reaching consequences outside the field of commercial law. Because we are prone to think of occidental feudalism, primarily as a system of socioeconomic ties, we are apt to overlook its peculiar origins and their significance.

Under the compelling military needs of the time of its origin, the feudal relationship made a free contract among sib strangers basic for the faith-bound relation between the lord and his vassals. Increasingly feudal lords developed the in-group feeling of a unitary status group. They developed eventually into the closed hereditary estate of chivalrous knights. We must not forget that this grew on the basis of sib estrangement among men who viewed themselves not as sib, clan, phratry, or tribe members but merely as status peers.

Indian development took quite a different turn. It is true that individual enfeoffment of retainers and officials with land or political rights occurred. Historically, this is clearly discernible. But it did not give the ruling stratum its stamp, and feudal status formation did not rest on land grants. Rather, as Baden-Powell has correctly emphasized, the character of Indian developments was derived from the sib, clan, phratry, and tribe.

Before continuing we shall have to clarify our terminology. The Irish term "clan" is ambiguous. In our terminology the typical organization of warrior communities consists of: (1) the tribe or a collectivity of "phratries"—in our terminology, primarily always associations of (originally, magically) trained warriors; (2) the sib, i.e., charismatically outstanding agnatic descendants of charismatic chieftains. The plain warrior did not necessarily have a "sib" but belonged to a "family" or a totemic (or quasi-totemic) association besides his phratry and possibly unitary age group.

A gens of overlords, however, had no totem; it had emancipated itself from it. The more the ruling tribes of India developed into a ruling class the more survivals of the totem (*devaks*) vanished and "sibs" emerged (or better, continued to exist). A blurring of charismatic clan differences occurred when the phratry began to develop "we-feeling" on the ground of common descent, rather than of joint defense, and hence became a quasi-sib.

In India the charismatic head of the phratry distributed conquered land; manorial prerogatives among fellow-sib members; open fields among the ordinary men of the phratry. The conquering classes must be conceived of as a circle of phratries and sibs of lords dispersing over the conquered territory under the rule of the tribe.

Prerogatives were enfeoffed by the head of the phratry (*raja*) or where one existed by the tribal king (*maharaja*) only, as a rule, to his agnates. It was not a freely contracted trusteeship. Fellow-sib members claimed this grant as a birthright. Each conquest produced, in the first place, new office fiefs for the sib of the king and its subsibs. Conquest was, therefore, the *dharma* of the king.

However different some details of the Indian from its occidental counterpart, the ascendency of the secular overlords and their estates had similar basis. No matter how often individual charismatic upstarts and their freely recruited followings shattered the firm structure of the sibs, the social process always resumed its firm course of charismatic clan organization of tribes, phratries, and sibs. Among the Aryans the ancient sacrificial priests, even at the time of the early Vedas, had become a distinguished priestly nobility. The various sibs of the priestly nobility divided according to hereditary function and appropriate clan charisma into hereditary "schools." Given the primacy of magical charisma claimed by the clans, they and their heirs—the Brahmans—became the primary propagators of this principle through Hindu society.

It is clear that the magical charisma of the clans contributed

greatly to the establishment of the firm structure of caste estrangement, actually containing it *in nuce*. On the other hand, the caste
order served greatly to stabilize the sib. All strata which raised
claims to distinction were forced to become stratified on the pattern of the ruling castes. The exogamous kinship order was based
on the sib. Social situation, ritual duty, way of life and occupational position in the end were determined by the charismatic clan
principle which extended to all positions of authority. As clan
charisma supported the caste so the caste, in turn, supported the
charisma of the sib.

15

SOCIAL STRATIFICATION
AND CLASS STRUCTURE
IN MODERN SOCIETY

The Concepts of Class and Class Status

THE TERM "class status"[1] will be applied to the typical probability that a given state of (a) provision with goods, (b) external conditions of life, and (c) subjective satisfaction or frustration will be possessed by an individual or a group. These probabilities define class status in so far as they are dependent on the kind and extent of control or lack of it which the individual has over goods or services and existing possibilities of their exploitation for the attainment of income or receipts within a given economic order.

A "class" is any group of persons occupying the same class status. The following types of classes may be distinguished: (a) A class is a "property class" when class status for its members is primarily determined by the differentiation of property holdings; (b) a class is an "acquisition class" when the class situation of its members is primarily determined by their opportunity for the exploitation of services on the market; (c) the "social class" struc-

---

Reprinted by permission of The Macmillan Company from *Theory of Social and Economic Organization* by Max Weber, trans. A. R. Henderson and Talcott Parsons. Copyright 1947 by Talcott Parsons.

1   Weber uses the term "class" (*Klasse*) in a special sense, which is defined in this paragraph and which, in particular, he contrasts with *Stand*. There seems no other alternative translation of *Klasse*, but it should be kept in mind that it is being used in a special sense.—T. PARSONS.

ture is composed of the plurality of class statuses between which an interchange of individuals on a personal basis or in the course of generations is readily possible and typically observable. On the basis of any of the three types of class status, associative relationships between those sharing the same class interests, namely, corporate class organizations may develop. This need not, however, necessarily happen. The concepts of class and class status as such designate only the fact of identity or similarity in the typical situation in which a given individual and many others find their interests defined. In principle control over different combinations of consumers goods, means of production, investments, capital funds or marketable abilities constitute class statuses which are different with each variation and combination. Only persons who are completely unskilled, without property and dependent on employment without regular occupation, are in a strictly identical class status. Transitions from one class status to another vary greatly in fluidity and in the ease with which an individual can enter the class. Hence the unity of "social" classes is highly relative and variable.

The primary significance of a positively privileged property class lies in the following facts: (i) Its members may be able to monopolize the purchase of high-priced consumers goods. (ii) They may control the opportunities of pursuing a systematic monopoly policy in the sale of economic goods. (iii) They may monopolize opportunities for the accumulation of property through unconsumed surpluses. (iv) They may monopolize opportunities to accumulate capital by saving, hence, the possibility of investing property in loans and the related possibility of control over executive positions in business. (v) They may monopolize the privileges of socially advantageous kinds of education so far as these involve expenditures.

Positively privileged property classes typically live from property income. This may be derived from property rights in human beings, as with slave owners, in land, in mining property, in fixed equipment such as plant and apparatus, in ships, and as creditors in loan relationships. Loans may consist of domestic animals, grain, or money. Finally they may live on income from securities.

Class interests which are negatively privileged with respect to property belong typically to one of the following types: (a) They are themselves objects of ownership, that is they are unfree. (b) They are "outcasts" that is "proletarians" in the sense meant in Antiquity. (c) They are debtor classes and, (d) the "poor."

In between stand the "middle" classes. This term includes groups who have all sorts of property, or of marketable abilities through training, who are in a position to draw their support from these sources. Some of them may be "acquisition" classes. Entrepreneurs are in this category by virtue of essentially positive privileges; proletarians, by virtue of negative privileges. But many types such as peasants, craftsmen and officials do not fall in this category. The differentiation of classes on the basis of property alone is not "dynamic," that is, it does not necessarily result in class struggles or class revolutions. It is not uncommon for very strongly privileged property classes such as slave owners, to exist side by side with such far less privileged groups as peasants or even outcasts without any class struggle. There may even be ties of solidarity between privileged property classes and unfree elements. However, such conflicts as that between land owners and outcast elements or between creditors and debtors, the latter often being a question of urban patricians as opposed to either rural peasants or urban craftsmen, may lead to revolutionary conflict. Even this, however, need not necessarily aim at radical changes in economic organization. It may, on the contrary, be concerned in the first instance only with a redistribution of wealth. These may be called "property revolutions."

A classic example of the lack of class antagonism has been the relation of the "poor white trash," originally those not owning slaves, to the planters in the Southern States of the United States. The "poor whites" have often been much more hostile to the negro than the planters who have frequently had a large element of patriarchal sentiment. The conflict of outcast against the property classes, of creditors and debtors, and of land owners and outcasts are best illustrated in the history of Antiquity.

The Significance of Acquisition Classes

The primary significance of a positively privileged acquisition class is to be found in two directions. On the one hand it is generally possible to go far toward attaining a monopoly of the management of productive enterprises in favour of the members of the class and their business interests. On the other hand, such a class tends to insure the security of its economic position by exercising influence on the economic policy of political bodies and other groups.

The members of positively privileged acquisition classes are typically entrepreneurs. The following are the most important types: merchants, ship owners, industrial and agricultural entrepreneurs, bankers and financiers. Under certain circumstances two other types are also members of such classes, namely, members of the "liberal" professions with a privileged position by virtue of their abilities or training, and workers with special skills commanding a monopolistic position, regardless of how far they are hereditary or the result of training.

Acquisition classes in a negatively privileged situation are workers of the various principal types. They may be roughly classified as skilled, semi-skilled and unskilled.

In this connexion as well as the above, independent peasants and craftsmen are to be treated as belonging to the "middle classes." This category often includes in addition officials, whether they are in public or private employment, the liberal professions, and workers with exceptional monopolistic assets or positions.

Examples of "social classes" are (a) the "working" class as a whole. It approaches this type the more completely mechanized the productive process becomes. (b) The "lower middle" classes[2]

---

[2]   Like the French "petit-bourgeoisie," the German term *Kleinbuergertum* has a somewhat more specific meaning than the English "lower-middle-class." It refers particularly to economically independent elements not employed in large-scale organizations. The typical example are the small shopkeeper and the proprietor of a small handicraft workshop.— T. PARSONS.

(c) The "intelligentsia" without independent property and the persons whose social position is primarily dependent on technical training such as engineers, commercial and other officials, and civil servants. These groups may differ greatly among themselves, in particular according to costs of training. (d) The classes occupying a privileged position through property and education.

The unfinished concluding section of Karl Marx's *Kapital* was evidently intended to deal with the problem of the class unity of the proletariat, which he held existed in spite of the high degree of qualitative differentiation. A decisive factor is the increase in the importance of semi-skilled workers who have been trained in a relatively short time directly on the machines themselves, at the expense of the older type of "skilled" labour and also of unskilled. However, even this type of skill may often have a monopolistic aspect. Weavers are said to attain the highest level of productivity only after five years experience.

At an earlier period every worker could be said to have been primarily interested in becoming an independent small bourgeois, but the possibility of realizing this goal is becoming progressively smaller. From one generation to another the most readily available path to advancement both for skilled and semi-skilled workers is into the class of technically trained individuals. In the most highly privileged classes, at least over the period of more than one generation, it is coming more and more to be true that money is overwhelmingly decisive. Through the banks and corporate enterprises members of the lower middle class and the salaried groups have certain opportunities to rise into the privileged class.

Organized activity of class groups is favoured by the following circumstances: (a) the possibility of concentrating on opponents where the immediate conflict of interests is vital. Thus workers organize against management and not against security holders who are the ones who really draw income without working. Similarly peasants are not apt to organize against landlords. (b) The existence of a class status which is typically similar for large masses of people. (c) The technical possibility of being easily brought together. This is particularly true where large numbers work together in a small area, as in the modern factory. (d) Leadership directed to readily understandable goals. Such goals are very generally imposed or at least are interpreted by persons, such as intelligentsia, who do not belong to the class in question.

Social Strata and their Status

The term of "social status"[3] will be applied to a typically effective claim to positive or negative privilege with respect to social prestige so far as it rests on one or more of the following bases: (a) mode of living, (b) a formal process of education which may consist in empirical or rational training and the acquisition of the corresponding modes of life, or (c) on the prestige of birth, or of an occupation.

The primary practical manifestations of status with respect to social stratification are connubium, commensality, and often monopolistic appropriation of privileged economic opportunities and also prohibition of certain modes of acquisition. Finally, there are conventions or traditions of other types attached to a social status.

Stratificatory status may be based on class status directly or related to it in complex ways. It is not, however, determined by this alone. Property and managerial positions are not as such sufficient to lend their holder a certain social status, though they may well lead to its acquisition. Similarly, poverty is not as such a disqualification for high social status though again it may influence it.

Conversely, social status may partly or even wholly determine

---

3   *Ständische Lage*. The term *stand* with its derivatives is perhaps the most troublesome single term in Weber's text. It refers to a social group the members of which occupy a relatively well-defined common status, particularly with reference to social stratification, though this reference is not always important. In addition to common status there is the further criterion that the members of the *stand* have a common mode of life and usually a more or less well-defined code of behavior. There is no English term which even approaches adequacy in rendering this concept. Hence it has been necessary to attempt to describe what Weber meant in whatever term the particular context has indicated.—T. PARSONS

class status, without, however, being identical with it. The class status of an officer, a civil servant, and a student as determined by their income may be widely different while their social status remains the same, because they adhere to the same mode of life in all relevant respects as a result of their common education.

A social "stratum" stand is a plurality of individuals who, within a larger group, enjoy a particular kind and level of prestige by virtue of their position and possibly also claim certain special monopolies.

The following are the most important sources of the development of distinct strata: (a) The most important is by the development of a peculiar style of life including, particularly, the type of occupation pursued. (b) The second basis is hereditary charisma arising from the successful claim to a position of prestige by virtue of birth. (c) The third is the appropriation of political or hierocratic authority as a monopoly by socially distinct groups.

The development of hereditary strata is usually a form of the hereditary appropriation of privileges by an organized group or by individual qualified persons. Every well-established case of appropriation of opportunities and abilities, especially of exercising imperative powers, has a tendency to lead to the development of distinct strata. Conversely, the development of strata has a tendency in turn to lead to the monopolistic appropriation of governing powers and of the corresponding economic advantages.

Acquisition classes are favoured by an economic system oriented to market situations, whereas social strata develop and subsist most readily where economic organization is of a monopolistic and liturgical character and where the economic needs of corporate groups are met on a feudal or patrimonial basis. The type of class which is most closely related to a stratum is the "social" class, while the "acquisition" class is the farthest removed. Property classes often constitute the nucleus of a stratum.

Every society where strata play a prominent part is controlled to a large extent by conventional rules of conduct. It thus creates economically irrational conditions of consumption and hinders the development of free markets by monopolistic appropriation and by restricting free disposal of the individual's own economic ability. This will have to be discussed further elsewhere.[4]

[4] This chapter breaks off at this point but is obviously incomplete. There is, however, no other part of Weber's published work in which the subject is systematically developed, although aspects of it are treated in different connexions at many points.—T. PARSONS

16

THE PRUSSIAN JUNKERS

As a carrier of political tradition, training, and balance in a polity, there is no doubt that a stratum of landlords cannot be replaced. We speak of such landlord strata as have existed in England and which, in a similar way, formed the kernel of ancient Rome's senatorial nobility.

How many such aristocrats are to be found in Germany, and especially in Prussia? Where is their political tradition? Politically, German aristocrats, particularly in Prussia, amount to almost nothing. And it seems obvious that today a state policy aimed at breeding such a stratum of large rentiers of genuinely aristocratic character is out of the question.

Even if it were still possible to let a number of great aristocratic estates emerge on woodland—land which alone qualifies socially and politically for the formation of entailed estates—it would still be impossible to obtain any significant results. *This* was precisely the abysmal dishonesty of the bill concerning entailed estates considered in Prussia at the beginning of 1917. The bill was intended to extend a legal institution appropriate for aristocratic holdings to the middle-class proprietors of the average East Elbian estate. It tried to make an 'aristocracy' out of a type which simply is not an aristocracy and never can be inflated into one.

The Junkers of the east are frequently (and often unjustly)

From *Max Weber: Essays in Sociology*, edited and translated by H. H. Gerth and C. Wright Mills. Copyright 1946 by Oxford University Press, Inc. Reprinted by permission.

vilified; they are just as frequently (and as often unjustly) idolized. Anyone who knows them personally will certainly enjoy their company at the hunt, over a good glass, or at cards; and in their hospitable homes, everything is genuine. But everything becomes spurious when one stylizes this essentially 'bourgeois' stratum of entrepreneurs into an 'aristocracy.' Economically, the Junkers are entirely dependent upon working as agricultural entrepreneurs; they are engaged in the struggle of economic interests. Their social and economic struggle is just as ruthless as that of any manufacturer. Ten minutes in their circle shows one that they are plebians. Their very virtues are of a thoroughly robust and plebeian nature. Minister von Miquel once stated (privately!) that 'Nowadays an East German feudal estate cannot support an aristocratic household,' and he was quite correct. If one tries to mold such a stratum into an aristocracy, replete with feudal gestures and pretensions, a stratum now dependent upon routine managerial work of a capitalistic nature, the only result which can be irrevocably attained is the *physiognomy of a parvenu*. Those traits of our political and general conduct in the world which bear this stamp are determined, though not exclusively, by the fact that we have fed aristocratic pretensions to strata which simply lack the qualifications.

The Junkers are only one instance of this point. Among us the absence of men of cosmopolitan education is, of course, not only due to the physiognomy of the Junkers; it is also a result of the pervasive 'petty bourgeois' character of all those strata which have been the specific bearers of the Prussian polity during the time of its poverized but glorious ascendancy. The old officers' families, in their highly honorific way, cultivate in their often extremely modest economic conditions the tradition of the old Prussian army. The civil-servant families are of the same hue. It does not matter whether or not these families are of noble birth; economically, socially, and according to their horizon, they constitute a bourgeois middle-class group. In general, the social forms of the German officer corps are absolutely appropriate to the nature of the stratum, and in their decisive features they definitely resemble those of the officer corps of the democracies (of France and also of

Italy). But these traits immediately become a caricature when non-military circles consider them as a model for their conduct. This holds, above all, when they are blended with social forms derived from the 'pennalism' of the schools for bureaucracy. Yet, such is the case with us.

It is well known that the student fraternities constitute the typical social education of aspirants for non-military offices, sinecures, and the liberal professions of high social standing. The 'academic freedom' of dueling, drinking, and class cutting stems from a time when other kinds of freedom did not exist in Germany and when only the stratum of literati and candidates for office was privileged in such liberties. The inroad, however, which these conventions have made upon the bearing of the 'academically certified man' of Germany cannot be eliminated even today. This type of man has always been important among us, and becomes increasingly so. Even if the mortgages on fraternity houses and the necessity for the alumni to bear their interest did not take care of the economic immortality of the student fraternities, this type would hardly disappear. On the contrary, the fraternity system is steadily expanding; for the social connections of the fraternities nowadays constitute a specific way of selecting officials. And the officers' commission with its prerequisite qualification for dueling, visibly guaranteed through the colored fraternity ribbon, gives access to 'society.'

To be sure, the drinking compulsions and dueling techniques of the fraternities are increasingly adjusted to the needs of the weaker constitutions of aspirants to the fraternity ribbon, who for the sake of connections become more and more numerous. Allegedly, there are even teetotalers in some of these dueling corps. The intellectual inbreeding of the fraternities, which has continuously increased during recent decades, is a decisive factor. Fraternities have reading rooms of their own and special fraternity papers, which the alumni provide exclusively with well-meant 'patriotic' politics of an unspeakably petty-bourgeois character. Social intercourse with classmates of a different social or intellectual background is shunned or at least made very difficult. With all this, fraternity connections are constantly expanding. A sales clerk who aspires to qualify for an officer's commission as a prerequisite of marriage into 'society' (particularly with the boss's daughter) will enroll in one of the business colleges which are frequented largely because of their fraternity life.

The yardstick of the moralist is not the yardstick of the politician. However one may judge all these student associations *per se*, they certainly do not provide an education for a cosmopolitan personality. On the contrary, their fagging system and pennalism are, after all, undeniably banal; and their subaltern social forms constitute the very opposite of such an education. The most stupid Anglo-Saxon club offers more of a cosmopolitan education, however empty one may find the organized sports in which the club often finds its fulfilment. The Anglo-Saxon club with its often very strict selection of members always rests upon the principle of the strict equality of gentlemen and not upon the principle of 'pennalism,' which bureaucracy cherishes so highly as a preparation for discipline in office. By cultivating such pennalism, the fraternities do not fail to recommend themselves to 'higher ups.'[1] In any case,

---

1   In the German *Korpszeitung*, No. 428, quoted here from Professor A. Messer's article in the *Weserzeitung* of 2 June 1917, we find the following remarks criticizing 'modern' proposals of reform: 'The proposals do not at all take into account the changing material of freshmen and active members of fraternities. To select only one item: The compulsion to drink should be abolished! There should be no compulsion to empty the glass! There should be no pumping full! Often enough I have experienced among various fraternities that kind of *Kneipen* [ceremonious drinking parties of student fraternities] without such reforms, sometimes for semesters. And later on I have spent evenings with the same fraternities when everybody was reeling drunk. Then they were simply different men who believed in drinking plenty. Quite often they even held it to be necessary. And it is necessary to provide an opportunity for drinking plenty and for making them drink a great deal. If we cancel the command for drinking "rests," any freshman who is a good drinker can at any time drink his fraternity seniors under the table, and authority is gone. Or if we abolish the obligation to honor each toast we thereby abolish the basis of *Kneipgemuetlichkeit* [tavern jollification]. If we forbid the pumping full of a member, we do away with a means of education! I beg that these words not be quoted out of their context. After all, our fraternity life shall constitute a chain of educational measures; and every member of a dueling corps will confirm that later in life he never again was told the

formalistic conventions and the pennalism of this so-called 'academic freedom' are imposed upon the aspirant to office in Germany. The more the candidates turn out to be parvenus, boastful of a full pocketbook—from the parents—as is unavoidably the case where-ever conditions allow for it, the less effective are these conventions in training aristocratic men of the world. Unless the young man who drifts into this conditioning is of an unusually independent character, a free spirit, the fatal traits of a varnished plebeian will be developed. We notice such plebeians quite often among dueling corps members, even among men who are otherwise quite excellent; for the interests cultivated by these fraternities are thoroughly plebeian and far from all 'aristocratic' interests, no matter in what sense one may interpret them. The salient point is simply that an essentially plebeian student life may formerly have been harmless; it was merely naive, youthful exuberance. But nowadays it pretends to be a means of aristocratic education qualifying one for leadership in the state. The simply incredible contradiction contained in this turns into a boomerang in that a parvenu physiognomy is the result.

We must beware of thinking that these parvenu features of the German countenance are politically irrelevant. Let us immediately consider a case. To go out for 'moral conquests' among enemies,

---

truth so unvarnished, so incredibly bluntly as sometimes in the dueling corps. How did it happen that he took it? However ridiculous it may sound, it was due to the *Kneipe*. To us the *Kneipe* is what the often abused barrack drill and the goose step are to the soldier. Just as the command "knees bent!" repeated hundreds of times on the drill ground makes the man overcome laziness, callousness, stubbornness, rage, sluggishness, and weariness, and just as this command makes discipline emerge from the sentiment of being utterly helpless and completely devoid of initiative in the face of a superior—in the same way with us the command "drink the rest!" always gives the senior the opportunity to show the junior his absolute superiority. He may punish, he may keep a distance, and maintain the atmosphere which is absolutely required for the educational endeavor of the dueling corps—lest they become clubs! Naturally the command "drink the rest!" is not always and not with everbody advisable, but it must be an imminent threat to the *Kneipe* as the "knees bent!" is on the drill ground. Nevertheless, in both situations men may have a jolly good time.' [M. W.]

that is, among opposed interest groups, is a vain enterprise, which Bismarck has rightly ridiculed. But does this hold for present or future allies? We and our Austrian allies are constantly depending upon one another politically. And this is known to them as well as to us. Unless great follies are committed, no danger of a break threatens. German achievement is acknowledged by them without reserve and without jealousy—the more so the less we brag about it. We do not always have a proper appreciation of difficulties which the Austrians have and which Germany is spared. Hence, we do not always appreciate Austrian achievement. But what everybody all over the world knows must also openly be said here. What could not be tolerated by the Austrians, or by any other nation with which we might ever wish to be friendly, are the manners of the parvenu as again displayed recently in an unbearable way. Such a bearing will meet with a silent and polite yet a determined rejection by any nation of good old social breeding, for instance, the Austrians. Nobody wants to be ruled by poorly educated parvenus. Any step beyond what is absolutely indispensable in foreign affairs, that is, anything which might be possible on the part of 'Central Europe' (in the inner meaning of the word), or which might be desirable for future solidarity of interests with other nations (no matter how one may feel about the idea of an economic rapprochement), may fail politically because of the absolute determination of the partner not to have imposed upon him what recently, with a boastful gesture, was proclaimed to be the 'Prussian spirit.' 'Democracy' allegedly endangers this Prussian spirit, according to the verbal assembly lines of the political phrasemongers. As is known, the same declamations have been heard, without exception, at every stage of internal reform for the last one hundred and ten years.

The genuine Prussian spirit belongs to the most beautiful blossoms of German culture. Every line we have of Scharnhorst, Gneisnau, Boyen, Moltke is inspired with this spirit, just as are the deeds and words of the great Prussian reform officials (a good many of whom, however, are of non-Prussian descent). We need not name them here. The same holds of Bismarck's eminent intellectuality, which is now so badly caricatured by the stupid and

Philistine representatives of *Realpolitik*. But occasionally it seems as if this old Prussian spirit is now stronger among the officialdom of *other* federal states than in Berlin. Abuse of the term 'Prussian spirit' by present conservative demagogues is only an abuse of these great men.

To repeat, no aristocracy of sufficient weight and political tradition exists in Germany. Such an aristocracy may at best have had a place in the *Freikonservative* party and in the Center party —although no longer now—but it has had no place in the Conservative party.

It is equally important that there is no social form of German gentility. For despite the occasional boasting of our literati, it is completely untrue that individualism exists in Germany in the sense of freedom from conventions, in contrast to the conventions of the Anglo-Saxon gentleman or of the Latin salon type of man. Nowhere are there more rigid and compelling conventions than those of the German 'fraternity man.' These conventions directly and indirectly control just as large a part of the progeny of our leading strata as do the conventions of any other country. Wherever the forms of the officer corps do not hold, these fraternity conventions constitute 'the German form'; for the effects of the dueling corps conventions largely determine the forms and conventions of the dominant strata of Germany: of the bureaucracy and of all those who wish to be accepted in 'society,' where bureaucracy sets the tone. And these forms are certainly not genteel.

From a political point of view, it is still more important that, in contrast to the conventions of Latin and Anglo-Saxon countries, these German forms are simply not suited to serve as a model for the whole nation down to the lowest strata. They are not suited to mold and unify the nation in its gesture as a *Herrenvolk*, self-assured in its overt conduct in the way in which Latin and Anglo-Saxon conventions have succeeded.

It is a grave error to believe that 'race' is the decisive factor in the striking lack of grace and dignity in the overt bearing of the German. The German-Austrian's demeanor is formed by a genuine aristocracy. He does not lack these qualities, in spite of identical race, whatever else his weaknesses may be.

The forms that control the Latin type of personality, down to the lowest strata, are determined by imitation of the cavalier as evolved since the sixteenth century.

The Anglo-Saxon conventions also mold personalities down into the lower strata. They stem from the social habits of the gentry stratum, which has set the tone in England since the seventeenth century. The gentry emerged during the later Middle Ages from a peculiar blend of rural and urban notables, namely 'gentlemen,' who became the bearers of 'self-government.'

In all these cases it has been of consequence that the decisive features of the relevant conventions and gestures could be easily and universally imitated and hence could be democratized. But the conventions of the academically examined candidates for office in Germany, of those strata which they influence, and, above all, the habits for which the dueling corps conditions its men—these were and are obviously not suited for imitation by any circles outside of the examined and certified strata. In particular, they cannot be imitated by the broad masses of the people; they cannot be democratized, although, or rather precisely because, in essence these conventions are by no means cosmopolitan or otherwise aristocratic. They are thoroughly plebeian in nature.

The neo-Latin code of honor, as well as the quite different Anglo-Saxon code, has been suitable for far-reaching democratization. The specifically German concept of qualification for dueling, however, is not suited for being democratized, as one can easily see. This concept is of great political bearing, but the politically and socially important point is not—as is frequently held —that a so-called 'code of honor' in the narrower sense exists in the officer corps. It is absolutely in place there. The fact that a Prussian *Landrat*[2] must qualify himself for dueling, in the sense of the pennalist duel corps, in order to maintain himself in his post—that is what is politically relevant. This also holds for any other administrative official who is easily removable. It is in contrast, for instance, to the *Amtsrichter*[3] who, by virtue of the law, is

2   Country executive.
3   Judge of a lower court.

'independent,' and who because of this independence is socially déclassé as compared to the *Landrat*. As with all other conventions and forms supported by the structure of bureaucracy and decisively fashioned by the idea of German student honor, from a formal point of view the concept of dueling qualification constitutes a caste convention because of its peculiar nature. None of these forms can be democratized. In substance, however, they are not of an aristocratic but of an absolutely plebeian character, because they lack all esthetic dignity and all genteel cultivation. It is this inner contradiction that invites ridicule and has such unfavorable political effects.

Germany is a nation of plebeians. Or, if it sounds more agreeable, it is a nation of commoners. Only on this basis could a specifically 'German form' grow.

Socially, democratization brought about or promoted by the new political order—and that is what should be discussed here—would not destroy the value of aristocratic forms, since there are no such forms. Nor could it deprive such values of their exclusiveness and then propagate them throughout the nation, as was done with the forms of the Latin and Anglo-Saxon aristocracies. The form values of the degree-hunter qualifying for duels are not sufficiently cosmopolitan to support personal poise even in their own stratum. As every test shows, these forms do not always suffice even to hide the actual insecurity before a foreigner who is educated as a man of the world. The endeavor to hide such insecurity often takes the form of 'pertness,' which, in the main, stems from awkwardness and appears as poor breeding.

We shall not discuss whether political 'democratization' would actually result in social democratization. Unlimited political 'democracy' in America, for instance, does not prevent the growth of a raw plutocracy or even an 'aristocratic' prestige group, which is slowly emerging. The growth of this 'aristocracy' is culturally and historically as important as that of plutocracy, even though it usually goes unnoticed.

The development of a truly cultured 'German form,' which is at the same time suitable for the character of the socially dominant stratum of commoners, lies in the future. The incipient development of such civil conventions in the Hanseatic cities has not been continued under the impact of political and economic changes since 1870. And the present war [World War I] has blessed us with a great many parvenus, whose sons will ardently acquire the usual duel corps conventions at the universities. These conventions do not raise any demands for a cultured tradition; they serve as a convenient way of taming men for qualifying as an applicant for officer commissions. Hence, for the time being there is no hope for a change. In any case, this much holds: if 'democratization' should result in eliminating the social prestige of the academically certified man—which is by no means certain and which cannot be discussed here—then no politically valuable social forms would be abolished in Germany. Since they do not exist, they cannot be eliminated. Democracy could perhaps then free the road for the development of valuable forms suitable to our civic, social, and economic structure, which therefore would be 'genuine' and cultured values. One cannot invent such values, just as one cannot invent a style. Only this much (in an essentially negative and formal way) can be said, and it holds for all values of this nature: such forms can never be developed on any other basis than upon an attitude of personal distance and reserve. In Germany this prerequisite of all personal dignity has frequently been lacking among both high and low. The latest literati, with their urge to brag about and to print their personal 'experiences' —erotical, religious, or what not—are the enemies of all dignity, no matter of what sort. 'Distance,' however, can by no means be gained exclusively on the 'cothurnus' of snobbishly setting one's self off from the 'far too many,' as is maintained by the various and misconceived 'prophecies' which go back to Nietzsche. On the contrary, when today it is in need of this inner support, distance is always spurious. Perhaps the necessity of maintaining one's inner dignity in the midst of a democratic world can serve as a test of the genuineness of dignity.

What we have said above shows that in this, as in so many other respects, the German fatherland is not and must not be the land of its fathers but rather the land of its children, as Alexander

Herzen has so beautifully said of Russia. And this holds particularly for political problems.

The 'German spirit' for solving political problems cannot be distilled from the intellectual work of our past, however valuable it may be. Let us pay deference to the great shadows of our spiritual ancestors and let us make use of their intellectual work for all formal training of the mind. Our literati, in their conceit, claim from the past the title to govern the working out of our political future, like schoolmasters with a rod, simply because it is their profession to interpret the past to the nation. Should they try to lay down the law, then let us throw the old books into the nearest corner! Nothing can be learned about the future from them. The German classics, among other things, can teach us that we could be a leading cultured nation in a period of material poverty and political helplessness and even foreign domination. Even where they concern politics and economics their ideas stem from this unpolitical epoch. The ideas of the German classics, inspired by discussion of the French Revolution, were projections into a political and economic situation that lacked popular passion. But in so far as any political passion inspired them, besides wrathful rebellion against foreign domination, it was the ideal enthusiasm for moral imperatives. What lies beyond that remain philosophical ideas, which we may utilize as stimulating means of defining our own stand according to our political reality and according to the requirements of our own day, but not as guides. The modern problems of parliamentary government and democracy, and the essential nature of our modern state in general, are entirely beyond the horizon of the German classics.

There are those who reproach universal suffrage as the victory of dull mass instincts incapable of reason, in contradistinction to judicious political conviction; they hold it to be a victory of emotional over rational politics. With reference to the latter—and this must be said—Germany's foreign policy is proof of the fact that a monarchy ruling by a system of class suffrage holds the record for purely personal emotion and an irrational mood influencing leadership. Prussia holds the hegemony and is always the decisive factor in German politics. To prove this we need only compare the zigzag path of this noisy policy, unsuccessful for decades, with the calm purposiveness, for instance, of English foreign policy.

And as for irrational crowd instincts, they rule politics only where the masses are tightly compressed and exert pressure: in the modern metropolis, particularly under the conditions of neo-Latin urban forms of life. There the civilization of the café, as well as climatic conditions, permit the policy of the 'street'—as it has fittingly been called—to lord it over the country from the capital. On the other hand, the role of the English 'man of the street' is linked with very specific characteristics of the structure of the urban masses, which are totally lacking in Germany. The Russian metropolitan street policy is connected with the underground organizations which exist there. All these preconditions are absent in Germany, and the moderation of German life makes it quite improbable that Germany should fall into this *occasional* danger—for it is an occasional one in contrast to what in Imperial Germany has influenced foreign policy as a *chronic* danger. Not labor tied to workshops, but the loafers and the café intellectuals in Rome and Paris have fabricated the war-mongering policy of the street—by the way, exclusively in the service of the government and *only* to the extent to which the government intended or allowed it.

In France and Italy the balance of the industrial proletariat was lacking. When it acts with solidarity, the industrial proletariat is certainly an immense power in dominating the street. In comparison, however, with entirely irresponsible elements, it is a force at least capable of order and of orderly leadership through its functionaries and hence through rationally thinking politicians. From the point of view of state policy, all that matters is to increase the power of these leaders, in Germany of trade-union leaders, over the passions of the moment. Beyond this, what matters is to increase the importance of the responsible leaders, the importance of political leadership *per se*. It is one of the strongest arguments for the creation of an orderly and responsible guidance of policy by a parliamentarian leadership that thereby the efficacy of purely emotional motives from 'above' and from 'below' is weakened as far as possible. The 'rule of the street' has nothing to do with equal suffrage; Rome and Paris have been dominated by the street even when in Italy the most plutocratic sufferance in the world and in Paris Napoleon III ruled with a fake parliament. *Only* the orderly guidance of the masses by responsible politicians can break the irregular rule of the street and the leadership of demagogues of the moment.

VI. The City as a Focus
of Charismatic Institutionalization

The city, as analyzed by Weber, forms a differentiated sociopolitical phenomenon of central importance in social development in general. The two outstanding features of the city were, first, the relatively active participation of its inhabitants in its various social spheres, economic, political, and cultural, and, second, the concomitant possibility of its becoming a center of social and cultural creativity. The possibility of such creativity was to no small degree related to the city's incomplete integration into the broader social system and its ability to be autonomous in its structure.

Thus the city could become the locus of different types of charismatic innovation in different social spheres. But in addition to its atmosphere often being conducive to such creativity in different spheres, one of the most crucial aspects of its innovative tendencies was the extension of participation of broader social groups in its most central activities and spheres of action.

Although cities were not always entirely integrated in the broader social system, neither were they entirely isolated from it. Thus they could sometimes transfer these innovations to the broader social structure and be of crucial importance in its transformation.

These special characteristics and functions of the city are analyzed in the excerpts from Weber's work presented in this section.

17

GENERAL CHARACTERISTICS
OF THE CITY

Economic Character of the City:
Market Settlement

THE MANY definitions of the city have only one element in common: namely that the city consists simply of a collection of one or more separate dwellings but is a relatively closed settlement. Customarily, though not exclusively, in cities the houses are built closely to each other, often, today, wall to wall. This massing of elements interpenetrates the everyday concept of the "city" which is thought of quantitatively as a large locality. In itself this is not imprecise for the city often represents a locality and dense settlement of dwellings forming a colony so extensive that personal reciprocal acquaintance of the inhabitants is lacking. However, if interpreted in this way only very large localities could qualify as cities; moreover it would be ambiguous, for various cultural factors determine the size at which "impersonality" tends to appear. Precisely this impersonality was absent in many historical localities possessing the legal character of cities. Even in contemporary Russia there are villages comprising many thousands of inhabitants which are, thus, larger than many old "cities" (for example, in the Polish colonial area of the German East) which had only a few hundred inhabitants. Both in terms

From *The City*, by Max Weber, translated and edited by Don Martindale and Gertrud Neuwirth. Published 1958 by The Free Press, Glencoe, Ill. Reprinted by permission.

of what it would include and what it would exclude size alone can hardly be sufficient to define the city.

Economically defined, the city is a settlement the inhabitants of which live primarily off trade and commerce rather than agriculture. However, it is not altogether proper to call all localities "cities" which are dominated by trade and commerce. This would include in the concept "city" colonies made up of family members and maintaining a single, practically hereditary trade establishment such as the "trade villages" of Asia and Russia. It is necessary to add a certain "versatility" of practiced trades to the characteristics of the city. However, this in itself does not appear suitable as the single distinguishing characteristic of the city either.

Economic versatility can be established in at least two ways: by the presence of a feudal estate or a market. The economic and political needs of a feudal or princely estate can encourage specialization in trade products in providing a demand for which work is performed and goods are bartered. However, even though the *oikos* of a lord or prince is as large as a city, a colony of artisans and small merchants bound to villein services is not customarily called a "city" even though historically a large proportion of important "cities" originated in such settlements.[1] In cities of such origin the products for a prince's court often remained a highly important, even chief, source of income for the settlers.

The other method of establishing economic versatility is more generally important for the "city"; this is the existence in the place of settlement of a regular rather than an occasional exchange of goods. The market becomes an essential component in the livelihood of the settlers. To be sure, not every "market" converted the locality in which it was found into a city. The periodic fairs and yearly foreign-trade markets at which traveling merchants met at fixed times to sell their goods in wholesale or retail lots to each other or to consumers often occurred in places which we would call "villages."

---

[1] For the place of the household or oikos-economy cf. Max Weber, *General Economic History*, trans. Frank H. Knight (Glencoe: The Free Press, 1950) pp. 48, 58, 124 ff., 131, 146, 162 and Johannes Hase Broek, *Griechische Wirtschaftsgeschichte* (Tübingen: J. C. B. Mohr, 1931) pp. 15, 24, 27, 29, 38, 46, 69, 284.

Thus, we wish to speak of a "city" only in cases where the local inhabitants satisfy an economically substantial part of their daily wants in the local market, and to an essential extent by products which the local population and that of the immediate hinterland produced for sale in the market or acquired in other ways. In the meaning employed here the "city" is a market place. The local market forms the economic center of the colony in which, due to the specialization in economic products, both the non-urban population and urbanites satisfy their wants for articles of trade and commerce. Wherever it appeared as a configuration different from the country it was normal for the city to be both a lordly or princely residence as well as a market place. It simultaneously possessed centers of both kinds, *oikos* and market and frequently in addition to the regular market it also served as periodic foreign markets of traveling merchants. In the meaning of the word here, the city is a "market settlement."

Often the existence of a market rests upon the concessions and guarantees of protection by a lord or prince. They were often interested in such things as a regular supply of foreign commercial articles and trade products, in tolls, in moneys for escorts and other protection fees, in market tariffs and taxes from law suits. However, the lord or prince might also hope to profit from the local settlement of tradesmen and merchants capable of paying taxes and, as soon as the market settlement arose around the market, from land rents arising therefrom. Such opportunities were of especial importance to the lord or prince since they represented chances for monetary revenues and the increase in his treasure of precious metal.

However, the city could lack any attachment, physical or otherwise, to a lordly or princely residence. This was the case when it originated as a pure market settlement at a suitable intersection point *(Umschlageplatz)*[2] where the means of transportation were changed by virtue of concession to non-resident lords or princes or usurpation by the interested parties themselves. This could assume the form of concessions to entrepreneurs—permitting

[2]   Charles H. Cooley's theory of transportation took the break in communication either physical or economic as the most critical of all factors for the formation of the city.

them to lay out a market and recruit settlers for it. Such capitalistic establishment of cities was especially frequent in medieval frontier areas, particularly in East, North, and Central Europe. Historically, though not as a rule, the practice has appeared throughout the world.

Without any attachment to the court of a prince or without princely concessions, the city could arise through the association of foreign invaders, naval warriors, or commercial settlers or, finally, native parties interested in the carrying trade. This occurred frequently in the early Middle Ages. The resultant city could be a pure market place. However, it is more usual to find large princely or patrimonial households and a market conjoined. In this case the eminent household as one contact point of the city could satisfy its want either primarily by means of a natural economy (that is by villein service or natural service or taxes placed upon the artisans and merchants dependent on it) or it could supply itself more or less secondarily by barter in the local market as that market's most important buyer. The more pronounced the latter relation the more distinct the market foundation of the city looms and the city ceases by degrees to be a mere appendaged market settlement alongside the *oikos*. Despite attachment to the large household it then became a market city. As a rule the quantitative expansion of the original princely city and its economic importance go hand in hand with an increase in the satisfaction of wants in the market by the princely household and other large urban households attached to that of the prince as courts of vassals or major officials.

Types of Consumer and Producer City

Similar to the city of the prince, the inhabitants of which are economically dependent upon the purchasing power of noble households are cities in which the purchasing power of other larger consumers, such as rentiers, determines the economic opportunities of resident tradesmen and merchants. In terms of the kind and source of their incomes such larger consumers may be of quite varied types. They may be officials who spend their legal and illegal income in the city or lords or other political power holders who spend their non-urban land rents or politically determined incomes there. In either of these cases the city closely approximates the princely city for it depends upon patrimonial and political incomes which supply the purchasing power of large consumers. Peking was a city of officials; Moscow, before suspension of serfdom, was a land-rent city.

Different in principle are the superficially similar cities in which urban land-rents are determined by traffic monopolies of landed property. Such cities originate in the trade and commerce consolidated in the hands of an urban aristocracy. This type of development has always been widespread: it appeared in Antiquity; in the Near East until the Byzantine Empire; and in the Middle Ages. The city that emerges is not economically of a rentier type but is, rather, a merchant or trade city the rents of which represent a tribute of acquisitors to the owners of houses. The conceptual differentiation of this case from the one in which rents are not determined by tributary obligations to monopolists but by non-urban sources, should not obscure the interrelation in the past of both forms. The large consumers can be rentiers spending their business incomes (today mainly interest on bonds, dividends or shares) in the city. Whereupon purchasing power rests on capitalistically conditioned monetary rentier sources as in the city of Arnheim. Or purchasing power can depend upon state pensions or other state rents as appears in a "pensionopolis" like Wiesbaden. In all similar cases one may describe the urban form as a consumer city, for the presence in residence of large consumers of special economic character is of decisive economic importance for the local tradesmen and merchants.

A contrasting form is presented by the producer city. The increase in population and purchasing power in the city may be due, as for example in Essen or Bochum, to the location there of factories, manufactures, or home-work industries supplying outside territories—thus representing the modern type. Or, again, the crafts and trades of the locality may ship their goods away as in cities of Asiatic, Ancient, and Medieval types. In either case the consumers for the local market are made up of large consumers if they are residents and/or entrepreneurs, workers and craftsmen who form the great mass, and merchants and benefactors of landrent supported indirectly by the workers and craftsmen.

The trade city and merchant city are confronted by the consumer city in which the purchasing power of its larger consumers rests on the retail for profit of foreign products on the local market (for example, the woolen drapers in the Middle Ages), the foreign sale for profit of local products or goods obtained by native producers (for example, the herring of the Hansa) or the purchase of foreign products and their sale with or without storage at the place to the outside (intermediate commercial cities). Very frequently a combination of all these economic activities occurred: the *commenda* and *societas maris* implied that a *tractator* (travelling merchant) journied to Levantine markets with products purchased with capital entrusted to him by resident capitalists. Often the *tractator* traveled entirely in ballast. He sold these products in the East and with the proceeds he purchased oriental articles brought back for sale in the local market. The profits of the undertaking were then divided between *tractator* and capitalist according to pre-arranged formulas.

The purchasing power and tax ability of the commercial city rested on the local economic establishment as was also the case for the producers' city in contrast to the consumers' city. The economic opportunities of the shipping and transport trade and of numerous secondary wholesale and retail activities were at the disposal of the merchants. However the economic activity of these establishments was not entirely executed for the local retail trade but in substantial measure for external trade. In principle, this state of affairs was similar to that of the modern city, which is the location of national and international financiers or large banks (London, Paris, Berlin) or of joint stock companies or cartels (Duesseldorf). It follows that today more than ever before a predominant part of the earnings of firms flow to localities other than the place of earning. Moreover, a growing part of business proceeds are not consumed by their rightful receivers at the metropolitan location of the business but in suburban villas, rural resorts or international hotels. Parallel with these developments "city-towns" or city-districts consisting almost exclusively of business establishments are arising.

There is no intention here of advancing the further casuistic distinctions required by a purely economic theory of the city. Moreover, it hardly needs to be mentioned that actual cities nearly always represent mixed types. Thus, if cities are to be economically classified at all, it must be in terms of their prevailing economic component.

Fraternization and the Formation of the Polis

More than anything else the fully developed ancient and medieval city was formed and interpreted as a fraternal association.[3] Therefore, as a rule these cities had a corresponding religious symbol standing for the associational cult of the burghers as such. There was usually a city-god or city-saint specifically available to the burghers. Such was not even lacking in China (often an apotheosized mandarin), though in China they retained the character of functional deities in the pantheon.

In the Occident the city association owned and controlled property. This contrasts with practice elsewhere such as is illustrated by the dispute of the Alides (Descendants of Ali, the fourth caliph) with the community over the "Gardens of Fadak"—a dispute which provided the first occasion for the economic separation of the *Schîah*. This was a dispute over family or communal property. The community in whose name the caliph claimed the land was a religious community of Islam and not a political community of Mecca—indeed, the latter did not exist. But in the Occident the political association itself appears as a property owner. Typical of such property was the commons of urban settlements which may have existed elsewhere and even for village communities. Similarly though the princes sometimes had urban tax sources, there is a unique finance structure for the urban community in the ancient and medieval city. At best only the

---

3   The classical study of the religious and civil institutions of the cities of Greece and Rome is Fustel de Coulanges, *The Ancient City* (Garden City: Doubleday, 1956).

barest rudiments appear elsewhere. Foremost among the reasons for the peculiar freedom of urbanites in the Mediterranean city in contrast to the Asiatic is the absence of magical and animistic caste and sib constraints. The social formations preventing fusion of urban dwellers into a homogeneous status group vary. In China it was the exogamous and endophratric sib; in India— since the victory of the patrimonial kings and the Brahmans—it has been the endogamous caste with its exclusive taboos which has prevented the fusion of city dwellers into a status group enjoying social and legal equality, into a connubium sharing table community and displaying solidarity toward the outgroup. Because of the intensity of exclusive caste taboos this possibility was even more remote in India than in China. Moreover, India possessed a population which was 90% rural in contrast to China where the city was of greater importance. While the inhabitants of India had no possibility for communal cult meals, the Chinese, due to their sib organization, had no occasion for them, particularly since the ancestor cult was more important to the Chinese than anything else. Of course, only a taboo-bound people like the Indians and (to a much lesser degree) the Jews went so far as to exclude even the private communal meal. In India, however, this was the case to such a degree that even the glance of one outside the caste was sufficient to defile the kitchen.

It was still true in Antiquity that the social ceremonies of the family were as inaccessible to non-members as was the Chinese ancestor cult. The historical evidence suggests that one component (real or fictitious) in the establishment of the community was the substitution of the city cult meal or prytaneium for that of the family.[4] The *prytaneium* of the polis was originally indispensable for the city, for it symbolized the community of urban families as a consequence of their fraternization.

Originally the ancient polis was officially based on an organization of families. Some were super-ordinate over others for purely local reasons which often (at least according to fiction) rested on

4   This is the central thesis of Fustel de Coulanges. The Feast of Synoikia was still celebrated in Athens in historical times.

communities of descent. Such communities of descent formed externally-strict, exclusive, cult associations. It is a significant fact that in the minds of their members the ancient cities were freely-willed associations. They were confederations of groups partly of consanguineous and partly—in the case of the phratries—of military character. The groups that composed them were later systematically reorganized into civic divisions of a technical administrative nature. Thus the cities of Antiquity were not only sacred structures closed to the outside but inwardly closed to anyone not belonging to the confederated families: closed to the plebeian. For this very reason, at first, they constituted exclusive cult associations.

The confederations of noble families in Southern European cities in the early Middle Ages, especially but not only in the martime cities, closely resemble those of the ancient city. Within the walls of the city each noble family had its own fortress or, if not, it shared a fortress with others, in which case its use (as in Siena) was regulated in detail. Feuds between families raged as violently within as outside the city and many of the oldest civic districts (for example the *alberghi*) were presumably such areas of feudal power. However, there were no residues—such as were still present in Antiquity—of sacred exclusiveness of families against each other and toward the outside. This was a consequence of the historically memorable precedent in Antioch justly thrust into the foreground by Paul in his letter to the Galatians. There Peter administered the (ritualistic) communal meal to uncircumcised brethren. Already in the ancient city ritualistic exclusiveness had begun to disappear. The clanless plebs accomplished ritualistic equalization in principle. In the medieval period, chiefly in Central and Northern European cities, the clans were weak from the beginning and they soon lost all importance as constituencies of the city. Thus the cities became confederations of individual burghers (house owners). In fact even in extra-civic affairs the exclusiveness of the burghers also lost all practical importance for the urban community.

It has been noted that the ancient polis increasingly tended to become an "institutionalized community" in the mind of its inhabitants. Even in Antiquity the concept of the "community" began to differentiate from that of the "state." To be sure this only occurred with incorporation into the large Hellenistic and Roman states which robbed the city communities of their political independence. By contrast, the medieval city was a "commune" from the beginning of its existence irrespective of the degree to which the legal concept of "corporation" as such was brought to clear consciousness.

Disruption of the Clans as a Prerequisite of Fraternization

Wherever it appeared the city was basically a resettlement of people previously alien to the place. Chinese, Mesopotamian, Egyptian and occasionally even Hellenistic war princes founded cities and transferred to them not only voluntary settlers but other kidnapped according to demand and possibility. This occurred most frequently in Mesopotamia where forced settlers had first to dig the irrigation canals which made possible the emergence of the city in the desert. The prince with his official apparatus and administrative officials remained absolute master of the city. This tended to prevent the appearance of any communal association whatsoever or, at best, permitted only the appearance of the rudiments of one. The people settled together in the area often remained as connubially segregated tribes.[5] Where this was not the case the newcomers remained members of their former locality and clan associations.

The urban resident in China normally belonged to his native rural community. So, too, did broad strata of the non-Hellenic population of the Hellenic Orient. Moreover, the legend of the New Testament locates the birth of the Nazarene at Bethlehem because the family of the father (using the German translation of Heliand) had its *Hantgemal* there; hence, according to the legend, it had to be counted there. Until recently the situation of

5   The Babylonian exile of the Jews was only a particularly famous case.

the Russian peasants who had migrated to the city was similar; they retained their right to the land as well as, upon demand of the village community, their duty to share in the village work. Under such circumstances no civic rights arose but only a duty-encumbered and privileged association of city residents. The Hellenic *synoecism* was based on clan groups. According to tradition the reconstitution of the city of Jerusalem by Esra and Nehemiah was affected by clans, namely the settling together of delegations from each rural resident clan possessing full political rights.

In the ancient city only the clan-less, politically-illegitimate plebs were organized in terms of local residence.[6] The individual could be a citizen in the ancient city, but only as a member of his clan. In early Antiquity, at least according to fiction, each Hellenic and Roman *synoecism* as well as each colonial establishment occurred in a manner similar to the reconstitution of Jerusalem. Even democracy was initially unable to disrupt the organization of the burghers into families, clans, phratries, and phyles. Purely personal, cult associations were in fact dominated by the noble families and democracy was able to render them politically innocuous only through indirect means. In Athens everyone wishing to qualify for office had to prove the existence of a cult center of his clan *(Zeus epkaios)* in Athens.

Roman legend also reports the appearance of the city through the conjoint settlement of natives with people alien to the tribes. Through ritualistic fraternal acts they were formed into a religious community with a communal hearth and a god serving as communal saint. However, they were simultaneously organized into gentes (clans), *curia* (phratries) and tribes (phyles). Such routine composition of the ancient city was initially imposed quite arbitrarily for tax purposes as is indicated by the round numbers of such associations (the cities were typically formed into 3, 30, or 12). But despite this in Rome participation in the *auspicia* remained the distinguishing mark of the burgher entitled to participation in the city cult and qualified for all offices requir-

---

6   The substitution of locality for kin groups was particularly emphasized by H. S. Maine.

ing communication with the gods. This was indispensable precisely for ritual purposes. A legitimate association could only rest on traditional or ritualistic forms such as the clan, the defense associations (phratry) or the political or tribal association (phyle).

All this was changed in the medieval city, particularly in the North. Here, in new civic creations burghers joined the citizenry as single persons. The oath of citizenship was taken by the individual. Personal membership, not that of kin groups or tribe, in the local association of the city supplied the guarantee of the individual's personal legal position as a burgher.

The North European city often expanded to include not only persons originally foreign to the locality, but merchants foreign to the tribes as well. New civic foundations extended the civic privilege as an attraction to newcomers. To some degree this also occurred incidental to the transformation of older settlements into cities. At times, to be sure, merchants such as are mentioned in Cologne, recruited from the entire circuit of the Occident from Rome to Poland, did not join the local oath-bound urban community, which was founded by the native propertied strata. However, enfranchisement of complete strangers also occurred.

A special position corresponding to that of Asiatic guest people was characteristically occupied in medieval cities only by the Jews. Although in Upper Rhine documents the bishop insists that he called in the Jews "for the greater glory of the city," and though in Cologne shrine-documents the Jews appear as landowners mingling with Christians, ritualistic exclusion of connubialism by the Jews in a manner foreign to the Occident as well as the actual exclusion of table community between Jews and non-Jews and the absence of the Lord's Supper, blocked fraternization. The city church, city saint, participation of the burghers in the Lord's Supper and official church celebrations by the city were all typical of the Occidental cities. Within them Christianity deprived the clan of its last ritualistic importance, for by its very nature the Christian community was a confessional association of believing individuals rather than a ritualistic association of clans. From the beginning, thus, the Jews remained outside the burgher association.

While it is true that the medieval city retained cult ties and

often (perhaps always) religious parishes were part of its constitution it was nevertheless a secular foundation like the ancient
city. The parishes were not incorporated as church associations by
their church representatives but by secular civic aldermen. The
decisive legal formalities were undertaken by lay presidents of
parochial communities and, eventually, guilds of merchants. Moreover, the qualification of an individual as a citizen was found in
communal religious equality rather than membership in the proper
clans as in antiquity.

Initially in the medieval city there was no fundamental religious difference from Asiatic conditions. The God of the Asiatic
city corresponds to the local saint of the Middle Ages; even
determination of citizenship in terms of the ritualistic community
was characteristic of the cities of Near Eastern Antiquity. However, the pacification policies following conquests by the great
Near Eastern kings tended to destroy the ritualistic community.
The great kings sought to pacify conquered areas by transplanting
whole populations, thus destroying systems of local ties which
could become nuclei of resistance. The effect of this policy was
to transpose the city into a mere administrative district within
which all inhabitants with differences of ritual and family membership shared similar life situations.

The effects of such Near Eastern policies of grafting populations on civic structures may be seen in the fate of the Jews who
were carried into exile. In their exile location only those public
offices which demanded knowledge of writing and thus, also,
ritualistic qualification[7] were closed to them. While the Jews were
permitted to enter without restriction almost every occupation
the Babylonian city offered they did not become "officials" of
the city.

In this area of the ancient world just as was the case among

[7]   Writing in considerable measure originated in the employment of
magical signs by magician priests and, in any case, remained a monopoly
of priestly strata for a long time in early civilization. Qualification for
religious ministrations, for public office, and possession of writing skills
thus were early linked phenomena still preserved in Babylonia at the time
of the Jewish exile.

the exiled Jews the individual members of foreign tribes had their own elders and priests. Thus they assumed the form of "guest tribes." In Israel before the exile, the metics (gerim) stood outside the ritualistic communities as indicated by the fact that they were not originally circumcised. The *gerim* comprised nearly all the craftsmen in Ancient Palestine. The counterpart to such craftsmen in India also were guest tribes, where ritualistic fraternization of city inhabitants was excluded by caste taboos.

Similar phenomena to these also appear in China where each city had its god, often a former mandarin of the city who had become transformed into a cultural hero and was the central object of a cult of worship. However, here, too, as in almost all Asiatic and Near Eastern cities the community is missing or, at best, rudimentary. When the urban community appears at all it is only in the form of a kin-association which also extends beyond the city. In the case of the Jews after the exile the confessional community was ruled in a purely theocratic manner.

18

THE CONCEPT OF CITIZENSHIP

IN THE CONCEPT of citizenship (*Bürgertum*) as it is used in social history are bound up three distinct significations. First, citizenship may include certain social categories or classes which have some specific communal or economic interest. As thus defined the class citizen is not unitary; there are greater citizens and lesser citizens; entrepreneurs and hand workers belong to the class. Second, in the political sense, citizenship signifies membership in the state, with its connotation as the holder of certain political rights. Finally, by citizens in the class sense, we understand those strata which are drawn together, in contrast with the bureaucracy or the proletariat and others outside their circle, as "persons of property and culture," entrepreneurs, recipients of funded incomes, and in general all persons of academic culture, a certain class standard of living, and a certain social prestige.

The first of these concepts is economic in character and is peculiar to western civilization. There are and have been everywhere hand laborers and entrepreneurs, but never and nowhere were they included in a unitary social class. The notion of the citizen of the state has its forerunners in antiquity and in the medieval city. Here there were citizens as holders of political rights, while outside of the occident only traces of this relation are met with, as in the Babylonian patriciate and the Josherim,

From *General Economic History*, by Max Weber, translated by Frank H. Knight. Published 1961 by Collier Books, New York. Reprinted by permission.

the inhabitants of a city with full legal rights, in the Old Testament. The farther east we go the fewer are these traces; the notion of citizens of the state is unknown to the world of Islam, and to India and China. Finally, the social class signification of citizen as the man of property and culture, or of one or the other, in contrast with the nobility, on the one hand, and the proletariat, on the other, is likewise a specifically modern and western concept, like that of the bourgeoisie. It is true that in antiquity and in the middle ages, citizen was a class concept; membership in specific class groups made the person a citizen. The difference is that in this case the citizen was privileged in a negative as well as a positive sense. In the positive sense in that he only—in the medieval city for example—might pursue certain occupations; negatively in that certain legal requirements were waived, such as the qualification for holding a fief, the qualification for the tourney, and that for membership in the religious community. The citizen in the quality of membership in a class is always a citizen of a particular city, and the city in this sense, has existed only in the western world, or elsewhere, as in the early period in Mesopotamia, only in an incipient stage.

The contributions of the city in the whole field of culture are extensive. The city created the party and the demagogue. It is true that we find all through history struggles between cliques, factions of nobles, and office-seekers, but nowhere outside the occidental cities are there parties in the present-day sense of the word, and as little are there demagogues in the sense of party leaders and seekers for ministerial posts. The city and it alone has brought forth the phenomena of the history of art. Hellenic and Gothic art, in contrast with Mycænean and Roman, are city art. So also the city produced science in the modern sense. In the city civilization of the Greeks the discipline out of which scientific thinking developed, namely mathematics, was given the form under which it continuously developed down to modern times. The city culture of the Babylonians stands in an analogous relation to the foundation of astronomy. Furthermore, the city is the basis of specific religious institutions. Not only was Judaism, in contrast with the religion of Israel, a thoroughly urban construction—a peasant could not conform with the ritual of the law—but early Christianity is also a city phenomenon; the larger the city the greater was the percentage of Christians, and the case of Puritanism and Pietism was also the same. That a peasant could function as a member of a religious group is a strictly modern phenomenon. In Christian antiquity the word *paganus* signified at the same time heathen and village dweller, just as in the post-exilic period the town-dwelling Pharisee looked with contempt on the Am-ha-aretz who was ignorant of the law. Even Thomas Aquinas, in discussing the different social classes and their relative worth, speaks with extreme contempt of the peasant. Finally, the city alone produced theological thought, and on the other hand again, it alone harbored thought untrammeled by priestcraft. The phenomenon of Plato, with his question of how to make men useful citizens as the dominant problem of his thought, is unthinkable outside the environment of a city.

The question whether a place is to be regarded as a city is not answered on the basis of its spatial extent.[1] From the economic standpoint, rather, both in the occident and elsewhere, the city is in the first place the seat of commerce and industry, and requires a continuous provision of the means of subsistence from without. From an economic standpoint, the various categories of large places are distinguished by the source from which supplies come and the means by which they are paid for. A large place which does not live on its own agricultural production may pay for its imports by its own products, that is industrial products, or through trade or rents, or finally by means of pensions. The "rents" represent salaries of officials or land rents; subsistence on pensions is illustrated by Wiesbaden, where the cost of imports is met by the pensions of political officials and army officers. Large places may be classified according to the dominance of these sources of income to pay for the imports of subsistence goods, but this is a

---

1   Otherwise Peking would have to be regarded as a "city" from the beginning, and at a time when nothing of the nature of a city existed in Europe. Officially, however, it is called "the five places," and is administratively handled in parts as five large villages: hence there are no "citizens" of Peking.

condition common to the world at large; it belongs to large places and does not distinguish a city.

A further general characteristic of a city is the fact that in the past it was generally a fortress; throughout long periods a place was recognized as a city only if and so long as it was a fortified point. In this connection the city was regularly the seat of government, both political and ecclesiastical. In some cases in the occident a *civitas* was understood to mean a place which was the seat of a bishop. In China it is a decisive characteristic that the city is the seat of a mandarin,[2] and cities are classified on the basis of the rank of their mandarins. Even in the Italian Renaissance the cities were distinguished by the grade of their officials and upper class residents, and the rank of the resident nobility.

It is true that outside the western world there were cities in the sense of a fortified point and the seat of political and hierarchical administration. But outside the occident there have not been cities in the sense of a unitary community. In the middle ages, the distinguishing characteristic was the possession of its own law and court and an autonomous administration of whatever extent. The citizen of the middle ages was a citizen because and insofar as he came under this law and participated in the choice of administrative officials. That cities have not existed outside the occident in the sense of a political community is a fact calling for explanation. That the reason was economic in character is very doubtful. As little is it the specific "Germanic spirit" which produced the unity, for in China and India there were unitary groups much more cohesive than those of the occident, and yet the particular union in cities is not found there.

The inquiry must be carried back to certain ultimate fundamental facts. We cannot explain the phenomena on the basis of the feudal or political grants of the middle ages or in terms of the founding of cities by Alexander the Great on his march to India. The earliest references to cities as political units designate rather their revolutionary character. The occidental city arose through

---

[2]   In contrast, the officials and princes in Japan resided in castles down to the modernization; places were distinguished according to size.

the establishment of a fraternity, the συνοικισμός in antiquity, the *coniuratio* in the middle ages. The juristic forms, always relating to externals, in which the resulting struggles and conflicts of the middle ages are clothed, and the facts which lie behind them, cannot be distinguished. The pronouncements of the Staufers against cities prohibit none of the specific presumptions of citizenship, but rather the *coniuratio*, the brotherhood in arms for mutual aid and protection, involving the usurpation of political power.

The first example in the middle ages is the revolutionary movement in 726 which led to the secession of Italy from the Byzantine rule and which centered in Venice. It was called forth especially by opposition to the attack on images carried out by the emperors under military pressure, and hence the religious element, although not the only factor, was the motive which precipitated the revolution. Previous to that time the *dux* (later *doge*) of Venice had been appointed by the emperor, although, on the other hand, there were certain families whose members were constantly to a predominant extent appointed military tribunes or district commandants. From then on the choice of the tribunes and of the *dux* was in the hands of persons liable to military service, that is, those who were in a position to serve as knights. Thus the movement was started. It requires 400 years longer before in 1143 the name *Commune Venetiarum* turns up. Quite similar was the "synœcism" of antiquity, as for example the procedure of Nehemiah in Jerusalem. This leader caused the leading families and a selected portion of the people on the land to band themselves together under oath for the purpose of administration and defense of the city. We must assume the same background for the origin of every ancient city. The *polis* is always the product of such a confraternity or synœcism, not always an actual settlement in proximity but a definite oath of brotherhood which signified that a common ritualistic meal is established and a ritualistic union formed and that only those had a part in this ritualistic group who buried their dead on the acropolis and had their dwellings in the city.

For the fact that this development took place only in the occident there are two reasons. The first is the peculiar character of the organization for defense. The occidental city is in its beginnings first of all a defense group, an organization of those economically competent to bear arms, to equip and train themselves. Whether the military organization is based on the principle of self-equipment or on that of equipment by a military overlord who furnishes horses, arms and provisions, is a distinction quite as fundamental for social history as is the question whether the means of economic production are the property of the worker or of a capitalistic entrepreneur. Everywhere outside the west the development of the city was prevented by the fact that the army of the prince is older than the city. The earliest Chinese epics do not, like the Homeric, speak of the hero who fares forth to battle in his own chariot, but only of the officer as a leader of the men. Likewise in India an army led by officers marched out against Alexander the Great. In the west the army equipped by the war lord, and the separation of soldier from the paraphernalia of war, in a way analogous to the separation of the worker from the means of production, is a product of the modern era, while in Asia it stands at the apex of the historical development. There was no Egyptian or Babylonian-Assyrian army which would have presented a picture similar to that of the Homeric mass army, the feudal army of the west, the city army of the ancient *polis*, or the medieval guild army.

The distinction is based on the fact that in the cultural evolution of Egypt, western Asia, India, and China the question of irrigation was crucial. The water question conditioned the existence of the bureaucracy, the compulsory service of the dependent classes, and the dependence of the subject classes upon the functioning of the bureaucracy of the king. That the king also expressed his power in the form of a military monopoly is the basis of the distinction between the military organization of Asia and that of the west. In the first case the royal official and army officer is from the beginning the central figure of the process, while in the west both were originally absent. The forms of religious brotherhood and self equipment for war made possible the origin and existence of the city. It is true that the beginnings of an analogous development are found in the east. In India we meet with relations which verge upon the establishment of a city in the western sense, namely, the combination of self equipment and legal citizenship; one who could furnish an elephant for the army is in the free city of Vaiçali a full citizen. In ancient Mesopotamia, too, the knights carried on war with each other and established cities with autonomous administration. But in the one case as in the other these beginnings later disappear as the great kingdom arises on the basis of water regulation. Hence only in the west did the development come to complete maturity.

The second obstacle which prevented the development of the city in the orient was formed by ideas and institutions connected with magic. In India the castes were not in a position to form ritualistic communities and hence a city, because they were ceremonially alien to one another. The same facts explained the peculiar position of the Jews in the middle ages. The cathedral and the eucharist were the symbols of the unity of the city, but the Jews were not permitted to pray in the cathedral or take part in the communion and hence were doomed to form diaspora-communes. On the contrary, the consideration which made it natural for cities to develop in the west was in antiquity the extensive freedom of the priesthood, the absence of any monopoly in the hands of the priests over communion with the gods, such as obtained in Asia. In western antiquity the officials of the city performed the rites, and the resultant proprietorship of the *polis* over the things belonging to the gods and the priestly treasures was carried to the point of filling the priestly offices by auction, since no magical limitations stood in the way as in India. For the later period in the west three great facts were crucial. The first was prophecy among the Jews, which destroyed magic within the confines of Judaism; magical procedure remained real but was devilish instead of divine. The second fact was the pentacostal miracle, the ceremonial adoption into the spirit of Christ which was a decisive factor in the extraordinary spread of the early Christian enthusiasm. The final factor was the day in Antioch (Gal. 2; 11 ff.) when Paul, in opposition to Peter, espoused fellowship with the uncircumcised. The magical barriers between clans, tribes, and peoples, which were still known in the ancient *polis* to a considerable degree, were thus set aside and the establishment of the occidental city was made possible.

Although the city in the strict sense is specifically a western institution, there are within the class two fundamental distinctions, first between antiquity and the middle ages and second between southern and northern Europe. In the first period of development of the city communities, the similarity between the ancient and medieval city is very great. In both cases it is those of knightly birth, the families leading an aristocratic existence, who alone are active members in the group, while all the remaining population is merely bound to obedience. That these knightly families became residents of the city is entirely the consequence of the possibility of sharing in trade opportunities. After the success of the Italian revolution against Byzantium, a portion of the Venetian upper class families collected in the Rialto because from that point commerce with the orient was carried on. It is to be remembered that in the sea trade and naval warfare Venice still formed a part of the Byzantine system although it was politically independent. Similarly in antiquity, the wealthy families did not carry on trade on their own account but in the capacity of ship owners or money lenders. It is characteristic that in antiquity there was no city of importance which lay more than a day's journey distant from the sea; only those places flourished which for political or geographical reasons possessed exceptional opportunities for trade. Consequently Sombart is essentially incorrect in asserting that ground rent is the mother of the city and of commerce. The facts stand in the reverse order; settlement in the city is occasioned by the possibility and the intention of employing the rents in trade, and the decisive influence of trade on the founding of cities stands out. . . .

Turning to the question as to the consequences of these relations in connection with the evolution of capitalism, we must emphasize the heterogeneity of industry in antiquity and in the middle ages, and the different species of capitalism itself. In the first place, we are met in the most widely separated periods with a multiplicity of non-rational forms of capitalism. These include first capitalistic enterprises for the purpose of tax farming—in the occident as well as in China and western Asia—and for the purpose of financing war, in China and India, in the period of small separate states; second, capitalism in connection with trade speculation, the trader being entirely absent in almost no epoch of history; third, money-lending capitalism, exploiting the necessities of outsiders. All these forms of capitalism relate to spoils, taxes, the pickings of office or official usury, and finally to tribute and actual need. It is noteworthy that in former times officials were financed as Cæsar was by Crassus and endeavored to recoup the sums advanced through misuse of their official position. All this, however, relates to occasional economic activity of an irrational character, while no rational system of labor organization developed out of these arrangements.

Rational capitalism, on the contrary, is organized with a view to market opportunities, hence to economic objectives in the real sense of the word, and the more rational it is the more closely it relates to mass demand and the provision for mass needs. It was reserved to the modern western development after the close of the middle ages to elevate this capitalism into a system, while in all of antiquity there was but one capitalistic class whose rationalism might be compared with that of modern capitalism, namely, the Roman knighthood. When a Greek city required credit or leased public land or let a contract for supplies, it was forced to incite competition among different interlocal capitalists. Rome, in contrast, was in possession of a rational capitalistic class which from the time of the Gracchi played a determining role in the state. The capitalism of this class was entirely relative to state and governmental opportunities, to the leasing of the *ager publicus* or conquered land, and of domain land, or to tax farming and the financing of political adventures and of wars. It influenced the public policy of Rome in a decisive way at times, although it had to reckon with the constant antagonism of the official nobility.

The capitalism of the late middle ages began to be directed toward market opportunities, and the contrast between it and the capitalism of antiquity appears in the development after the cities have lost their freedom. Here again we find a fundamental distinction in the lines of development as between antiquity and medieval and modern times. In antiquity the freedom of the cities was swept away by a bureaucratically organized world empire within which there was no longer a place for political capitalism. In the beginning the emperors were forced to resort to the financial power of the knighthood but we see them progressively emancipate themselves and exclude the knightly class from the farming of the taxes and hence from the most lucrative source of wealth—just as the Egyptian kings were able to make the provisions for political and military requirements in their realms independent of the capitalist powers and reduce the tax farmers to the position of tax officials. In the imperial period of Rome the leasing of domain land everywhere decreased in extent in favor of permanent hereditary appropriation. The provision for the economic needs of the state was taken care of through compulsory contributions and compulsory labor of servile persons instead of competitive contracts. The various classes of the population became stratified along occupational lines and the burden of state requirements was imposed on the newly created groups on the principle of joint liability.

This development means the throttling of ancient capitalism. A conscript army takes the place of the mercenaries and ships are provided by compulsory service. The entire harvest of grain, insofar as regions of surplus production are concerned, is distributed among the cities in accordance with their needs, with the exclusion of private trade. The building of roads and every other service which has to be provided for is laid on the shoulders of specific personal groups who become attached by inheritance to the soil and to their occupations. At the end the Roman urban communities, acting through their mayors in a way not very different from the village community through its common meeting, demand the return of the rich city councilmen on property grounds, because the population is jointly responsible for the payments and services due to the state. These services are subject to the principle of the *origo* which is erected on the pattern of the ἴδια of Ptolemaic Egypt; the compulsory dues of servile persons can only be rendered in their home commune. After this system became established the political opportunities for securing gain were closed to capitalism; in the late Roman state, based on compulsory contributions (*Leiturgiestaat*) there was as little place for capitalism as in the Egyptian state organized on the basis of compulsory labor service (*Fronstaat*).

Quite different was the fate of the city in the modern era. Here again its autonomy was progressively taken away. The English city of the 17th and 18th centuries had ceased to be anything but a clique of guilds which could lay claim only to financial and social class significance. The German cities of the same period, with the exception of the imperial cities, were merely geographical entities (*Landstadt*) in which everything was ordered from above. In the French cities this development appeared even earlier, while the Spanish cities were deprived of their power by Charles V, in the insurrection of the *communeros*. The Italian cities found themselves in the power of the "signory" and those of Russia never arrived at freedom in the western sense. Everywhere the military, judicial, and industrial authority was taken away from the cities. In form the old rights were as a rule unchanged, but in fact the modern city was deprived of its freedom as effectively as had happened in antiquity with the establishment of the Roman dominion, though in contrast with antiquity they came under the power of competing national states in a condition of perpetual struggle for power in peace or war. This competitive struggle created the largest opportunities for modern western capitalism. The separate states had to compete for mobile capital, which dictated to them the conditions under which it would assist them to power. Out of this alliance of the state with capital, dictated by necessity, arose the national citizen class, the bourgeoisie in the modern sense of the word. Hence it is the closed national state which afforded to capitalism its chance for development—and as long as the national state does not give place to a world empire capitalism also will endure.

VII. Charisma and Institutionalization in the Sphere of Religion and Culture

More than others, the sphere of religion and cultural activities, both art and science, is prone to the manifestations of charismatic creativity and innovation. But at the same time, in this sphere the importance of organizational exigencies in making such creativity enduring becomes most fully evident. It was the combination of these two aspects of charisma that made Weber emphasize so strongly the institutional implication of religious charisma, both in the religious sphere as well as in other institutional spheres. It was also in this sphere that the problem of the simultaneous development of rationality and of *Entzauberung* (demystification) becomes most prominent.

The following selections present Weber's analysis of these processes. The excerpts from *Sociology of Religion* show the relationship between charisma and its routinization within the religious sphere and its impact on the broader social structure, especially on social stratification. Weber's analysis of the religious sphere does not separate the analytical discussion from the analysis of concrete societies. Because of this, unlike in the former chapters, there is no division between the general discussion of religion and the analysis of actual case studies of different types of societies. At the end of this part is an extract from Weber's "Science as a Vocation," an analysis of some of the results of the process of secularization, and *Entzauberung* in modern culture and society.

19

THE PROPHET

WHAT IS a prophet, from the perspective of sociology?
We shall forego here any consideration of the general question
regarding the "bringer of salvation" (*Heilbringer*) as raised by
Breysig. Not every anthropomorphic god is a deified bringer of
salvation, whether external or internal salvation. And certainly
not every provider of salvation became a god or even a savior,
although such phenomena were widespread.

We shall understand "prophet" to mean a purely individual
bearer of charisma, who by virtue of his mission proclaims a religious doctrine or divine commandment. No radical distinction will
be drawn between a "renewer of religion" who preaches an older
revelation, actual or supposititious, and a "founder of religion"
who claims to bring completely new deliverances. The two types
merge into one another. In any case, the formation of a new religious community need not be the result of doctrinal preaching by
prophets, since it may be produced by the activities of non-pro-
phetic reformers. Nor shall we be concerned in this context with
the question whether the followers of a prophet are more attracted
to his person, as in the cases of Zoroaster, Jesus, and Muhammad,

From *The Sociology of Religion* by Max Weber, first published in German
as "Religionssoziologie," from *Wirtschaft und Gesellschaft*, copyright ©
1922 by J. C. B. Mohr (Paul Siebeck). Fourth edition, revised by Johannes Winckelmann, copyright © 1956 by J. C. B. Mohr (Paul Siebeck).
English translation (from the fourth edition) by Ephraim Fischoff, copyright © 1963 by Beacon Press. All rights reserved. Reprinted by permission
of Beacon Press.

or to his doctrine, as in the cases of Buddha and the prophets of Israel.

For our purposes here, the personal call is the decisive element distinguishing the prophet from the priest. The latter lays claim to authority by virtue of his service in a sacred tradition, while the prophet's claim is based on personal revelation and charisma. It is no accident that almost no prophets have emerged from the priestly class. As a rule, the Indian teachers of salvation were not Brahmins, nor were the Israelite prophets priests. Zoroaster's case is exceptional in that there exists a possibility that he may have descended from the hieratic nobility. The priest, in clear contrast, dispenses salvation by virtue of his office. Even in cases in which personal charisma may be involved, it is the hierarchical office that confers legitimate authority upon the priest as a member of a corporate enterprise of salvation.

But the prophet, like the magician, exerts his power simply by virtue of his personal gifts. Unlike the magician, however, the prophet claims definite revelations, and the core of his mission is doctrine or commandment, not magic. Outwardly, at least, the distinction is fluid, for the magician is frequently a knowledgeable expert in divination, and sometimes in this alone. At this stage, revelation functions continuously as oracle or dream interpretation. Without prior consultation with the magician, no innovations in communal relations could be adopted in primitive times. To this day, in certain parts of Australia, it is the dream revelations of magicians that are set before the councils of clan heads for adoption, and it is a mark of secularization that this practice is receding.

On the other hand, it was only under very unusual circumstances that a prophet succeeded in establishing his authority without charismatic authentication, which in practice meant magic. At least the bearers of new doctrine practically always needed such validation. It must not be forgotten for an instant that the entire basis of Jesus' own legitimation, as well as his claim that he and only he knew the Father and that the way to God led through faith in him alone, was the magical charisma he felt within himself. It was doubtless this consciousness of power, more than anything else, that enabled him to traverse the road of the prophets. During the apostolic period of early Christianity and thereafter the figure of the wandering prophet was a constant phenomenon. There was always required of such prophets a proof of their possession of particular gifts of the spirit, of special magical or ecstatic abilities. Prophets very often practiced divination as well as magical healing and counseling. This was true, for example, of the prophets (*nabi, nebim*) so frequently mentioned in the Old Testament, especially in the prophetic books and Chronicles. But what distinguishes the prophet, in the sense that we are employing the term, from the types just described is an economic factor, i.e., that his prophecy is unremunerated. Thus, Amos indignantly rejected the appellation of *nabi*. This criterion of gratuitous service also distinguishes the prophet from the priest. The typical prophet propagates ideas for their own sake and not for fees, at least in any obvious or regulated form. The provisions enjoining the non-remunerative character of prophetic propaganda have taken various forms. Thus developed the carefully cultivated postulate that the apostle, prophet, or teacher of ancient Christianity must not professionalize his religious proclamations. Also, limitations were set upon the length of the time he could enjoy the hospitality of his friends. The Christian prophet was enjoined to live by the labor of his own hands or, as among the Buddhists, only from alms which he had not specifically solicited. These injunctions were repeatedly emphasized in the Pauline epistles, and in another form, in the Buddhist monastic regulations. The dictum "whosoever will not work, shall not eat" applied to missionaries, and it constitutes one of the chief mysteries of the success of prophetic propaganda itself.

The period of the older Israelitic prophecy at about the time of Elijah was an epoch of strong prophetic propaganda throughout the Near East and Greece. It is likely that prophecy in all its forms arose, especially in the Near East, in connection with the growth of great world empires in Asia, and the resumption and intensification of international commerce after a long interruption. At that time Greece was exposed to the invasion of the Thracian cult of Dionysos, as well as to the most diverse types of prophecies. In addition to the semiprophetic social reformers, certain purely religious movements now broke into the magical and cultic lore of the Homeric priests. Emotional cults, emotional prophecy based on "speaking with tongues," and highly valued intoxicating ecstasy vied with the evolving theological rationalism (Hesiod); the incipient cosmogonic and philosophic speculation was intersected by philosophical mystery doctrines and salvation religions. The growth of these emotional cults paralleled both overseas colonization and, above all, the formation of cities and the transformation of the *polis* which resulted from the development of a citizen army.

It is not necessary to detail here these developments of the eighth and seventh centuries, so brilliantly analyzed by Rohde, some of which reached into the sixth and even the fifth century. They were contemporary with Jewish, Persian, and Hindu prophetic movements, and probably also with the achievements of Chinese ethics in the pre-Confucian period, although we have only scant knowledge of the latter. These Greek "prophets" differed widely among themselves in regard to the economic criterion of professionalism, and in regard to the possession of a "doctrine." The Greeks also made a distinction between professional teaching and unremunerated propagandizing of ideas, as we see from the example of Socrates. In Greece, furthermore, there existed a clear differentiation between the only real congregational type of religion, namely Orphism with its doctrine of salvation, and every other type of prophecy and technique of salvation, especially those of the mysteries. The basis of this distinction was the presence in Orphism of a genuine doctrine of salvation.

Our primary task is to differentiate the various types of prophets from the sundry purveyors of salvation, religious or otherwise. Even in historical times the transition from the prophet to the legislator is fluid, if one understands the latter to mean a personage who in any given case has been assigned the responsibility of codifying a law systematically or of reconstituting it, as was the case notably with the Greek *aisymnete* (e.g., Solon, Charondas, etc.). In no case did such a legislator or his labor fail to receive divine approval, at least subsequently.

A legislator is quite different from the Italian *podesta*, who is summoned from outside the group, not for the purpose of creating a new social order, but to provide a detached, impartial arbitrator, especially for cases in which the adversaries are of the same social status. On the other hand, legislators were generally, though not always, called to their office when social tensions were in evidence. This was apt to occur with special frequency in the one situation which commonly provided the earliest stimulus to a planned social policy. One of the conditions fostering the need for a new planned policy was the economic development of a warrior class as a result of growing monetary wealth and the debt enslavement of another stratum; an additional factor was the dissatisfaction arising from the unrealized political aspirations of a rising commercial class which, having acquired wealth through economic activity, was now challenging the old warrior nobility. It was the function of the *aisymnete* to resolve the conflicts between classes and to produce a new sacred law of eternal validity, for which he had to secure divine approbation.

It is very likely that Moses was a historical figure, in which case he would be classified functionally as an *aisymnete*. For the prescriptions of the oldest sacred legislation of the Hebrews presuppose a money economy and hence sharp conflicts of class interests, whether impending or already existing, within the confederacy. It was Moses' great achievement to find a compromise solution of, or prophylactic for, these class conflicts (e.g., the *seisachthie* of the year of release) and to organize the Israelite confederacy by means of an integral national god. In essence, his work stands midway between the functioning of an ancient *aisymnete* and that of Muhammad. The reception of the law formulated by Moses stimulated a period of expansion of the new unified people in much the same way that the leveling of classes stimulated expansion in so many other cases, particularly in Athens and Rome. The scriptural dictum that "after Moses there arose not in Israel any prophet like unto him" means that the Jews never had another *aisymnete*.

Not only were none of the prophets *aisymnetes* in this sense, but in general what normally passes for prophecy does not belong to this category. To be sure, even the later prophets of Israel were concerned with social reform. They hurled their "woe be unto you" against those who oppressed and enslaved the poor, those who joined field to field, and those who deflected justice by bribes. These were the typical actions leading to class stratification everywhere in the ancient world, and were everywhere intensified by the development of the city-state (*polis*). Jerusalem too had been organized into a city-state by the time of these later prophets. A distinctive concern with social reform is characteristic of Israelite prophets. This concern is all the more notable, because such a trait is lacking in Hindu prophecy of the same period, although the conditions in India at the time of the Buddha have been described as relatively similar to those in Greece during the sixth century.

An explanation for Hebrew prophecy's unique concern for social reform is to be sought in religious grounds, which we shall set forth subsequently. But it must not be forgotten that in the motivation of the Israelite prophets these social reforms were only means to an end. Their primary concern was with foreign politics, chiefly because it constituted the theater of their god's activity. The Israelite prophets were concerned with social and other types of injustice as a violation of the Mosaic code primarily in order to explain god's wrath, and not in order to institute a program of social reform. It is noteworthy that the real theoretician of social reform, Ezekiel, was a priestly theorist who can scarcely be categorized as a prophet at all. Finally, Jesus was not at all interested in social reform as such.

Zoroaster shared with his cattle-raising people a hatred of the despoiling nomads, but the heart of his message was essentially religious. His central concerns were his faith in his own divine mission and his struggle against the magical cult of ecstasy. A similar primary focus upon religion appeared very clearly in the case of Muhammad, whose program of social action, which Umar carried through consistently, was oriented almost entirely to the goal of the psychological preparation of the faithful for battle in order to maintain a maximum number of warriors for the faith.

It is characteristic of the prophets that they do not receive their mission from any human agency, but seize it, as it were. To be sure, usurpation also characterized the assumption of power by tyrants in the Greek *polis*. These Greek tyrants remind one of the legal *aisymnetes* in their general functioning, and they frequently pursued their own characteristic religious policies, e.g., supporting the emotional cult of Dionysos, which was popular with the masses rather than with the nobility. But the aforementioned assumption of power by the prophets came about as a consequence of divine revelation, essentially for religious purposes. Furthermore, their characteristic religious message and their struggle against ecstatic cults tended to move in an opposite direction from that taken by the typical religious policy of the Greek tyrants. The religion of Muhammad, which is fundamentally political in its orientation, and his position in Medina, which was in between that of an Italian *podesta* and that of Calvin at Geneva, grew primarily out of his purely prophetic mission. A merchant, he was first a leader of pietistic conventicles in Mecca, until he realized more and more clearly that the organization of the interests of warrior clans in the acquisition of booty was the external basis provided for his missionizing.

On the other hand, there are various transitional phases linking the prophet to the teacher of ethics, especially the teacher of social ethics. Such a teacher, full of a new or recovered understanding of ancient wisdom, gathers disciples about him, counsels private individuals in personal matters and nobles in questions relating to public affairs, and purports to mold ethical ways of life, with the ultimate goal of influencing the crystallization of ethical regulations. The bond between the teacher of religious or philosophical wisdom and his disciple is uncommonly strong and is regulated in an authoritarian fashion, particularly in the sacred laws of Asia. Everywhere the disciple-master relationship is classified among those involving reverence. Generally, the doctrine of magic, like that of heroism, is so regulated that the novice is assigned to a particularly experienced master or is required to seek him out. This is comparable to the relationship in German fraternities, in which the junior member (the *Leibbursche*) is attached by a kind of personal piety to the senior member (the *Leibfuchs*), who watches over his training. All the Greek poetry of pederasty derives from such a relationship of respect, and similar phenomena are to be found among Buddhists and Confucianists, indeed in all monastic education.

The most complete expression of this disciple-master relationship is to be found in the position of the *guru* in Hindu sacred law. Every young man belonging to polite society was unconditionally required to devote himself for many years to the instruction and direction of life provided by such a Brahminic teacher. The obligation of obedience to the *guru*, who had absolute power over his charges, a relationship comparable to that of the occidental *famulus* to his *magister*, took precedence over loyalty to family, even as the position of the court Brahmin (*purohita*) was officially regulated so as to raise his position far above that of the most powerful father confessor in the Occident. Yet the *guru* is, after all, only a teacher who transmits acquired, not revealed, knowledge, and this by virtue of a commission and not on his own authority.

The philosophical ethicist and the social reformer are not prophets in our sense of the word, no matter how closely they may seem to resemble prophets. Actually, the oldest Greek sages, who like Empedocles are wreathed in legend, and other Greek sages such as Pythagoras stand closer to the prophets. They have left at least some legacy of a distinctive doctrine of salvation and conduct of life, and they laid some claim to the status of savior. Such intellectual teachers of salvation have parallels in India, but the Greek teachers fell far short of the Hindu teachers in consistently focusing both life and doctrine on salvation.

Even less can the founders and heads of actual "schools of philosophy" be regarded as prophets in our sense, no matter how closely they may approach this category in some respects. From Confucius, in whose temple even the emperor made obeisance, graded transitions lead to Plato. But both of them were simply academic teaching philosophers, who differed chiefly in that Confucius was centrally concerned and Plato only occasionally concerned to influence princes in the direction of particular social reforms.

What primarily differentiates such figures from the prophets is their lack of that vital emotional preaching which is distinctive of prophecy, regardless of whether this is disseminated by the spoken word, the pamphlet, or any other type of literary composition (e.g., the *suras* of Muhammad). The enterprise of the prophet is closer to that of the popular orator (*demagogue*) or political publicist than to that of the teacher. On the other hand, the activity of a Socrates, who also felt himself opposed to the professional teaching enterprise of the Sophists, must be distinguished in theory from the activities of a prophet, by the absence of a directly revealed religious mission in the case of Socrates. Socrates' daemon (*daimonion*) reacted only to concrete situations, and then only to dissuade and admonish. For Socrates, this was the outer limit of his ethical and strongly utilitarian rationalism, which occupied for him the position that magical divination assumed for Confucius. For this reason, Socrates' daemon cannot be compared at all to the conscience of a genuine religious ethic; much less can it be regarded as the instrument of prophecy.

Such a divergence from the characteristic traits of the Hebrew prophets holds true of all philosophers and their schools as they were known in China, India, ancient Hellas, and in the medieval period among Jews, Arabs, and Christians alike. All such philosophies had the same sociological form. But philosophic teaching, as in the case of the Cynics, might take the form of an exemplary prophecy of salvation (in the sense presently to be explained) by virtue of practicing the pattern of life achieved and propagated by a particular school. These prophets and their schools might, as in the case of the Cynics, who protested against the sacramental grace of the mysteries, show certain outer and inner affinities to Hindu and Oriental ascetic sects. But the prophet, in our special sense, is never to be found where the proclamation of a religious truth of salvation through personal revelation is lacking. In our view, this qualification must be regarded as the decisive hallmark of prophecy.

Finally, the Hindu reformers of religion such as Shankara and Ramanuja and their occidental counterparts like Luther, Zwingli, Calvin, and Wesley are to be distinguished from the category of prophets by virtue of the fact that they do not claim to be offering a substantively new revelation or to be speaking in the name of a special divine injunction. This is what characterized the founder of the Mormon church, who resembled, even in matters of detail, Muhammad and above all the Jewish prophets. The prophetic type is also manifest in Montanus and Novitianus, and in such figures as Mani and Manus, whose message had a more rational doctrinal content than did that of George Fox, a prophet type with emotional nuances.

When we have separated out from the category of prophet all the aforementioned types, which sometimes abut very closely, various others still remain. The first is that of the mystagogue. He performs sacraments, i.e., magical actions that contain the boons of salvation. Throughout the entire world there have been saviors of this type whose difference from the average magician is only one of degree, the extent of which is determined by the formation of a special congregation around him. Very frequently dynasties of mystagogues developed on the basis of a sacramental charisma which was regarded as hereditary. These dynasties maintained their prestige for centuries, investing their disciples with great authority and thus developing a kind of hierarchical position. This was especially true in India, where the title of *guru* was also used to designate distributors of salvation and their plenipotentiaries. It was likewise the case in China, where the hierarch of the Taoists and the heads of certain secret sects played just such hereditary roles. Finally, one type of exemplary prophet to be discussed presently was also generally transformed into a mystagogue in the second generation.

The mystagogues were also very widely distributed throughout the Near East, and they entered Greece in the prophetic age to which reference was made earlier. Yet the far more ancient noble families, who were the hereditary incumbents of the Eleusinian mysteries, also represented at least another marginal manifestation of the simple hereditary priestly families. Ethical doctrine was lacking in the mystagogue, who distributed magical salvation, or at least doctrine played only a very subordinate role in his work. Instead, his primary gift was hereditarily transmitted magical art. Moreover, he normally made a living from his art, for which there was a great demand. Consequently we must exclude

him too from the conception of prophet, even though he sometimes revealed new ways of salvation.

Thus, there remain only two kinds of prophets in our sense,
one represented most clearly by the Buddha, the other with especial clarity by Zoroaster and Muhammad. The prophet may be
primarily, as in the cases just noted, an instrument for the proclamation of a god and his will, be this a concrete command or an
abstract norm. Preaching as one who has received a commission
from god, he demands obedience as an ethical duty. This type we
shall term the "ethical prophet." On the other hand, the prophet
may be an exemplary man who, by his personal example, demonstrates to others the way to religious salvation, as in the case of the
Buddha. The preaching of this type of prophet says nothing about
a divine mission or an ethical duty of obedience, but rather directs
itself to the self-interest of those who crave salvation, recommend-
ing to them the same path as he himself traversed. Our designation
for this second type of prophecy is "exemplary."

The exemplary type is particularly characteristic of prophecy
in India, although there have been a few manifestations of it in
China (e.g., Lao Tzu) and the Near East. On the other hand, the
ethical type is confined to the Near East, regardless of racial differences there. For neither the Vedas nor the classical books of
the Chinese—the oldest portions of which in both cases consist of
songs of praise and thanksgiving by sacred singers, and of magical rites and ceremonies—makes it appear at all probable that
prophecy of the ethical type, such as developed in the Near East
or Iran, could ever have arisen in India or China. The decisive
reason for this is the absence of a personal, transcendental, and
ethical god. In India this concept was found only in a sacramental
and magical form, and then only in the later and popular faiths.
But in the religions of those social classes within which the decisive prophetic conceptions of Mahavira and Buddha were developed, ethical prophecy appeared only intermittently and was
constantly subjected to reinterpretations in the direction of pan-
theism. In China the notion of ethical prophecy was altogether
lacking in the ethics of the class that exercised the greatest influence in the society. To what degree this may presumably be as-

sociated with the intellectual distinctiveness of such classes, which was of course determined by various social factors, will be discussed later.

As far as purely religious factors are concerned, it was decisive for both India and China that the conception of a rationally regulated world had its point of origin in the ceremonial order of sacrifices, on the unalterable sequence of which everything depended. In this regard, crucial importance was attached to the indispensable regularity of meteorological processes, which were thought of in animistic terms. What was involved here was the normal activity or inactivity of the spirits and demons. According to both classical and heterodox Chinese views, these processes were held to be insured by the ethically proper conduct of government, that followed the correct path of virtue, the Tao; without this everything would fail, even according to Vedic doctrine. Thus, in India and China, rita and Tao respectively represented similar superdivine, impersonal forces.

On the other hand, the personal, transcendental and ethical god is a Near-Eastern concept. It corresponds so closely to that of an all-powerful mundane king with his rational bureaucratic regime that a causal connection can scarcely be overlooked. Throughout the world the magician is in the first instance a rainmaker, for the harvest depends on timely and sufficient rain, though not in excessive quantity. Until the present time the pontifical Chinese emperor has remained a rainmaker, for in northern China, at least, the uncertainty of the weather renders dubious the operation of irrigation procedures, no matter how extensive they are. Of greater significance was the construction of dams and internal canals, which became the real source of the imperial bureaucracy. The emperor sought to avert meteorological disturbances through sacrifices, public atonement, and various virtuous practices, e.g., the termination of abuses in the administration, or the organization of a raid on unpunished malefactors. For it was always assumed that the reason for the excitation of the spirits and the disturbances of the cosmic order had to be sought either in the personal derelictions of the monarch or in some manifestation of social disorganization. Again, rain was one of the rewards promised by Yahweh to his devotees, who were at that time primarily agriculturalists, as is clearly apparent in the older portions of the tradition. God promised neither too scanty rain nor yet excessive precipitation or deluge.

But throughout Mesopotamia and Arabia, however, it was not rain that was the creator of the harvest, but artificial irrigation alone. In Mesopotamia, irrigation was the sole source of the absolute power of the monarch, who derived his income by compelling his conquered subjects to build canals and cities adjoining them, just as the regulation of the Nile was the source of the Egyptian monarch's strength. In the desert and semiarid regions of the Near East this control of irrigation waters was indeed one source of the conception of a god who had created the earth and man out of nothing and not merely fashioned them, as was believed elsewhere. A riparian economy of this kind actually did produce a harvest out of nothing, from the desert sands. The monarch even created law by legislation and rationalization, a development the world experienced for the first time in Mesopotamia. It seems quite reasonable, therefore, that as a result of such experiences the ordering of the world should be conceived as the law of a freely acting, transcendental and personal god.

Another, and negative, factor accounting for the development in the Near East of a world order that reflected the operation of a personal god was the relative absence of those distinctive classes who were the bearers of the Hindu and Chinese ethics, and who created the godless religious ethics found in those countries. But even in Egypt, where originally Pharaoh himself was a god, the attempt of Ikhnaton to produce an astral monotheism foundered because of the power of the priesthood, which had by then systematized popular animism and become invincible. In Mesopotamia the development of monotheism and demagogic prophecy was opposed by the ancient pantheon, which was politically organized and had been systematized by the priests, and was further opposed and limited by the rigid development of the state.

The kingdom of the Pharaohs and of Mesopotamia made an even more powerful impression upon the Israelites than the great Persian monarch, the *basileus kat exochen,* made upon the Greeks (the strong impact of Cyrus upon the Greeks is mirrored in the eulogistic account of him formulated in the pedagogical treatise, the *Cyropaidia*, despite the defeat of this monarch). The Israelites had gained their freedom from the "house of bondage" of the earthly Pharaoh only because a divine king had come to their assistance. Indeed, their subsequent establishment of a worldly monarchy was expressly declared to be a declension from Yahweh, the real ruler of the people. Hebrew prophecy was completely oriented to a relationship with the great political powers of the time, the great kings, who as the rods of God's wrath first destroy Israel and then, as a consequence of divine intervention, permit Israelites to return from the Exile to their own land. In the case of Zoroaster too it can be asserted that the range of his vision was also oriented to the views of the civilized lands of the West.

Thus, the distinctive character of the earliest prophecy, in both its dualistic and monotheistic forms, seems to have been determined decisively—aside from the operation of certain other concrete historical influences—by the pressure of relatively contiguous great centers of rigid social organization upon less developed neighboring peoples. The latter tended to see in their own continuous peril from the pitiless bellicosity of terrible nations the anger and grace of a heavenly king.

Regardless of whether a particular religious prophet is predominantly of the ethical or predominantly of the exemplary type, prophetic revelation involves for both the prophet himself and for his followers—and this is the element common to both varieties—a unified view of the world derived from a consciously integrated and meaningful attitude toward life. To the prophet, both the life of man and the world, both social and cosmic events, have a certain systematic and coherent meaning. To this meaning the conduct of mankind must be oriented if it is to bring salvation, for only in relation to this meaning does life obtain a unified and significant pattern. Now the structure of this meaning may take varied forms, and it may weld together into a unity motives that are logically quite heterogeneous. The whole conception is dominated, not by logical consistency, but by practical valuations. Yet it always denotes, regardless of any variations in scope and in measure of success, an effort to systematize all the manifestations of life; that is, to organize practical behavior into a direction of life, regardless of the form it may assume in any individual case. Moreover, it always contains the important religious conception of the world as a cosmos which is challenged to produce somehow a "meaningful," ordered totality, the particular manifestations of which are to be measured and evaluated according to this requirement.

The conflict between empirical reality and this conception of the world as a meaningful totality, which is based on a religious postulate, produces the strongest tensions in man's inner life as well as in his external relationship to the world. To be sure, this problem is by no means dealt with by prophecy alone. Both priestly wisdom and all completely nonsacerdotal philosophy, the intellectualist as well as the popular varieties, are somehow concerned with it. The ultimate question of all metaphysics has always been something like this: if the world as a whole and life in particular were to have a meaning, what might it be, and how would the world have to look in order to correspond to it? The religious problem-complex of prophets and priests is the womb from which non-sacerdotal philosophy emanated, wherever it developed. Subsequently, non-sacerdotal philosophy was bound to take issue with the antecedent thought of the religious functionaries; and the struggle between them provided one of the very important components of religious evolution. Hence, we must now examine more closely the mutual relationships of priests, prophets, and non-priests.

20

THE DIFFERENT ROADS
TO SALVATION

THE INFLUENCE any religion exerts on the conduct of life, and especially on the conditions of rebirth, varies in accordance with the particular path to salvation which is desired and striven for, and in accordance with the psychological quality of the salvation in question. We may first note that salvation may be the accomplishment of the individual himself without any assistance on the part of supernatural powers, e.g., in ancient Buddhism.

One path to salvation leads through the purely ritual activities and ceremonies of cults, both within religious worship and in everyday behavior. Pure ritualism as such is not very different from magic in its effect on the conduct of life. Indeed, ritualism may even lag behind magic, inasmuch as magical religion occasionally produced a definite and rather thorough methodology of rebirth, which ritualism did not always succeed in doing. A religion of salvation may systematize the purely formal and specific activities of ritual into a devotion with a distinctive religious mood, in which the rites to be performed are symbols of the divine. In such a case the religious mood is the true instrument of salvation. Once emphasis has been placed on this inward aspect

From *The Sociology of Religion* by Max Weber, first published in German as "Religionssoziologie," from *Wirtschaft und Gesellschaft*, copyright © 1922 by J. C. B. Mohr (Paul Siebeck). Fourth edition, revised by Johannes Winckelmann, copyright © 1956 by J. C. B. Mohr (Paul Siebeck). English translation (from the fourth edition) by Ephraim Fischoff, copyright © 1963 by Beacon Press. All rights reserved. Reprinted by permission of Beacon Press.

of salvation, the bare and formal magical ritualism becomes super-
fluous. This happened as a matter of course again and again in the
routinization of all devotional religions.

The consequences of a ritualistic religion of devotion may be
quite diversified. The comprehensive ritualistic regimentation of
life among pious Hindus, which by European standards placed extraordinary daily demands upon the devout, actually rendered virtually impossible any intensive acquisitive economic activity in
communities which followed faithfully the religious injunctions for
a meritorious life in this world. Such extreme devotional piety is
diametrically opposite to Puritanism in one respect: such a program of ritualism could be executed completely only by a man of
means, who is free from the burden of hard work. But this circumstance limiting the number of those whose conduct of life can be
influenced by ritualism is to some extent avoidable, whereas another inherent limiting circumstance is even more basic to the
nature of ritualism.

Ritualistic salvation, especially when it limits the layman to a
spectator role, confines his participation to simple or essentially
passive manipulations, or sublimates the ritual mood into the most
emotional sort of piety, stresses the mood content of the particular
devotional factor that appears to bring the salvation. Consequently, the possession of an essentially ephemeral subjective state
is striven after, and this subjective state—because of the idiosyncratic irresponsibility characterizing, for example, the hearing of
a mass or the witnessing of a mystical play— has only a negligible
effect on behavior once the ceremony is over. The meager influence such experiences frequently have upon everyday ethical living may be compared to the insignificant influence of a beautiful
and inspiring play upon the theater public which has witnessed it.
All salvation deriving from mysteries has such an inconstant character. Mysteries purport to produce their effect *ex opere operato*
by means of a pious occasional devotion. They provide no inner
motivation for any such requirement as the believer's demonstration in his life pattern of a religious norm, such as a rebirth might
entail.

On the other hand, when the occasional devotion induced by

ritual is escalated into a continuing piety and the effort is made to incorporate this piety into everyday living, this ritualistic piety most readily takes on a mystical character. This transition is facilitated by the requirement that religious devotion lead to the participant's possession of a subjective state. But the disposition to mysticism is an individual charisma. Hence, it is no accident that the great mystical prophecies of salvation, like the Hindu and others in the Orient, have tended to fall into pure ritualism as they have become routinized. What is of primary concern to us is that in ritualism the psychological condition striven for ultimately leads directly away from rational activity. Virtually all mystery cults have this effect. Their typical intention is the accomplishment, by the sheer sacredness of their manipulations, of redemption from guilt and the distribution of sacramental grace. Like every form of magic, this process has a tendency to become diverted from everyday life, thereby failing to exert any influence upon it.

But a sacrament might have a very different effect if its distribution and administration were linked to the presupposition that the sacrament could bring salvation only to those who have become ethically purified in the sight of god, and might indeed bring ruin to all others. Even up to the threshold of the present time, large groups of people have felt a terrifying fear of the Lord's Supper (the sacrament of the Eucharist) because of the doctrine that "whoever does not believe and yet eats, eats and drinks himself to judgment." Such factors could exert a strong influence upon everyday behavior wherever, as in ascetic Protestantism, there was no central source for the provision of absolution, and where further participation in the sacramental communion occurred frequently, providing a very important index of piety. . . .

A developing systematization of an ethic of "good works" may assume either of two very different forms. In the first major form of systematization of an ethic of good works, the particular actions of an individual in quest of salvation, whether virtuous or wicked actions, can be evaluated singly and credited to or subtracted from the individual's account. Each individual is regarded as the carrier of his own behavior pattern and as possessing ethical standards only tenuously; he may turn out to be a weaker or a stronger creature in the face of temptation, according to the force of the subjective or external situation. Yet it is held that his religious fate depends upon his actual achievements, in their relationship to one another.

This first type of systematization is consistently followed in Zoroastrianism, particularly in the oldest Gathas by the founder himself, which depict the judge of all the dead balancing the guilt and merit of individual actions in a very precise bookkeeping and determining the religious fate of the individual person according to the outcome of this accounting. This notion appears among the Hindus in an even more heightened form, as a consequence of the doctrine of *karma*. It is held that within the ethical mechanism of the world not a single good or evil action can ever be lost. Each action, being ineradicable, must necessarily produce, by an almost automatic process, inevitable consequences in this life or in some future rebirth. This essential principle of life-accounting also remained the basic view of popular Judaism regarding the individual's relationship to God. Finally, Roman Catholicism and the oriental Christian churches held views very close to this, at least in practice. The *intentio*, to which reference must be made for the ethical evaluation of behavior in Catholicism, is more than a simple and uniform quality of personality, of which conduct is the expression. Rather, it is the "significance" (*Meinung*) in the mind of the person (in the sense of the *bona fides, mala fides, culpa*, and *dolus* of the Roman law) which leads him to perform any particular action. This view, when consistently maintained, eschews the yearning for rebirth in the strict sense of an ethic of inwardness. A result is that the conduct of life remains, from the viewpoint of ethics, an unmethodical and miscellaneous succession of discrete actions.

The second major form of systematization of an ethic of good works treats individual actions as symptoms and expressions of an underlying ethical total personality. It is instructive to recall the attitude of some of the more rigorous Spartans toward one of their comrades who had fallen in battle after having sought such a death as a purification measure which would atone for an earlier manifestation of cowardice. They did not regard him as having rehabilitated his ethical status, since he had acted bravely for a specific reason and not "out of the totality of his personality," as we would term it. In the religious sphere too, formal sanctification by the good works shown in external actions is supplanted by the value of the total personality pattern, which in the Spartan example would be an habitual temper of heroism. A similar principle applies to social actions of all sorts. If they demonstrate "love for one's fellow man," then ethical systematization of this kind requires that the actor possess the charisma of "goodness."

It is of ultimate importance that the specific action be really symptomatic of the total character and that no significance be attached to it when it is a result of accident. This ethic of inwardness, in its most highly systematized forms, may make increased demands at the level of the total personality and yet be more tolerant in regard to particular transgressions. But this is not always the case, and the ethic of inwardness is generally the most distinctive form of ethical rigorism. On the one hand, a total personality pattern with positive religious qualifications may be regarded as a divine gift, the presence of which will manifest itself in a general orientation to whatever is demanded by religion, namely a pattern of life integrally and methodically oriented to the values of religion. On the other hand, a religious total personality pattern may be envisaged as something which may in principle be acquired through training in goodness. Of course this training itself will consist of a rationalized, methodical direction of the entire pattern of life, and not an accumulation of single, unrelated actions. Although these two views of the origin of a religious total personality pattern produce very similar practical results, yet one particular result of the methodical training of the total personality pattern is that the social and ethical quality of actions falls into secondary importance, while the religious effort expended upon oneself becomes of primary importance. Consequently, religious good works with a social orientation become mere instruments of *self-perfection*.

Perfecting of the self is of course equivalent to a planned procedure for attaining religious consecration. Now ethical religions are by no means the first to produce such a planned procedure. On the contrary, highly systematized planned procedures frequently played significant roles in those awakenings to charismatic rebirth which promised the acquisition of magical powers. This animistic trend of thinking entailed belief in the incarnation of a new soul within one's own body, the possession of one's soul by a powerful demon, or the removal of one's soul to a realm of spirits. In all cases the possibilty of attaining superhuman actions and powers was involved. "Other-worldly" goals were of course completely lacking in all this. What is more, this capacity for ecstasy might be used for the most diverse purposes. Thus, only by acquiring a new soul through rebirth can the warrior achieve superhuman deeds of heroism. The original sense of "rebirth" as producing either a hero or a magician remains present in all vestigial initiation ceremonies, e.g., the reception of youth into the religious brotherhood of the phratry and their equipment with the paraphernalia of war, or the decoration of youth with the insignia of manhood in China and India (where the members of the higher castes are termed the "twice-born"). All these ceremonies were originally associated with activities which produced or symbolized ecstasy, and the only purpose of the associated training regimens is the testing or arousing of the capacity for ecstasy.

Ecstasy as an instrument of salvation or self-deification, our exclusive interest here, may have the essential character of an acute mental aberration or possession, or else the character of a chronically heightened idiosyncratic religious mood, tending either toward greater intensity of life or toward alienation from life. This escalated, intensified religious mood can be of either a more contemplative or a more active type. It should go without saying that a planned methodology of sanctification was not the means used to produce the state of acute ecstasy. The various methods for breaking down organic inhibitions were of primary importance in producing ecstasy. Organic inhibitions were broken down by the production of acute toxic states induced by alcohol, tobacco, or other drugs which have intoxicating effects; by music and dance; by sexuality; or by a combination of all three—in short by orgies. Ecstasy was also produced by the provocation of hysterical or epileptoid seizures among those with predispositions toward such paroxysms, which in turn produced orgiastic states in others. However, these acute ecstasies are transitory in their nature and apt to leave but few positive traces on everyday behavior. Moreover, they lack the meaningful content revealed by prophetic religion.

It would appear that a much more enduring possession of the charismatic condition is promised by those milder forms of euphoria which may be experienced as either a dreamlike mystical illumination or a more active and ethical conversion. Furthermore, they produce a meaningful relationship to the world, and they correspond in quality to evaluations of an eternal order or an ethical god such as are proclaimed by prophecy. We have already seen that magic is acquainted with a systematic procedure of sanctification for the purpose of evoking charismatic qualities, in addition to its last resort to the acute orgy. For professional magicians and warriors need permanent states of charisma as well as acute ecstasies.

Not only do the prophets of ethical salvation not need orgiastic intoxication, but it actually stands in the way of the systematic ethical patterning of life they require. For this reason, the primary target of Zoroaster's indignant ethical rationalism was orgiastic ecstasy, particularly the intoxicating cult of the soma sacrifice, which he deemed unworthy of man and cruel to beasts. For the same reason, Moses directed his rationalized ethical attack against the orgy of the dance, just as many founders or prophets of ethical religion attacked "whoredom," i.e., orgiastic temple prostitution. As the process of rationalization went forward, the goal of methodically planned religious sanctification increasingly transformed the acute intoxication induced by orgy into a milder but more permanent *habitus*, and moreover one that was consciously possessed. This transformation was strongly influenced by, among other things, the particular concept of the divine that was entertained. The ultimate purpose to be served by the planned procedure of sanctification remained everywhere the same purpose which was served in an acute way by the orgy, namely the incarnation within man of a supernatural being, and therefore presently of a god. Stated differently, the goal was self-deification. Only now this incarnation had to become a continuous personality pattern, so far as possible. Thus, the entire planned procedure for achieving consecration was directed to attaining this possession of the god himself here on earth.

But wherever there is belief in a transcendental god, all-powerful in contrast to his creatures, the goal of methodical sanctification can no longer be self-deification (in the sense in which the transcendental god is deified) and must become the acquisition of those religious qualities the god demands in men. The goal of sanctification becomes oriented to the world beyond and to ethics. The aim is no longer to possess god, for this cannot be done, but either to become his instrument or to be spiritually suffused by him. Spiritual suffusion is obviously closer to self-deification than is instrumentality. This difference had important consequences for the planned procedure of sanctification itself, as we shall later explain. But in the beginning of this development there were important points of agreement between the methods directed at instrumentality and those directed at spiritual suffusion. In both cases the average man had to eliminate from his everyday life whatever was not godlike, so that he himself might become more like god. The primary ungodlike factors were actually the average *habitus* of the human body and the everyday world, as those are given by nature. . . .

Yet the gap between unusual and routine religious experiences tends to be eliminated by evolution towards the systematization and rationalization of the methods for attaining religious sanctification. Out of the unlimited variety of subjective conditions which may be engendered by methodical procedures of sanctification, certain of them may finally emerge as of central importance, not only because they represent psycho-physical states of extraordinary quality, but because they also appear to provide a secure and continuous possession of the distinctive religious acquirement. This is the *assurance of grace* (*certitudo salutis, perseverantia gratia*). This certainly may be characterized by a more mystical or by a more actively ethical coloration, about which more will be said presently. But in either case, it constitutes the conscious possession of a lasting, integrated foundation for the conduct of life.

To heighten the conscious awareness of this religious possession, orgiastic ecstasy and irrational, emotional, and merely irritating methods of deadening sensation are replaced, principally by planned reductions of bodily functioning, such as can be achieved by continuous malnutrition, sexual abstinence, regulation of respiration, and the like. In addition, thinking and other psychological processes are trained in a systematic concentration of the soul upon whatever is alone essential in religion. Examples of such psychological training are found in the Hindu techniques of Yoga, the continuous repetition of sacred syllables (e.g., *Om*), meditation focused on circles and other geometrical figures, and various exercises designed to effect a planned evacuation of the consciousness.

But in order to further secure continuity and uniformity in the possession of the religious good, the rationalization of the methodology of sanctification finally evolved even beyond the methods just mentioned to an apparent inversion, a planned limitation of the exercises to those devices which tend to insure continuity of the religious mood. This meant the abandonment of all techniques that are irrational from the viewpoint of hygiene. For just as every sort of intoxication, whether it be the orgiastic ecstasy of heroes in erotic orgies or the ecstasy of terpsichorean frenzies, inevitably culminates in physical collapse, so hysterical suffusion with religious emotionalism leads to psychic collapse, which in religious terminology is termed a state of profound abandonment by god. . . .

When methodical techniques for attaining sanctification stressed ethical conduct based on religious sentiment, one practical result was the transcendence of particular desires and emotions of raw human nature which had not hitherto been controlled by religion. We must determine for each particular religion whether it regarded cowardice, brutality, selfishness, sensuality, or some other natural drive as the one most prone to divert the individual from his charismatic character. This matter belongs among the most important substantive characteristics of any particular religion. But the methodical religious doctrine of sanctification always remains, in this sense of transcending human nature, an ethic of virtuosi. Like magical charisma, it always requires demonstration by the virtuosi. As we have already established, religious virtuosi possess authentic certainty of their sanctification only as long as their own virtuoso religious temper continues to maintain itself in spite of all temptations. This holds true whether the religious adept is a brother in a world-conquering order like that of the Muslims at the time of Umar or whether he is a world-fleeing ascetic like most monks of either the Christian or the less consistent Jainist type. It is equally true of the Buddhist monk, a virtuoso of world-rejecting contemplation, and the ancient Christian, who was sometimes an exponent of passive martyrdom and sometimes, like the ascetic Protestant, a virtuoso of the demonstration of religious merit in one's calling. Finally, this holds true of the formal legalism of the Pharisaic Jew and of the acomistic goodness of such persons as St. Francis. This maintenance of the certainty of sanctification varied in its specific character, depending on the type of religious salvation involved, but it always—both in the case of the Buddhist *arhat* and the case of the pristine Christian—required the upholding of religious and ethical standards, and hence the avoidance of at least the most venal sins.

Demonstration of the certainty of grace takes very different forms, depending on the concept of religious salvation in the particular religion. In pristine Christianity, a person of positive religious qualification, namely one who had been baptized, was bound never again to fall into any mortal sin. "Mortal sin" designates the type of sin which destroys religious qualification. Therefore, it is unpardonable, or at least capable of remission only at the hands of someone specially qualified by virtue of his possession of charisma to endow the sinner anew with religious charisma (the loss of which constituted mortal sin). When this virtuoso doctrine became untenable in practice within the ancient Christian communities, the Montanist group clung firmly and consistently to one virtuoso requirement, that the sin of cowardice remain unpardonable, quite as the Islamic religion of heroic warriors unfailingly punished apostasy with death. Accordingly, the Montanists segregated themselves from the mass church of the average Christians when the persecutions under Decius and Diocletian made even this virtuoso requirement impractical, in view of the interest of the priests in maintaining the largest possible membership in the community.

As we have already stated at a number of points, the specific character of the certification of salvation and also of the associated practical conduct is completely different in religions which differently represent the character of the promised salvation, the possession of which assures blessedness. Salvation may be viewed as the distinctive gift of active ethical behavior performed in the awareness that god directs this behavior, i.e., that the actor is an instrument of god. We shall designate this type of attitude toward salvation, which is characterized by a methodical procedure for achieving religious salvation, as "ascetic." This designation is for our purposes here, and we do not in any way deny that this term may be and has been used in another and wider sense. The contrast between our usage and the wider usage may become clearer later on in this work.

Religious virtuosity, in addition to subjecting the natural drives to a systematic patterning of life, always leads to the control of relationships within communal life, the conventional virtues of which are inevitably unheroic and utilitarian, and leads further to an altogether radical religious and ethical criticism. Not only do the simple, "natural" virtues within the world not guarantee salvation, but they actually place salvation in hazard by producing illusions as to that which alone is indispensable. The "world" in the religious sense, i.e., the domain of social relationships, is therefore a realm of temptations. The world is full of temptations, not only because it is the site of sensual pleasures which are ethically irrational and completely diverting from things divine, but even more because it fosters in the religiously average person complacent self-sufficiency and self-righteousness in the fulfillment of common obligations, at the expense of the uniquely necessary concentration on active achievements leading to salvation.

21

ASCETICISM, MYSTICISM, AND SALVATION RELIGION

THE CONTRAST between the ascetic and mystical modes of behavior is clearest when the full implications of world-rejection and world-flight are not drawn. The ascetic, when he wishes to act within the world, that is, to practice inner-worldly asceticism, must become afflicted with a sort of happy stupidity regarding any question about the meaning of the world, for he must not worry about such questions. Hence, it is no accident that inner-worldly asceticism reached its most consistent development on the foundation of the Calvinist god's absolute inexplicability, utter remoteness from every human criterion, and unsearchableness as to his motives. Thus, the inner-worldly ascetic is the recognized "man of a vocation," who neither inquires about nor finds it necessary to inquire about the meaning of his actual practice of a vocation within the world, the total framework of which is not his responsibility but his god's. For him it suffices that through his rational actions in this world he is personally executing the will of god, which is unsearchable in its ultimate significance.

On the other hand, the contemplative mystic is not in a position to realize his primary aim of perceiving the essential meaning

---

From *The Sociology of Religion* by Max Weber, first published in German as "Religionssoziologie," from *Wirtschaft und Gesellschaft*, copyright © 1922 by J. C. B. Mohr (Paul Siebeck). Fourth edition, revised by Johannes Winckelmann, copyright © 1956 by J. C. B. Mohr (Paul Siebeck). English translation (from the fourth edition) by Ephraim Fischoff, copyright © 1963 by Beacon Press. All rights reserved. Reprinted by permission of Beacon Press.

of the world and then comprehending it in a rational form, for the very reason that he has already conceived of the essential meaning of the world as a unity beyond all empirical reality. Mystical contemplation has not always resulted in a flight from the world in the sense of an avoidance of every contact with the social milieu. On the contrary, the mystic may also require of himself the maintenance of his state of grace against every pressure of the mundane order, as an index of the enduring character of that very state of grace. In that case, even the mystic's position within the institutional framework of the world becomes a vocation, but one leading in an altogether different direction from any vocation produced by inner-worldly asceticism.

Neither asceticism nor contemplation affirms the world as such. The ascetic rejects the world's empirical character of creatureliness and ethical irrationality, and rejects its ethical temptations to sensual indulgence, to epicurean satisfaction, and to reliance upon natural joys and gifts. But at the same time he affirms individual rational activity within the institutional framework of the world, affirming it to be his responsibility as well as his means for securing certification of his state of grace. On the other hand, the contemplative mystic living within the world regards action, particularly action performed within the world's institutional framework, as in its very nature a temptation against which he must maintain his state of grace.

The contemplative mystic minimizes his activity by resigning himself to the order of the world as it is, and lives incognito, so to speak, as humble people have always done, since god has ordained once and for all that man must live in the world. The activity of the contemplative mystic within the world is characterized by a distinctive brokenness, colored by humility. He is contantly striving to escape from activity in the world back to the quietness and inwardness of his god. Conversely, the ascetic, whenever he acts in conformity with his type, is certain to become god's instrument. For this reason the ascetic's humility, which he considers a necessary obligation incumbent upon a creature of god, is always of dubious genuineness. Therefore the success of the ascetic's action is a success of the god himself, who has contributed to the action's success, or at the very least the success is a special sign of divine blessing upon the ascetic and his activity. But for the genuine mystic, no success which may crown his activity within the world can have any significance with respect to salvation. For him, his maintenance of true humility within the world is his sole warranty for the conclusion that his soul has not fallen prey to the snares of the world. As a rule, the more the genuine mystic remains within the world, the more broken his attitude toward it becomes, in contrast to the proud aristocratic feeling with respect to salvation entertained by the contemplative mystic who lives apart from the world.

For the ascetic, the certainty of salvation always demonstrates itself in rational action, integrated as to meaning, end, and means, and governed by principles and rules. Conversely, for the mystic who actually possesses a subjectively appropriated state of salvation the result of this subjective condition may be antinomianism. His salvation manifests itself not in any sort of activity but in a subjective condition and its idiosyncratic quality. He feels himself no longer bound by any rule of conduct; regardless of his behavior, he is certain of salvation. Paul had to struggle with this consequence, among others, of mystical contemplation (*panta moi eksestin*); and in numerous other contexts the abandonment of rules for conduct has been an occasional result of the mystical quest for salvation.

For the ascetic, moreover, the divine imperative may require of human creatures an unconditional subjection of the world to the norms of religious virtue, and indeed a revolutionary transformation of the world for this purpose. In that event, the ascetic will emerge from his remote and cloistered cell to take his place in the world as a prophet in opposition to the world. But he will always demand of the world an ethically rational order and discipline, corresponding to his own methodical self-discipline. Now a mystic may arrive at a similar position in relation to the world. His sense of divine inwardness, the chronic and quiet euphoria of his solitary contemplative possession of substantively divine salvation, may become transformed into an acute feeling of sacred possession by or possession of the god who is speaking in and through him. He will then wish to bring eternal salvation to men as soon as they have prepared, as the mystic himself has done, a place for god upon earth, i.e., in their souls. But in this case the result will be the emergence of the mystic as a magician who causes his power to be felt among gods and demons; and this may have the practical consequence of the mystic's becoming a mystagogue, something which has actually happened very often.

If the mystic does not follow this path towards becoming a mystagogue, for a variety of reasons which we hope to discuss later, he may bear witness to his god by doctrine alone. In that case his revolutionary preaching to the world will be chiliastically irrational, scorning every thought of a rational order in the world. He will regard the absoluteness of his own universal acosmistic feeling of love as completely adequate for himself, and indeed regard this feeling as the only one acceptable to his god as the foundation for a mystically renewed community among men, because this feeling alone derives from a divine source. The transformation of a mysticism remote from the world into one characterized by chiliastic and revolutionary tendencies took place frequently, most impressively in the revolutionary mysticism of the sixteenth-century Baptists. The contrary transformation has also occurred, as in the conversion of John Lilburne to Quakerism.

To the extent that an inner-worldly religion of salvation is determined by contemplative features, the usual result is the acceptance of the secular social structure which happens to be at hand, an acceptance that is relatively indifferent to the world but at least humble before it. A mystic of the type of Tauler completes his day's work and then seeks contemplative union with his god in the evening, going forth to his usual work the next morning, as Tauler movingly suggests, in the correct inner state. Similarly, Lao Tzu taught that one recognizes the man who has achieved union with the Tao by his humility and by his self-depreciation before other men. The mystic component in Lutheranism, for which the highest bliss available in this world is the ultimate *unio mystica,* was responsible along with other factors for the indifference of the Lutheran church towards the external organization of the preaching of the gospel, and also for that church's anti-ascetic and traditionalistic character.

In any case, the typical mystic is never a man of conspicuous social activity, nor is he at all prone to accomplish any rational transformation of the mundane order on the basis of a methodical pattern of life directed toward external success. Wherever genuine mysticism did give rise to communal action, such action was characterized by the acosmism of the mystical feeling of love. Mysticism may exert this kind of psychological effect, thus tending— despite the apparent demands of logic—to favor the creation of communities (*gemeinschaftsbildend*).

The core of the mystical concept of the oriental Christian church was a firm conviction that Christian brotherly love, when sufficiently strong and pure, must necessarily lead to unity in all things, even in dogmatic beliefs. In other words, men who sufficiently love one another, in the Johannine sense of love, will also think alike and, because of the very irrationality of their common feeling, act in a solidary fashion which is pleasing to God. Because of this concept, the Eastern church could dispense with an infallibly rational authority in matters of doctrine. The same view is basic to the Slavophile conception of the community, both within and beyond the church. Some forms of this notion were also common in ancient Christianity. The same conception is at the basis of Muhammad's belief that formal doctrinal authorities can be dispensed with. Finally, this conception along with other factors accounts for the minimization of organization in the monastic communities of early Buddhism.

Conversely, to the extent that an inner-worldly religion of salvation is determined by distinctively ascetical tendencies, the usual result is practical rationalism, in the sense of the maximization of rational action as such, the maximization of a methodical systematization of the external conduct of life, and the maximization of the rational organization and institutionalization of mundane social systems, whether monastic communities or theocracies.

22

CASTES, ESTATES, CLASSES, AND RELIGION

THE LOT of peasants is so strongly tied to nature, so dependent on organic processes and natural events, and economically so little oriented to rational systematization that in general the peasantry will become a carrier of religion only when it is threatened by enslavement or proletarization, either by domestic forces (financial, agrarian, or seignorial) or by some external political power.

Ancient Israelite religious history already manifested both major threats to the peasant class: first, pressures from foreign powers that threatened enslavement, and second, opposition between peasants and domestic land owners (who in antiquity resided in the cities). The oldest documents, particularly the *Song of Deborah*, reveal the typical essential elements of the struggle of a peasant confederacy, involving associative processes comparable to those of the Aetolians, Samnites, and Swiss. Another point of similarity with the Swiss situation is that Palestine possessed the geographical character of a land bridge, being situated on a great trade route which spanned the terrain from Egypt to the Euphrates. This facilitated culture contacts, and accordingly, Pal-

estine produced a money economy fairly early. The Israelite confederacy directed its efforts against both the Philistines and the
Canaanite land magnates who dwelt in the cities. These latter were
knights who fought with iron chariots, "warriors trained from
their very youth," as Goliath was described, who sought to enslave
and render tributary the peasantry of the mountain slopes through
which flowed milk and honey.

It was a most significant constellation of historical factors that
this struggle, as well as the unification of the tribes and the expansion of the Mosaic period, was constantly renewed under the leadership of the Yahweh religion's saviors ("messiahs," from *ma-
shiah*, which means "the anointed one"—like Gideon and like
others termed "judges"). Because of this distinctive leadership,
a religious concern that far transcended the level of the usual
agrarian cults entered very early into the ancient religion of the
Palestinian peasantry. But not until the city of Jerusalem had been
conquered did the cult of Yahweh, with its Mosaic social legislation, become a genuinely ethical religion. Indeed, as the social
admonitions of the prophets demonstrate, even here this took
place partly under the influence of agrarian social reform movements directed against the urban land magnates and financial
nabobs, and by reference to the social prescriptions of the Mosaic
law regarding the equalization of classes.

But prophetic religion has by no means been the product of
agrarian influences alone. A typically plebeian urban destiny was
one of the primary dynamic factors in the social reform doctrine
of the first and only theologian of official Greek literature, Hesiod.
The more agrarian the essential social pattern of a culture, e.g.,
Rome, India, or Egypt, the more likely it is that the agrarian element of the population will fall into a pattern of traditionalism
and that religion, at least that of the masses, will lack ethical rationalization. Thus, in the later development of Judaism and
Christianity, the peasants never appeared as the carriers of rational ethical movements. This statement is completely true of
Judaism, while in Christianity the participation of the peasantry
in rational ethical movements took place only in exceptional cases
and then in a communist, revolutionary form. The puritanical sect

of the Donatists in Roman Africa, the Roman province of greatest land accumulation, appears to have been very popular among the peasantry, but this was the sole example of peasant concern for a rational ethical movement in antiquity. The Taborites, who were partially derived from peasant groups, the German peasant protagonists of "divine right" in peasant wars, the English radical communist farmers, and above all the Russian peasant sectarians —all these have points of contact with agrarian communism by virtue of their more or less explicit development of institutionalized communal ownership of land. All these groups felt themselves threatened by proletarization, and they turned against the official church in the first instance because it was the recipient of tithes and served as a bulwark of the financial and landed magnates. The association of the aforementioned peasant groups with religious demands was possible only on the basis of an already existing ethical religion which contained specific prophecies or promises that might suggest and justify a revolutionary "law of nature." More will be said about this in another context.

Hence, manifestations of a close relationship between peasant religion and agrarian reform movements did not occur in Asia, where the combination of religious prophecy with revolutionary currents, e.g., as in China, took a different direction altogether, and did not assume the form of a real peasant movement. Only rarely does the peasant class serve as the carrier of any other sort of religion than their original magic. . . .

In early Christianity, it will be recalled, the rustic was simply regarded as the heathen (*paganus*). Even the official doctrine of medieval churches, as formulated by Thomas Aquinas, treated the peasant essentially as a Christian of lower rank, and at best accorded him very little esteem. The religious glorification of the peasant and the belief in the special worth of his piety is the result of a very modern development. It was characteristic of Lutheranism in particular—in rather strongly marked contrast to Calvinism and to most of the other Protestant sects—as well as of modern Russian religion, which manifest Slavophile influences. These are ecclesiastical communities which, by virtue of their type or organization, are very closely tied to the authoritarian interests of princes and noblemen upon whom they are dependent. In modern Lutheranism (for this was not the position of Luther himself) the dominant interest is the struggle against the rationalism of the intellectuals, and against political liberalism. In the ideology of the Slavophile religious peasant, the primary concern was the struggle against capitalism and modern socialism. Finally, the glorification of the Russian sectarians by the *Narodniki* combined an anti-rationalist protest against intellectualism with the revolt of a proletarized class of farmers against a bureaucratic church that was serving the interests of the ruling classes, thereby surrounding both components of the social struggle with a religious aura. Thus, what was involved in all cases was very largely a reaction against the development of modern rationalism, of which the cities were regarded as the carriers.

In striking contrast to all this is the fact that it was the city which, in earlier times, was regarded as the site of piety. As late as the seventeenth century, Baxter saw in the relationships of the weavers of Kidderminster to the metropolis of London (made possible by the development of domestic industry) a definite enhancement of the weavers' piety. Actually, early Christianity was an urban religion, and as Harnack decisively demonstrated, its importance in any particular city was in direct proportion to the size of the urban community. In the Middle Ages too, fidelity to the church, as well as sectarian movements in religion, characteristically developed in the cities. It is highly unlikely that an organized congregational religion, such as early Christianity became, could have developed as it did apart from the community life of a city (notably in the sense found in the Occident). For early Christianity presupposed as already extant certain conceptions, viz., the transcendence of taboo barriers between clans, the concept of office, and the concept of the community as an institution (*Anstalt*), an organized corporate entity serving specific realistic functions. To be sure, Christianity, on its part, strengthened these conceptions, and greatly facilitated the renewed reception of them by the growing European cities during the Middle Ages. But actually these notions reached their fullest development exclusively within the Mediterranean culture, particularly in Greek and then definitely in Roman urban law. What is more, the specific qualities of Christianity as an ethical religion of salvation and as personal piety found their real nurture in the urban environment; and it is there that they constantly set in motion new stimuli in contrast to the ritualistic, magical or formalistic re-interpretation favored by the dominant feudal powers.

As a rule, the class of warrior nobles, and indeed feudal powers generally, have not readily become the carriers of a rational religious ethic. The life pattern of a warrior has very little affinity with the notion of a beneficent providence, or with the systematic ethical demands of a transcendental god. Concepts like sin, salvation, and religious humility have not only seemed remote from all elite political classes, particularly the warrior nobles, but have indeed appeared reprehensible to its sense of honor. To accept a religion that works with such conceptions and to genuflect before the prophet or priest would appear plebeian and dishonorable to any martial hero or noble person, e.g., the Roman nobility of the age of Tacitus, or the Confucian mandarins. It is an everyday psychological event for the warrior to face death and the irrationalities of human destiny. Indeed, the chances and adventures of mundane existence fill his life to such an extent that he does not require of his religion (and accepts only reluctantly) anything beyond protection against evil magic or such ceremonial rites as are congruent with his caste, such as priestly prayers for victory or for a blissful death leading directly into the hero's heaven.

As has already been mentioned in another connection, the educated Greek always remained a warrior, at least in theory. The simple animistic belief in spirits which left vague the qualities of existence after death and finally dropped the entire question (though remaining certain that the most miserable status here on earth was preferable to ruling over Hades), remained the normal faith of the Greeks until the time of the complete destruction of their political autonomy. The only developments beyond this were the mystery religions, which provided means for ritualistic improvement of the human condition in this world and in the next. The only radical departure from this position was the Orphic congregational religion, with its doctrine of metempsychosis.

Periods of strong prophetic or reformist religious agitation have frequently pulled the nobility in particular into the path of prophetic ethical religion, because this type of religion breaks through all classes and estates, and because the nobility has generally been the first carrier of lay education. But presently the routinization of prophetic religion had the effect of eliminating the nobility from the circle of groups characterized by religious enthusiasm. This is already evident at the time of the religious wars in France in the conflicts of the Huguenot synods with a leader like Condé over ethical questions. Ultimately, the Scotch nobility, like the British and the French, was completely extruded from the Calvinist religion in which it, or at least some of its groups, had originally played a considerable role.

As a rule, prophetic religion is naturally compatible with the class feeling of the nobility when it directs its promises to the warrior in the cause of religion. This conception assumes the exclusiveness of a universal god and the moral depravity of unbelievers who are his adversaries and whose untroubled existence arouses his righteous indignation. Hence, such a notion is absent in the Occident of ancient times, as well as in all Asiatic religion until Zoroaster. Indeed, even in Parsism a direct connection between religious promises and war against religious infidelity is still lacking. It was Islam that first produced this conjunction of ideas. . . .

The distinctive attitude of a bureaucracy to religious matters has been classically formulated in Confucianism. Its hallmark is an absolute lack of feeling of a need for salvation or for any transcendental anchorage for ethics. In its place resides what is substantively an opportunistic and utilitarian (though aesthetically attractive) doctrine of conventions appropriate to a bureaucratic caste. Other factors in the bureaucratic attitude toward religion include the elimination of all those emotional and irrational manifestations of personal religion which go beyond the traditional belief in spirits, and the maintenance of the ancestral cult and of filial piety as the universal basis for social subordination. Still another ingredient of bureaucratic religions is a certain distance from the spirits, the magical manipulation of which is scorned by the enlightened official (but in which the superstitious one may participate, as is the case with spiritualism among us today). Yet both types of bureaucratic officials will, with contemptuous indifference, permit such spiritualistic activity to flourish as the religion of the masses (*Volksreligiosität*). Insofar as this popular religion comes to expression in recognized state rites, the official continues to respect them, outwardly at least, as a conventional obligation appropriate to his status. The continuous retention of magic, especially of the ancestral cult, as the guarantee of social obedience, enabled the Chinese bureaucracy to completely suppress all independent ecclesiastical development and all congregational religion. As for the European bureaucracy, although it generally shared such subjective disesteem for any serious concern with religion, it found itself compelled to pay more official respect to the existing churches in the interest of control over the masses.

If certain fairly uniform tendencies are normally apparent, in spite of all differences in the religious attitude of the nobility and bureaucracy, the classes with the maximum social privilege, the real "middle" classes evince striking contrasts. Moreover, this is something quite apart from the rather sharp differences of status which these classes manifest within themselves. Thus, in some instances, merchants may be members of the most highly privileged class, as in the case of the ancient urban patriciate, while in others they may be pariahs, like impecunious wandering peddlers. Again, they may be possessed of considerable social privilege, though occupying a lower social status than the nobility or officialdom; or they may be without privilege, or indeed dispriviledged, yet actually exerting great social power. Examples of the latter would be the Roman knights, the Hellenic *metoikoi,* the medieval tailors and other merchant groups, the financiers and great merchant princes of Babylonia, the Chinese and Hindu traders, and finally the bourgeoisie of the modern period.

Apart from these differences of social position, the attitude of the commercial patriciate toward religion shows characteristic contrasts in all periods of history. In the nature of the case, the strongly mundane orientation of their life precludes their having much inclination for prophetic or ethical religion. The activity of the great merchants of antiquity and medieval times represented a distinctive kind of specifically occasional and unprofessional acquisition of money, e.g., by providing capital for traveling traders who required it. Originally rural dwellers possessing landed estates, these merchants became, in historical times, an urbanized nobility which had grown rich from such occasional trade. On the other hand, they might have started as tradesmen who having acquired landed property were seeking to climb into the families of the nobility. To the category of the commercial patriciate there were added, as the financing of public enterprises developed, the representatives of finance whose primary business was to meet the financial needs of the state by supplying necessary material and governmental credit, together with the financiers of colonial capitalism, an enterprise that has existed in all periods of history. None of these classes has ever been the primary carrier of an ethical or salvation religion. At any rate, the more privileged the position of the commercial class, the less it has evinced any inclination to develop an other-worldly religion. . . .

But as against these easily understandable phenomena, the acquisition of new capital or, more correctly, capital continuously and rationally employed in a productive enterprise for the acquisition of profit, especially in industry (which is the characteristically modern employment of capital) has in the past been combined frequently and in a striking manner with a rational, ethical congregational religion among the classes in question. In the business life of India there was even a (geographical) differentiation between the Parsees and the Jain sect. The former, adherents of the religion of Zoroaster, retained their ethical rigorism, particularly its unconditional injunction regarding truthfulness, even after modernization had caused a reinterpretation of the ritualistic commandments of purity as hygienic prescriptions. The economic morality of the Parsees originally recognized only agriculture as acceptable to God, and abominated all urban acquisitive pursuits. On the other hand, the sect of the Jains, the most ascetic of the religions of India, along with the aforementioned Vallabhacharis represented a salvation doctrine that was constituted as congregational religion, despite the anti-rational character of the cults. It is difficult to prove that the Islamic commercial religion of traders was particularly widespread among the dervishes, but it is not unlikely. As for Judaism, the ethical rational religion of the Jewish community was already in antiquity largely a religion of traders or financiers.

To a lesser but still notable degree, the religion of the medieval Christian community, particularly of the sectarian type or of the heretical circles was, if not a religion appropriate to traders, nonetheless a middle-class religion, and that in direct proportion to its ethical rationalism. The closest connection between ethical religion and rational economic development—particularly capitalism—was effected by all the forms of ascetic Protestantism and sectarianism in both Western and Eastern Europe, viz., Zwinglians, Calvinists, Reformed Baptists, Mennonites, Quakers, Methodists, and Pietists (both of the Reformed and, to a lesser degree, Lutheran varieties); as well as by Russian schismatic, heretical, and rational pietistic sects, especially the Stundists and Skoptzi, though in very different forms. Indeed, generally speaking, the inclination to join an ethical, rational, congregational religion becomes more strongly marked the farther away one gets from those social classes which have been the carriers of the type of capitalism which is primarily political in orientation. Since the time of Hammurabi this situation has existed wherever there has been tax farming, the profitable provision of the state's political needs, war, piracy, large-scale usury, and colonization. The tendency toward affiliation with an ethical, rational, congregational religion is more apt to be found the closer one gets to those classes which have been the carriers of modern rational productive economic activity, i.e., those classes with middle-class economic characteristics, in the sense to be expounded later.

Obviously, the mere existence of capitalism of some sort is not sufficient, by any means, to produce a uniform ethic, not to speak of an ethical congregational religion. Indeed, it does not automatically produce any uniform consequences. For the time being, no analysis will be made of the kind of causal relationship subsisting between a rational religious ethic and a particular type of commercial rationalism, where such a connection exists at all. At this point, we desire only to establish the existence of an affinity between economic rationalism and certain types of rigoristic ethical religion, to be discussed later. This affinity comes to light only occasionally outside the Occident, which is the distinctive seat of economic rationalism. In the West, this phenomenon is very clear and its manifestations are the more impressive as we approach the classical bearers of economic rationalism.

23

SCIENCE AS A VOCATION

A REALLY DEFINITIVE and good accomplishment is today always a specialized accomplishment. And whoever lacks the capacity to put on blinders, so to speak, and to come up to the idea that the fate of his soul depends upon whether or not he makes the correct conjecture at this passage of this manuscript may as well stay away from science. He will never have what one may call the 'personal experience' of science. Without this strange intoxication, ridiculed by every outsider; without this passion, this 'thousands of years must pass before you enter into life and thousands more wait in silence'—according to whether or not you succeed in making this conjecture; without this, you have *no* calling for science and you should do something else. For nothing is worthy of man as man unless he can pursue it with passionate devotion.

Yet it is a fact that no amount of such enthusiasm, however sincere and profound it may be, can compel a problem to yield scientific results. Certainly enthusiasm is a prerequisite of the 'inspiration' which is decisive. Nowadays in circles of youth there is a widespread notion that science has become a problem in calculation, fabricated in laboratories or statistical filing systems just as 'in a factory,' a calculation involving only the cool intellect and not one's 'heart and soul.' First of all one must say that such comments lack all clarity about what goes on in a factory or in a

From *Max Weber: Essays in Sociology*, edited and translated by H. H. Gerth and C. Wright Mills. Copyright 1946 by Oxford University Press, Inc. Reprinted by permission.

laboratory. In both some idea has to occur to someone's mind, and it has to be a correct idea, if one is to accomplish anything worthwhile. And such intuition cannot be forced. It has nothing to do with any cold calculation. Certainly calculation is also an indispensable prerequisite. No sociologist, for instance, should think himself too good, even in his old age, to make tens of thousands of quite trivial computations in his head and perhaps for months at a time. One cannot with impunity try to transfer this task entirely to mechanical assistants if one wishes to figure something, even though the final result is often small indeed. But if no 'idea' occurs to his mind about the direction of his computations and, during his computations, about the bearing of the emergent single results, then even this small result will not be yielded.

Normally such an 'idea' is prepared only on the soil of very hard work, but certainly this is not always the case. Scientifically, a dilettante's idea may have the very same or even a greater bearing for science than that of a specialist. Many of our very best hypotheses and insights are due precisely to dilettantes. The dilettante differs from the expert, as Helmholtz has said of Robert Mayer, only in that he lacks a firm and reliable work procedure. Consequently he is usually not in the position to control, to estimate, or to exploit the idea in its bearings. The idea is not a substitute for work; and work, in turn, cannot substitute for or compel an idea, just as little as enthusiasm can. Both, enthusiasm and work, and above all both of them *jointly*, can entice the idea.

Ideas occur to us when they please, not when it pleases us. The best ideas do indeed occur to one's mind in the way in which Ihering describes it: when smoking a cigar on the sofa; or as Helmholtz states of himself with scientific exactitude: when taking a walk on a slowly ascending street; or in a similar way. In any case, ideas come when we do not expect them, and not when we are brooding and searching at our desks. Yet ideas would certainly not come to mind had we not brooded at our desks and searched for answers with passionate devotion.

However this may be, the scientific worker has to take into his bargain the risk that enters into all scientific work: Does an 'idea' occur or does it not? He may be an excellent worker and yet never have had any valuable idea of his own. It is a grave error to believe that this is so only in science, and that things for instance in a business office are different from a laboratory. A merchant or a big industrialist without 'business imagination,' that is, without ideas or ideal intuitions, will for all his life remain a man who would better have remained a clerk or a technical official. He will never be truly creative in organization. Inspiration in the field of science by no means plays any greater role, as academic conceit fancies, than it does in the field of mastering problems of practical life by a modern entrepreneur. On the other hand, and this also is often misconstrued, inspiration plays no less a role in science than it does in the realm of art. It is a childish notion to think that a mathematician attains any scientifically valuable results by sitting at his desk with a ruler, calculating machines or other mechanical means. The mathematical imagination of a Weierstrass is naturally quite differently oriented in meaning and result than is the imagination of an artist, and differs basically in quality. But the psychological processes do not differ. Both are frenzy (in the sense of Plato's 'mania') and 'inspiration.'

Now, whether we have scientific inspiration depends upon destinies that are hidden from us, and besides upon 'gifts.' Last but not least, because of this indubitable truth, a very understandable attitude has become popular, especially among youth, and has put them in the service of idols whose cult today occupies a broad place on all street corners and in all periodicals. These idols are 'personality' and 'personal experience.' Both are intimately connected, the notion prevails that the latter constitutes the former and belongs to it. People belabor themselves in trying to 'experience' life—for that befits a personality, conscious of its rank and station. And if we do not succeed in 'experiencing' life, we must at least pretend to have this gift of grace. Formerly we called this 'experience,' in plain German, 'sensation'; and I believe that we then had a more adequate idea of what personality is and what it signifies.

Ladies and gentlemen. In the field of science only he who is devoted *solely* to the work at hand has 'personality.' And this holds not only for the field of science; we know of no great artist who has ever done anything but serve his work and only his work. As far as his art is concerned, even with a personality of Goethe's rank, it has been detrimental to take the liberty of trying to make his 'life' into a work of art. And even if one doubts this, one has to be a Goethe in order to dare permit oneself such liberty. Everybody will admit at least this much: that even with a man like Goethe, who appears once in a thousand years, this liberty did not go unpaid for. In politics matters are not different, but we shall not discuss that today. In the field of science, however, the man who makes himself the impresario of the subject to which he should be devoted, and steps upon the stage and seeks to legitimate himself through 'experience,' asking: How can I prove that I am something other than a mere 'specialist' and how can I manage to say something in form or in content that nobody else has ever said? —such a man is no 'personality.' Today such conduct is a crowd phenomenon, and it always makes a petty impression and debases the one who is thus concerned. Instead of this, an inner devotion to the task, and that alone, should lift the scientist to the height and dignity of the subject he pretends to serve. And in this it is not different with the artist.

In contrast with these preconditions which scientific work shares with art, science has a fate that profoundly distinguishes it from artistic work. Scientific work is chained to the course of progress; whereas in the realm of art there is no progress in the same sense. It is not true that the work of art of a period that has worked out new technical means, or, for instance, the laws of perspective, stands therefore artistically higher than a work of art devoid of all knowledge of those means and laws—if its form does justice to the material, that is, if its object has been chosen and formed so that it could be artistically mastered without applying those conditions and means. A work of art which is genuine 'fulfilment' is never surpassed; it will never be antiquated. Individuals may differ in appreciating the personal significance of works of art, but no one will ever be able to say of such a work that it is 'outstripped by another work which is also "fulfilment."'

In science, each of us knows that what he has accomplished will be antiquated in ten, twenty, fifty years. That is the fate to which science is subjected; it is the very *meaning* of scientific work, to which it is devoted in a quite specific sense, as compared with other spheres of culture for which in general the same holds. Every scientific 'fulfilment' raises new 'questions'; it *asks* to be 'surpassed' and outdated. Whoever wishes to serve science has to resign himself to this fact. Scientific works certainly can last as 'gratifications' because of their artistic quality, or they may remain important as a means of training. Yet they will be surpassed scientifically—let that be repeated—for it is our common fate and, more, our common goal. We cannot work without hoping that others will advance further than we have. In principle, this progress goes on *ad infinitum*. And with this we come to inquire into the *meaning* of science. . . .

It means the knowledge or belief that if one but wished one *could* learn it at any time. Hence, it means that principally there are no mysterious incalculable forces that come into play, but rather that one can, in principle, master all things by calculation. This means that the world is disenchanted. One need no longer have recourse to magical means in order to master or implore the spirits, as did the savage, for whom such mysterious powers existed. Technical means and calculations perform the service. This above all is what intellectualization means.

Now, this process of disenchantment, which has continued to exist in Occidental culture for millennia, and, in general, this 'progress,' to which science belongs as a link and motive force, do they have any meanings that go beyond the purely practical and technical? You will find this question raised in the most principled form in the works of Leo Tolstoi. He came to raise the question in a peculiar way. All his broodings increasingly revolved around the problem of whether or not death is a meaningful phenomenon. And his answer was: for civilized man death has no meaning. It has none because the individual life of civilized man, placed into an infinite 'progress,' according to its own imminent meaning should never come to an end; for there is always a further step ahead of one who stands in the march of progress. And no man who comes to die stands upon the peak which lies in infinity. Abraham, or some peasant of the past, died 'old and satiated with life' because he stood in the organic cycle of life; because his life, in terms of its meaning and on the eve of his days, had given to him what life had to offer; because for him there remained no puzzles he might wish to solve; and therefore he could have had 'enough' of life. Whereas civilized man, placed in the midst of the continuous enrichment of culture by ideas, knowledge, and problems, may become 'tired of life' but not 'satiated with life.' He catches only the most minute part of what the life of the spirit brings forth ever anew, and what he seizes is always something provisional and not definitive, and therefore death for him is a meaningless occurrence. And because death is meaningless, civilized life as such is meaningless; by its very 'progressiveness' it gives death the imprint of meaninglessness. Throughout his late novels one meets with this thought as the keynote of the Tolstoyan art.

What stand should one take? Has 'progress' as such a recognizable meaning that goes beyond the technical, so that to serve it is a meaningful vocation? The question must be raised. But this is no longer merely the question of man's calling *for* science, hence, the problem of what science as a vocation means to its devoted disciples. To raise this question is to ask for the vocation of science within the total life of humanity. What is the value of science?

Here the contrast between the past and the present is tremendous. You will recall the wonderful image at the beginning of the seventh book of Plato's *Republic:* those enchained cavemen whose faces are turned toward the stone wall before them. Behind them lies the source of the light which they cannot see. They are concerned only with the shadowy images that this light throws upon the wall, and they seek to fathom their interrelations. Finally one of them succeeds in shattering his fetters, turns around, and sees the sun. Blinded, he gropes about and stammers of what he saw. The others say he is raving. But gradually he learns to behold the light, and then his task is to descend to the cavemen and to lead them to the light. He is the philosopher; the sun, however, is the truth of science, which alone seizes not upon illusions and shadows but upon the true being.

Well, who today views science in such a manner? Today youth feels rather the reverse: the intellectual constructions of science constitute an unreal realm of artificial abstractions, which with their bony hands seek to grasp the blood-and-the-sap of true life without ever catching up with it. But here in life, in what for Plato was the play of shadows on the walls of the cave, genuine reality is pulsating; and the rest are derivatives of life, lifeless ghosts, and nothing else. How did this change come about?

Plato's passionate enthusiasm in *The Republic* must, in the last analysis, be explained by the fact that for the first time the *concept,* one of the great tools of all scientific knowledge, had been consciously discovered. Socrates had discovered it in its bearing. He was not the only man in the world to discover it. In India one finds the beginnings of a logic that is quite similar to that of Aristotle. But nowhere else do we find this realization of the significance of the concept. In Greece, for the first time, appeared a handy means by which one could put the logical screws upon somebody so that he could not come out without admitting either that he know nothing or that this and nothing else was truth, the *eternal* truth that never would vanish as the doings of the blind men vanish. That was the tremendous experience which dawned upon the disciples of Socrates. And from this it seemed to follow that if one only found the right concept of the beautiful, the good, or, for instance, of bravery, of the soul—or whatever—that then one could also grasp its true being. And this, in turn, seemed to open the way for knowing and for teaching how to act rightly in life and, above all, how to act as a citizen of the state; for this question was everything to the Hellenic man, whose thinking was political throughout. And for these reasons one engaged in science.

The second great tool of scientific work, the rational experiment, made its appearance at the side of this discovery of the Hellenic spirit during the Renaissance period. The experiment is a means of reliably controlling experience. Without it, present-day empirical science would be impossible. There were experiments earlier; for instance, in India physiological experiments were made in the service of ascetic yoga technique; in Hellenic antiquity, mathematical experiments were made for purposes of war technology; and in the Middle Ages, for purposes of mining. But to raise the experiment to a principle of research was the achievement of the Renaissance. They were the great innovators in *art*, who were the pioneers of experiment. Leonardo and his like and, above all, the sixteenth-century experimenters in music with their experimental pianos were characteristic. From these circles the experiment entered science, especially through Galileo, and it entered theory through Bacon; and then it was taken over by the various exact disciplines of the continental universities, first of all those of Italy and then those of the Netherlands.

What did science mean to these men who stood at the threshold of modern times? To artistic experimenters of the type of Leonardo and the musical innovators, science meant the path to *true* art, and that meant for them the path to true *nature*. Art was to be raised to the rank of a science, and this meant at the same time and above all to raise the artist to the rank of the doctor, socially and with reference to the meaning of his life. This is the ambition on which, for instance, Leonardo's sketch book was based. And today? 'Science as the way to nature' would sound like blasphemy to youth. Today, youth proclaims the opposite: redemption from the intellectualism of science in order to return to one's own nature and therewith to nature in general. Science as a way to art? Here no criticism is even needed.

But during the period of the rise of the exact sciences one expected a great deal more. If you recall Swammerdam's statement, 'Here I bring you the proof of God's providence in the anatomy of a louse,' you will see what the scientific worker, influenced (indirectly) by Protestantism and Puritanism, conceived to be his task: to show the path to God. People no longer found this path among the philosophers, with their concepts and deductions. All pietist theology of the time, above all Spener, knew that God was not to be found along the road by which the Middle Ages had sought him. God is hidden, His ways are not our ways, His thoughts are not our thoughts. In the exact sciences, however, where one could physically grasp His works, one hoped to come upon the traces of what He planned for the world. And today? Who—aside from certain big children who are indeed found in the natural sciences—still believes that the findings of astronomy, biology, physics, or chemistry could teach us anything about the *meaning* of the world? If there is any such 'meaning,' along what road could one come upon its tracks? If these natural sciences lead to anything in this way, they are apt to make the belief that there is such a thing as the 'meaning' of the universe die out at its very roots.

And finally, science as a way 'to God'? Science, this specifically irreligious power? That science today is irreligious no one will doubt in his innermost being, even if he will not admit it to himself. Redemption from the rationalism and intellectualism of science is the fundamental presupposition of living in union with the divine. This, or something similar in meaning, is one of the fundamental watchwords one hears among German youth, whose feelings are attuned to religion or who crave religious experiences. They crave not only religious experience but experience as such. The only thing that is strange is the method that is now followed: the spheres of the irrational, the only spheres that intellectualism has not yet touched, are now raised into consciousness and put under its lens. For in practice this is where the modern intellectualist form of romantic irrationalism leads. This method of emancipation from intellectualism may well bring about the very opposite of what those who take to it conceive as its goal.

After Nietzsche's devastating criticism of those 'last men' who 'invented happiness,' I may leave aside altogether the naive optimism in which science—that is, the technique of mastering life which rests upon science—has been celebrated as the way to happiness. Who believes in this?—aside from a few big children in university chairs or editorial offices. Let us resume our argument.

Under these internal presuppositions, what is the meaning of science as a vocation, now after all these former illusions, the 'way to true being,' the 'way to true art,' the 'way to true nature,' the 'way to true God,' the 'way to true happiness,' have been dispelled? Tolstoi has given the simplest answer, with the words: 'Science is meaningless because it gives no answer to our question, the only question important for us: "What shall we do and how shall we live?" ' That science does not give an answer to this is indisputable. The only question that remains is the sense in which science gives 'no' answer, and whether or not science might yet be of some use to the one who puts the question correctly.

Today one usually speaks of science as 'free from presuppositions.' Is there such a thing? It depends upon what one understands thereby. All scientific work presupposes that the rules of logic and method are valid; these are the general foundations of our orientation in the world; and, at least for our special question, these presupposition are the least problematic aspect of science. Science further presupposes that what is yielded by scientific work is important in the sense that it is 'worth being known.' In this, obviously, are contained all our problems. For this presupposition cannot be proved by scientific means. It can only be *interpreted* with reference to its ultimate meaning, which we must reject or accept according to our ultimate position towards life.

Furthermore, the nature of the relationship of scientific work and its presuppositions varies widely according to their structure. The natural sciences, for instance, physics, chemistry, and astronomy, presuppose as self-evident that it is worth while to know the ultimate laws of cosmic events as far as science can construe them. This is the case not only because with such knowledge one can attain technical results but for its own sake, if the quest for such knowledge is to be a 'vocation.' Yet this presupposition can by no means be proved. And still less can it be proved that the existence of the world which these sciences describe is worth while, that it has any 'meaning,' or that it makes sense to live in such a world. Science does not ask for the answers to such questions.

Consider modern medicine, a practical technology which is highly developed scientifically. The general 'presupposition' of the medical enterprise is stated trivially in the assertion that medical science has the task of maintaining life as such and of diminishing suffering as such to the greatest possible degree. Yet this is problematical. By his means the medical man preserves the life of the mortally ill man, even if the patient implores us to relieve him of life, even if his relatives, to whom his life is worthless and to whom the costs of maintaining his worthless life grow unbearable, grant his redemption from suffering. Perhaps a poor lunatic is involved, whose relatives, whether they admit it or not, wish and must wish for his death. Yet the presuppositions of medicine, and the penal code, prevent the physician from relinquishing his therapeutic efforts. Whether life is worth while living and when— this question is not asked by medicine. Natural science gives us an answer to the question of what we must do if we wish to master life technically. It leaves quite aside, or assumes for its purposes, whether we should and do wish to master life technically and whether it ultimately makes sense to do so.

Consider a discipline such as aesthetics. The fact that there are works of art is given for aesthetics. It seeks to find out under what conditions this fact exists, but it does not raise the question whether or not the realm of art is perhaps a realm of diabolical grandeur, a realm of this world, and therefore, in its core, hostile to God and, in its innermost and aristocratic spirit, hostile to the brotherhood of man. Hence, aesthetics does not ask whether there *should* be works of art.

Consider jurisprudence. It establishes what is valid according to the rules of juristic thought, which is partly bound by logically compelling and partly by conventionally given schemata. Juridical thought holds when certain legal rules and certain methods of interpretations are recognized as binding. Whether there should be law and whether one should establish just these rules—such questions jurisprudence does not answer. It can only state: If one wishes this result, according to the norms of our legal thought, this legal rule is the appropriate means of attaining it.

Consider the historical and cultural sciences. They teach us how to understand and interpret political, artistic, literary, and social phenomena in terms of their origins. But they give us no answer to the question, whether the existence of these cultural phenomena have been and are *worth while*. And they do not answer the further question, whether it is worth the effort required to know them. They presuppose that there is an interest in partaking, through this procedure, of the community of 'civilized men.' But they cannot prove 'scientifically' that this is the case; and that they presuppose this interest by no means proves that it goes without saying. In fact it is not at all self-evident.

Finally, let us consider the disciplines close to me: sociology, history, economics, political science, and those types of cultural philosophy that make it their task to interpret these sciences. It is said, and I agree, that politics is out of place in the lecture-room. It does not belong there on the part of the students. If, for instance, in the lecture-room of my former colleague Dietrich Schäfer in Berlin, pacifist students were to surround his desk and make an uproar, I should deplore it just as much as I should deplore the uproar which anti-pacifist students are said to have made against Professor Förster, whose views in many ways are as remote as could be from mine. Neither does politics, however, belong in the lecture-room on the part of the docents, and when the docent is scientifically concerned with politics, it belongs there least of all.

To take a practical political stand is one thing, and to analyze political structures and party positions is another. When speaking in a political meeting about democracy, one does not hide one's personal standpoint; indeed, to come out clearly and take a stand is one's damned duty. The words one uses in such a meeting are not means of scientific analysis but means of canvassing votes and winning over others. They are not plowshares to loosen the soil of contemplative thought; they are swords against the enemies: such words are weapons. It would be an outrage, however, to use words in this fashion in a lecture or in the lecture-room. If, for instance, 'democracy' is under discussion, one considers its various forms, analyzes them in the way they function, determines what results for the conditions of life the one form has as compared with the other. Then one confronts the forms of democracy with non-democratic forms of political order and endeavors to come to a position where the student may find the point from which, in terms of his ultimate ideals, he can take a stand. But the true teacher will beware of imposing from the platform any political position upon the student, whether it is expressed or suggested. 'To let the facts speak for themselves' is the most unfair way of putting over a political position to the student.

Why should we abstain from doing this? I state in advance that some highly esteemed colleagues are of the opinion that it is not possible to carry through this self-restraint and that, even if it were possible, it would be a whim to avoid declaring oneself. Now one cannot demonstrate scientifically what the duty of an academic teacher is. One can only demand of the teacher that he have the intellectual integrity to see that it is one thing to state facts, to determine mathematical or logical relations or the internal structure of cultural values, while it is another thing to answer questions of the *value* of culture and its individual contents and the question of how one should act in the cultural community and in political associations. These are quite heterogeneous problems. If he asks further why he should not deal with both types of problems in the lecture-room, the answer is: because the prophet and the demagogue do not belong on the academic platform.

To the prophet and the demagogue, it is said: 'Go your ways out into the streets and speak openly to the world,' that is, speak where criticism is possible. In the lecture-room we stand opposite our audience, and it has to remain silent. I deem it irresponsible to exploit the circumstance that for the sake of their career the students have to attend a teacher's course while there is nobody present to oppose him with criticism. The task of the teacher is to serve the students with his knowledge and scientific experience and not to imprint upon them his personal political views. It is certainly possible that the individual teacher will not entirely succeed in eliminating his personal sympathies. He is then exposed to the sharpest criticism in the forum of his own conscience. And this deficiency does not prove anything; other errors are also possible, for instance, erroneous statements of fact, and yet they prove nothing against the duty of searching for the truth. I also reject this in the very interest of science. I am ready to prove from the works of our historians that whenever the man of science introduces his personal value judgment, a full understanding of the facts *ceases*. But this goes beyond tonight's topic and would require lengthy elucidation.

I ask only: How should a devout Catholic, on the one hand, and a Freemason, on the other, in a course on the forms of church and state or on religious history ever be brought to evaluate these subjects alike? This is out of the question. And yet the academic teacher must desire and must demand of himself to serve the one as well as the other by his knowledge and methods. Now you will rightly say that the devout Catholic will never accept the view of the factors operative in bringing about Christianity which a teacher who is free of his dogmatic presuppositions presents to him. Certainly! The difference, however, lies in the following: Science 'free from presuppositions,' in the sense of a rejection of religious bonds, does not know of the 'miracle' and the 'revelation.' If it did, science would be unfaithful to its own 'presuppositions.' The believer knows both, miracle and revelation. And science 'free from presuppositions' expects from him no less—and no more—than acknowledgment that *if* the process can be explained without those supernatural interventions, which an empirical explanation has to eliminate as causal factors, the process has to be explained the way science attempts to do. And the believer can do this without being disloyal to his faith.

But has the contribution of science no meaning at all for a man who does not care to know facts as such and to whom only the practical standpoint matters? Perhaps science nevertheless contributes something.

The primary task of a useful teacher is to teach his students to recognize 'inconvenient' facts—I mean facts that are inconvenient for their party opinions. And for every party opinion there are facts that are extremely inconvenient, for my own opinion no less than for others. I believe the teacher accomplishes more than a mere intellectual task if he compels his audience to accustom itself to the existence of such facts. I would be so immodest as even to apply the expression 'moral achievement,' though perhaps this may sound too grandiose for something that should go without saying.

Thus far I have spoken only of practical reasons for avoiding the imposition of a personal point of view. But these are not the only reasons. The impossibility of 'scientifically' pleading for practical and interested stands—except in discussing the means for a firmly given and presupposed end—rests upon reasons that lie far deeper.

'Scientific' pleading is meaningless in principle because the various value spheres of the world stand in irreconcilable conflict with each other. The elder Mill, whose philosophy I will not praise otherwise, was on this point right when he said: If one proceeds from pure experience, one arrives at polytheism. This is shallow in formulation and sounds paradoxical, and yet there is truth in it. If anything, we realize again today that something can be sacred not only in spite of its not being beautiful, but rather because and in so far as it is not beautiful. You will find this documented in the fifty-third chapter of the book of Isaiah and in the twenty-first Psalm. And, since Nietzsche, we realize that something can be beautiful, not only in spite of the aspect in which it is not good, but rather in that very aspect. You will find this expressed earlier in the *Fleurs du mal*, as Baudelaire named his volume of poems. It is commonplace to observe that something may be true although it is not beautiful and not holy and not good. Indeed it may be true in precisely those aspects. But all these are only the most elementary cases of the struggle that the gods of the various orders and values are engaged in. I do not know how one might wish to decide 'scientifically' the value of French and German culture; for here, too, different gods struggle with one another, now and for all times to come.

We live as did the ancients when their world was not yet disenchanted of its gods and demons, only we live in a different sense. As Hellenic man at times sacrificed to Aphrodite and at other times to Apollo, and, above all, as everybody sacrificed to the gods of his city, so do we still nowadays, only the bearing of man has been disenchanted and denuded of its mystical but inwardly genuine plasticity. Fate, and certainly not 'science,' holds sway over these gods and their struggles. One can only understand what the godhead is for the one order or for the other, or better, what godhead is in the one or in the other order. With this understanding, however, the matter has reached its limit so far as it can be discussed in a lecture-room and by a professor. Yet the great and vital problem that is contained therein is, of course, very far from being concluded. But forces other than university chairs have their say in this matter.

What man will take upon himself the attempt to 'refute scientifically' the ethic of the Sermon on the Mount? For instance, the sentence, 'resist no evil,' or the image of turning the other cheek? And yet it is clear, in mundane perspective, that this is an ethic of undignified conduct; one has to choose between the religious dignity which this ethic confers and the dignity of manly conduct which preaches something quite different; 'resist evil— lest you be co-responsible for an overpowering evil.' According to our ultimate standpoint, the one is the devil and the other the God, and the individual has to decide which is God for him and which is the devil. And so it goes throughout all the orders of life.

The grandiose rationalism of an ethical and methodical conduct of life which flows from every religious prophecy has dethroned this polytheism in favor of the 'one thing that is needful.' Faced with the realities of outer and inner life, Christianity has deemed it necessary to make those compromises and relative judgments, which we all know from its history. Today the routines of everyday life challenge religion. Many old gods ascend from their graves; they are disenchanted and hence take the form of impersonal forces. They strive to gain power over our lives and again they resume their eternal struggle with one another. What is hard for modern man, and especially for the younger generation, is to measure up to *workaday* existence. The ubiquitous chase for 'experience' stems from this weakness; for it is weakness not to be able to countenance the stern seriousness of our fateful times.

Our civilization destines us to realize more clearly these struggles again, after our eyes have been blinded for a thousand years —blinded by the allegedly or presumably exclusive orientation towards the grandiose moral fervor of Christian ethics.

Bibliography

I SELECTED WORKS BY MAX WEBER
IN ENGLISH TRANSLATION

Economy and Society, an Outline of Interpretive Sociology. Edited by
Guenther Roth and Claus Wittich. New York: The Bedminster
Press, 1968.

The Theory of Social and Economic Organization. Translated by A. M.
Henderson and Talcott Parsons. Edited with an introduction by Talcott Parsons. New York: Oxford University Press, 1947.

From Max Weber: Essays in Sociology. Translated and edited and with
an introduction by Hans H. Gerth and C. Wright Mills. New York:
Oxford University Press, 1946; new eds., 1953, 1958.

Basic Concepts in Sociology. Translated by H. P. Secher. New York:
Citadel Press, 1962.

The Methodology of the Social Sciences. Translated and edited by Edward
A. Shils and Henry A. Finch, with a foreword by Edward A. Shils.
Glencoe, Ill.: Free Press, 1949.

General Economic History. Translated by Frank H. Knight. Glencoe, Ill.:
Free Press, 1950.

The City. Translated and edited by Don Martindale and Gertrude Neuwirth. Glencoe, Ill.: Free Press, 1958.

Max Weber on Law in Economy and Society. Edited with an introduction
by Max Rheinstein. Translated by Edward Shils and Max Rheinstein. Cambridge, Mass.: Harvard University Press, 1954.

The Sociology of Religion. Translated by Ephraim Fischoff. Introduction
by Talcott Parsons. Boston: Beacon Press, 1963.

The Protestant Ethic and the Spirit of Capitalism. Translated by Talcott
Parsons. London: Allen & Unwin, 1930; New York: Scribner, 1958.

311

The Religion of China: Confucianism and Taoism. Translated and edited by Hans H. Gerth. Glencoe, Ill.: Free Press, 1951.

The Religion of India: The Sociology of Hinduism and Buddhism. Translated and edited by Hans H. Gerth and Don Martindale. Glencoe, Ill.: Free Press, 1958.

Ancient Judaism. Translated and edited by Hans H. Gerth and Don Martindale. Glencoe, Ill.: Free Press, 1952.

The Rational and Social Foundations of Music. Translated and edited by Don Martindale, Johannes Riedel and Gertrude Neuwirth. Carbondale: Southern Illinois University Press, 1958.

See also the introductions to the different translations of Weber's works in English.

II Selected Works on Max Weber in English

Abel, Theodore F. *Systematic Sociology in Germany.* Studies in History, Economics and Public Law, edited by the Faculty of Political Science of Columbia University, no. 310. New York: Columbia University Press, 1929.

Aron, Raymond. *Main Currents in Sociological Thought.* Translated by Richard Howard and Helen Weaver. Pp. 177–252. New York, London: Basic Books, 1967.

Bendix, Reinhard. *Max Weber: An Intellectual Portrait.* Garden City, N. Y.: Doubleday, 1962.

————. "Max Weber's Sociology Today." *International Social Science Journal* 17, no. 1 (1965): 9–22.

Eisenstadt, S. N., ed. *The Protestant Ethic and Modernization: A Comparative View.* New York, London: Basic Books, 1968.

Knight, Frank H. "Historical and Theoretical Issues in the Problem of Modern Capitalism." *Journal of Economic and Business History* 1 (1928): 119–36.

Kolko, Gabriel. "A Critique of Max Weber's Philosophy of History." *Ethics* 10 (October 1959): 21–35.

Lazarsfeld, Paul F., and Oberschall, Anthony R. "Max Weber and Empirical Social Research." *American Sociological Review* 30 (April 1965): 185–99.

Merton, R. K. "Science, Technology, and Society in XVIIth Century

England." In *Osiris Studies on the History and Philosophy of Science and on the History of Learning and Culture,* edited by George Sarton, vol. 4. Bruges, Belgium: Saint Catherine Press, 1938.

Mommsen, W. "Max Weber's Political Sociology and His Philosophy of World History." *International Social Science Journal* 17, no. 1 (1965) : 23–45.

Parsons, Talcott. "Evaluation and Objectivity in Social Science: An Interpretation of Max Weber's Contribution." *International Social Science Journal* 17, no. 1 (1965) : 46–63.

————. *The Structure of Social Action: A Study in Social Theory with Special Reference to a Group of Recent European Writers.* Pp. 500–694, 714–19. New York: The Free Press of Glencoe; London: Collier-Macmillan, 1967.

Rossi, Pietro. "Scientific Objectivity and Value Hypotheses." *International Social Science Journal* 17, no. 1 (1965) : 64–70.

Salomon, Albert. "Max Weber's Methodology." Social Research 1 (May 1934) : 147–68.

————. "Max Weber's Political Ideas." *Social Research* 2 (August 1935) : 368–84.

————. "Max Weber's Sociology." *Social Research* 2 (February 1935) : 60–73.

Sorokin, Pitirim. *Contemporary Sociological Theories.* New York and London: Harper & Brothers, 1928.

Tawney, R. H. *Religion and the Rise of Capitalism: A Historical Study.* New York: Harcourt, Brace & Co., 1926.